A Renewable World
Energy, Ecology, Equality
A Report for the World Future Council

A Renewable World
Energy, Ecology, Equality
A Report for the World Future Council

Herbert Girardet & Miguel Mendonça

green books

First published in the UK in 2009
by Green Books Ltd
Foxhole, Dartington, Totnes, Devon TQ9 6EB
www.greenbooks.co.uk

on behalf of
The World Future Council
Trafalgar House, 11 Waterloo Place, London SW1Y 4AU
www.worldfuturecouncil.org

Designed by Rick Lawrence   www.samskara-design.com

"Peace Sells" words and music by David Mustaine © 1987,
reproduced by permission of EMI Music Publishing Ltd, London W8 5SW

Printed by Cambrian Printers, Aberystwyth, Wales, UK
The text is printed on 100% recycled paper
The covers are printed on 75% recycled material

A catalogue record for this book is available from the British Library

ISBN 9781 900322 49 2

Contents

Dedication

To the children of the world, and those not as yet born:
We have tried our best to speak up for you.

Acknowledgements

Herbert Girardet thanks:

Hans and Ann Zulliger and the Foundation for the Third Millennium Foundation, Zürich, whose generosity has made the production of this book possible;

The Royal Commission for the Exhibition of 1851, London, whose generous support enabled me to gather my thoughts and to start writing the text;

The councillors, staff members and advisers of the World Future Council who have helped to shape the content of this book;

Rick Lawrence of Samskara Design for his outstanding creativity, for his patience and for giving us much moral support;

John Elford and his colleagues at Green Books for taking on this project, being such wonderful partners, and for bringing the book out so quickly;

My co-author Miguel Mendonça who has worked tirelessly over many months, determined to make this book a success;

My wife Barbara for her astonishing patience and support, and for her meticulous proof-reading and stylistic advice.

Miguel Mendonça thanks:

All those who have made this work possible through direct support, input and assistance: Herbie and Barbara Girardet, Azad Shivdasani, Hans and Ann Zulliger and the Foundation for the Third Millennium, the staff, funders, advisors and councillors of the World Future Council, the city of Hamburg and its people, Dr Michael Otto, Frances Moore Lappé and Jared Duval, Vala Ragnarsdottir, Alan Champneys and Bristol University, Walt Patterson, Eric Martinot, Lynda O'Malley, Stephen Lacey, Lily Riahi, Janet Sawin, Michael Renner and Worldwatch Institute, Julian Caldecott, David Jacobs, Benjamin Sovacool, Dave Mustaine, and Guido Glania.

In production, the greatest thanks go to Rick Lawrence at Samskara Design, for his endless creativity and patience; John Elford at Green Books for his fantastic attention to detail and his patience; and Daphne Christelis and Angela Glienicke at Greenpeace UK for their generosity with their time and photo library.

I am deeply indebted to innumerable thinkers, writers, musicians, actors, activists and many other individuals who have inspired, educated and encouraged me. Without them, I would not have written a word.

My special thanks to my nearest and dearest: Louise and Joe Applegate, Mike Wallis, Fiona Balkham, Daphne Kourkounaki, Phillip Elsmore, Dennis Keogh, Daniel Oliver, Jo Gate-Eastley and Katie Aartse-Tuyn, the Mendonças, the Blachfords, and the late great Dexter Banks.

Oh yes, we can

By BIANCA JAGGER

Chair, World Future Council Climate and Energy Commission
Chair, Bianca Jagger Human Rights Foundation

There is no doubt that today we stand at a crossroads in history. The warnings from our most respected scientists are loud and clear: we have less than a decade left to address climate change before reaching a point of no return. We have already reached the stage of *dangerous* climate change. Now the task is to prevent *catastrophic* climate chaos. And yet, government leaders continue to ignore the scale of the threat.

The reality is that failure to act will be far more costly and damaging to the world economy over the long term than if we act immediately. The costs of acting soon are manageable, especially when compared with the projected loss of human life, natural disasters and economic collapse in the coming decades. With the current financial meltdown and global economic recession, we failed to heed the signs before it was too late, and we have been forced to deal with the consequences and to bear the burden of bailouts. We are making the same mistake with our environment, but when this system breaks, it may not be possible to fix it at all.

At the Bali climate summit in 2007 I called on the world community to agree legally binding measures on climate protection, and to replace a carbon-driven economy with a carbon-absorbing economy instead. Will this be feasible? This ground-breaking book indicates that, yes, we can.

The earth's atmosphere today has a concentration of nearly 390 carbon dioxide molecules per million. This number is rising by around 2 parts per million every year. Professor Jim Hansen at NASA is unequivocal that 'official targets' of 450 parts per million of CO_2 should be slashed to 350 parts per million. He argues that cuts of atmospheric carbon concentrations, rather than just emissions reductions, are now needed "if humanity wishes to preserve a planet similar to that on which civilization developed". This is probably the first book that indicates how such cuts may be achieved.

The time has come to recognize the true economic asset value of natural resources – rainforests, oceans, barrier reefs and much more. The long-term economic value of these global ecosystems is best enhanced through conservation, innovation and efficiency, and not by reckless exploitation.

Climate change is no longer just an environmental issue: it touches every part of our lives: security, human rights, poverty, hunger, health, economics and mass migration.

We need to address the question of 'climate justice': developing countries suffer most from the impacts of climate change, even though they have barely contributed to the problem.

Justice is the litmus test for any measure designed to combat climate change. This includes justice between countries, within countries and between generations, and justice for Mother Nature. Climate justice means rich countries providing poorer countries with access to modern clean technologies to help them raise their living standards by enabling them to embark on a renewable energy revolution.

Given the scale of the impending climate disaster, we need to rapidly replace our carbon-driven economy with a renewable energy economy, switching to a secure, low-carbon energy system that does not undermine economic and social development, and that addresses the risks of energy insecurity and global inequality.

Renewable energy is substantially cheaper than nuclear power, particularly in the long term. Rather than threatening geopolitical stability, a renewable energy solution enables and empowers communities and individuals, offering clean energy security for the people of both the developed and the developing world. Renewable energy creates a plethora of new opportunities – economic, environmental and social.

As Professor Nicholas Stern says, "Investments in . . . [these] technologies could provide sustainable and well-founded economic growth, in contrast to the recent booms, and eventual busts, driven by flaky dotcom ventures or inflated house prices."

The arguments that renewable energy does not provide sufficient or affordable alternatives to conventional energy sources have been exposed as false. The German renewable energy industry has thrived and now employs around 280,000 people. Spain's employment figure in the sector is around 100,000. A recent study by the European Commission predicts that a 20 percent share for renewable energy in Europe's total energy mix by 2020 would lead to a net gain of around 410,000 jobs.

As this book shows, renewable solutions are affordable, available and a moral imperative. They are less complex to operate than conventional energy facilities and can be managed by local workforces as part of a decentralized system.

A renewable energy revolution will have crucial economic and social benefits for the poorest countries in the world, enabling them to insulate themselves against rising energy prices and to fuel their development with a decentralized energy network without expensive grid solutions. Decentralized energy will also help to prevent conflicts sparked by scarcity of resources, and some countries' control over limited resources. This will give the developing world true and lasting energy security.

The International Renewable Energy Agency, IRENA, which has recently been established, represents a crucial step towards decentralizing and democratizing energy. It will work towards improved regulatory frameworks for renewable energy; provide policy guidance to governments; address the enormous need for research, development and technology transfer; enhance capacity building; and provide advice on financing renewable energy across the world.

Wealthy countries must live up to their responsibilities and set up an international investment fund for technology transfer from the Global North to the Global South. According to the McKinsey Global Institute, at least one trillion dollars must be invested in developing countries over the next decade to enable them to expand their economies through renewable energy, resource efficiency and clean technologies.

In order to bring about A Renewable World we must embark upon a global programme of forest protection, reforestation and soil restoration. Deforestation currently contributes nearly 20 percent of overall carbon emissions. It is now widely recognized that curbing deforestation is a highly cost-effective way of reducing greenhouse gas emissions. Planting large areas of land with new forests and enriching soils with organic matter will further help to stabilize the concentration of CO_2 in the earth's atmosphere at 350 parts per million.

At this critical juncture in history it is well to remember the words of President Abraham Lincoln: "You cannot avoid the responsibility of tomorrow by evading it today." The time has come for decision-makers to embrace this opportunity. There is no time for further excuses, postponement or procrastination. This is a time for courage and leadership, and for positive and immediate action.

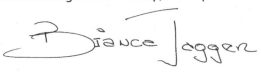

We can and we must

By ASHOK KHOSLA

President, International Union for the Conservation of Nature
Co-President, The Club of Rome
Chairman, Development Alternatives
Councillor, World Future Council

A Sustainable World must, by definition, be a Renewable World. A renewable world is one in which materials and energy are used without being used up. It draws its sustenance freely from nature's resources, but without depleting them to a point where they are no longer available or affordable.

A Renewable World must, in practice, be a Fair World. Extremes of affluence and poverty are not compatible with the imperatives of a renewable or sustainable world. The very rich tend to over-utilize those resources (usually of ancient origin, such as minerals, fossil fuels, virgin forests and environmental sinks) that cannot be replaced; and the very poor have to survive by over-dependence on living resources (such as soils, waters and biomass) that can then no longer regenerate themselves. The limits of nature are inherently and inexorably transgressed by both these diseases – *affluenza* and *povertitis* – conditions that are now possibly terminal.

So, a sustainable world must be both renewable and fair. This means that we must make use of nature and the planet's resources in a manner that leaves them intact and fully productive for future generations; and that the peoples and economies of the world must all benefit from the positive changes we succeed in making through the use of these resources.

This timely book addresses the specific issues of our energy systems, and seeks to find ways by which the global economy can effectively and speedily make the transition from a heavy dependence on non-renewable energy sources to one predominantly based on renewable ones. Its focus is on achieving this in a manner that is good for all people and beneficial for our ecosystems.

The current model of social and economic development is no longer tenable. It is too mechanistic, narrowly conceived and short-sighted. It is too costly for human values and too destructive for nature. It leads to a 'civilization' that is uncaring, inequitable and highly unjust. And now, we find, it is also about to destroy the very life-support systems that make our existence possible. Giving up bad habits is not, however, easy. And the foot-dragging by the world's major economies on dealing with life-threatening matters like climate change and species extinction indicates that the transition advocated in this book is going to face major hurdles. In the past, only major wars and catastrophes have been able to inspire the activity needed to meet challenges of such magnitude.

But perhaps the developing countries and emerging economies have a chance to do something that has not happened before. Could they demonstrate that other models of development not only work but are even better and more fulfilling in human terms? Could they move more quickly to an energy system based on benign renewable energy, and remove the millstone of fuel imports from around their necks? Some poor nations spend almost as much on fossil fuels as they produce in GDP per annum; on top of the debts owed to the north, this is an unacceptable burden to carry. Totally new solutions are needed to deal with these problems, and it is a matter of survival for not just the two-thirds who live in the global south but for all of humanity that we find them quickly.

It is easy for people in the developed world to take for granted basic services such as lighting, heating, cooling and running water; yet billions of their counterparts in poorer nations cannot meet even these basic needs on a daily basis. Rural and off-grid areas can benefit greatly from access to energy from technologies like solar, wind or small hydro. With battery back-up, they can provide lighting into the night, and allow education, work and health activities to continue. This can improve literacy, livelihoods and longevity.

Indeed, the biosphere is equally deserving of such investment. Many efforts are underway globally to restore the health of ecosystems, to retrieve productive land from desert areas, to replant forests and mangroves, to allow fish stocks to recover, and to restore people's livelihoods in a sustainable way. Those closest to the natural world understand the need for balance, as their lives depend on it. City dwellers, who from this year make up more than half of the world's population, are insulated from this knowledge. But they will soon have to master it when disaster strikes, when food prices skyrocket, when water becomes scarce and when rising tides flood coastal cities. It will not be long before we will be forced to relearn how to respect, and understand, our place within nature.

As my World Future Council colleague Tim Flannery has predicted, Perth, in Western Australia, may become the world's first ghost metropolis, due to water scarcity resulting from climate change. Perth's 1.6 million residents, looking for new homes, could join the millions of other climate refugees that may soon be displaced the world over. Bangladesh, with its low-lying flood plains, may well have 30 million or more. The next 40 years could see the numbers of eco-refugees increase globally to as many as a billion. Resettling and rehabilitating these people, providing food and water for them and creating green jobs will become the central concern of all economies; the alternative is alienation, violence and terrorism on a scale never before seen.

The only sane choice we have, as summarized in this book, is to take advantage of the positive economic opportunities that are offered by the industrial transformation which must occur to move to a low-carbon society. This will enable us to protect and restore the carbon-absorbing ecosystems which have been decimated over the centuries. And it will create meaningful jobs, substantial tax receipts, healthy economies and a sense of civilizational purpose. This is our burden in this most unique of centuries, but also the exciting challenge which can bring this divided world closer together, both among peoples, and between humanity and the natural world that is our home. As this important book outlines, it can be a renewable, and therefore a just and sustainable world, if we so choose.

A Renewable World
Introduction and executive summary

It's time for the human race to enter the solar system.
– Dan Quayle

The living planet we inhabit has effectively become a *disposable* world. We have been using resources as though there were no tomorrow. We have been dumping our wastes in the air, on land and in the sea, with little concern about the consequences. We have been living off nature's *capital* rather than its annual *income*. It is time to take the right steps to make it *a renewable world*.

In this book we are trying to address a number of urgent issues in a holistic way, acknowledging that those alive today have a greater responsibility to future life than any generation before – because of our unprecedented numbers and the enormous global impacts of our ubiquitous uses of energy and technology. These issues prompt questions such as:

- How can we decarbonize the global economy by implementing enabling policies and business practices as well as changes in personal behaviour patterns?
- How can we make clean, efficient, renewable and decentralized energy the basis for a new, sustainable global economy?
- How can we prevent run-away climate change, assure secure livelihoods for all, and restore the world's natural life-support systems?

In recent years climate change has received much international attention. Al Gore, Nicholas Stern and the Intergovernmental Panel on Climate Change (IPCC) have all told us about the urgent need to minimize carbon *emissions*. But now leading climate researchers such as Jim Hansen are saying that the challenge is no longer just to reduce annual carbon emissions, but to reduce their actual *concentrations* in the atmosphere.

The evidence of the 'earth emergency' facing us, that has presented itself clearly in recent years, is simply too compelling to ignore. This is a time for bold thinking, about doing everything possible to build a new, positive and sustainable relationship between people and planet.

In this book we have attempted to draw together strands of thought and action to indicate that *another world is possible*. The good news is that in recent years the earth has acquired a sort of nervous system, with millions of people on every continent seeking to share knowledge about ways of dealing with the climate crisis and other urgent matters. As scientists link up with journalists and NGOs, and as politicians and business leaders are presented with the evidence, new options for creating a renewable world are emerging.

The primary focus of this book is on turning the quadruple crisis facing us – of climate, energy, finance and poverty – into an opportunity for building a new, global green energy economy, and for renewing the earth's living systems. This is closely linked to improving the environmental performance of our cities – now the primary human habitat – and to a dramatic increase in the use of renewable energy. It is a book about turning vision into practical reality.

The overarching theme of this book is to clearly define climate stabilization as a fundamental necessity for long-term human security, and also as an opportunity for creating a more just, peaceful and sustainable world for present and future generations.

First and foremost, we seek to sketch out what measures are necessary, what is actually possible today, and beyond this, how we can extend the boundaries of what is politically, economically and culturally feasible to achieve the desired outcomes.

Dealing with climate change – and its environmental, economic and social consequences – is the greatest challenge for human security in the 21st century – especially when one takes into account tackling poverty and truly sustainable development at the same time. There has been a great deal of research and much recent publicity about the huge problems facing us, but plausible proposals on how to deal with these are, so far, woefully inadequate. A few reports have given some indication about what can actually done about climate change, but very little has so far been written about *how* the necessary changes can be brought about. This book deals with its chosen subject as an ethical problem that needs to be addressed on behalf of future generations, as well as those alive today.

Chapter 1 –
Energy Change, Climate Change

For hundreds of thousands of years relatively small numbers of humans led a relatively modest existence on Planet Earth, using only the renewable energy income available to them. The tools they used for supplying their necessities were limited in scope. Then, 300 years ago, the industrial revolution changed everything. For the first time, people were able to exploit the rich stores of subterranean fossil fuels that had accumulated over some 300 million years. The exponential growth of human power, human numbers, and economic and urban development that resulted, and the impacts of the ever-greater range of human activities, qualitatively changed the human presence on earth.

At the start of the 21st century, we are burning the earth's fossil-fuel deposits at the rate of some two million years' worth every year.

Until recently, air pollution in the form of urban smog and acid rain has been treated as a local or regional problem, and carbon dioxide was not even regarded as a pollutant.

Now the transfer of carbon from the earth's crust into the atmosphere, combined with a pronounced reduction in the earth's vegetation cover and the carbon content of the world's soils, is known to significantly contribute to climate change. Thousands of scientists across the world have been piecing together an increasingly irrefutable case that climate change is an immediate threat.

The process of fossil-fuel combustion has recently been accelerating rapidly as industrial and urban development has spread across the planet. To deal with the increased combustion of fossil fuels, and to stop the earth from becoming an uninhabitable planet, all kinds of technical options are being proposed, such as Carbon Capture and Storage (CCS) or geological sequestration of carbon dioxide in underground caverns. Whilst this may succeed in a few places, there is little evidence that it can be made to work effectively or cost-efficiently for the thousands of power stations that already exist or that are being planned.

Chapter 2 –
Carbon and the Biosphere

The main argument of Chapter 2 is that carbon dioxide should be regarded not simply as a *bad*, to be stored underground out of harm's way, but that it can be turned into a *good*, for the benefit of both the biosphere and humanity. Life is carbon-based, and instead of trying to sequester it by technical means, can we do so by biological means? Instead of geo-sequestration, major bio-sequestration initiatives are needed. This means improving the condition of soils, forests and aquatic vegetation to absorb carbon dioxide. Some of these measures will have the additional benefit of protecting watersheds, enhancing biodiversity and countering soil erosion and desertification.

Conservation of forests needs to be put on a new footing by supporting rural communities to protect forests rather than to allow them to deteriorate. In addition, large-scale reforestation initiatives are urgently required. An impressive start has been made by the Billion Tree Programme initiated by UNEP and Kenya's Green Belt movement, but much more needs to be done. Adequate funding also needs to be provided to assure substantial efforts to restore carbon-depleted soils. To this purpose, biochar – charcoal made from waste organic matter – can be incorporated in soils for long-term carbon storage for the benefit of local communities as well as the stability of the world's climate.

In this context, modern food production needs to be closely scrutinized. Our food supplies are extraordinarily dependent on huge inputs of fossil fuels, artificial fertilizers and pesticides. At least 10 times more fossil-fuel energy goes into modern food production than is contained in the calorific content of the food we buy in the shops. As an additional problem, the transfer of ever-larger amounts of food from rural areas to cities has led to the depletion of carbon from the world's farmland. This trend urgently needs to be reversed.

The carbon-storage potential of healthy soils is very significant indeed. Large-scale soil sequestration of carbon is very cost-effective and could take effect very quickly. We discuss how rural populations across the world could benefit by becoming carbon stewards. Support for sustainable farming practices that enhance the potential for soils to sequester from the atmosphere in large quantities must now be given very serious consideration.

Chapter 3 – Renewable Energy

As we were writing this book, we could hardly keep up with announcements about new policy initiatives on renewable energy and on new technical breakthroughs in renewable energy technologies and energy storage. As the development of renewable energy and supporting technologies is accelerated, it seems entirely feasible for us to wean ourselves off our systemic dependence on fossil fuels.

In Europe, wherever forward-looking policies such as Feed-In Tariffs (FITs) have been introduced, the scale of the creation of new jobs and businesses has been astounding. Renewables have had a transformative effect on the economies of countries such as Germany, Spain and Portugal. There, very rapid renewable energy development – encouraged by appropriate government policies – has become a spur to technological innovation that, in turn, increases the plausibility of renewables becoming the basis for future human endeavour.

Germany: having a FIT

- **280,000 jobs created, €30 bn turnover for renewable energy companies, €8.7bn investment per year**
- **€4.3 billion of fuel imports saved**
- **117 million tonnes of CO_2 saved**
- **Eco-benefit: €5.40 less environmental damage per household/month**
- **Total cost: €3.10 per household/month**
- **15% share of electricity consumption**
- **At current growth rates, renewables will provide 40% of electricity by 2020 and 100% by 2050**

Supplying the bulk of humanity's energy needs entirely from renewable energy is becoming a plausible prospect: living in a world where we can switch on a low-voltage light or drive an electric car without being complicit in warming the planet; where we are no longer tempted to start international conflicts to secure oil and gas supplies; where future generations no longer have to depend on electricity supplies from nuclear and coal power plants.

We introduce the concept of energy subsidiarity, aiming to supply as much renewable energy from local and regional sources as possible. Whilst the technical feasibility of electricity 'supergrids' – linking countries and even continents together – has been proved, the question whether such a scheme is also socially and economically desirable needs to be discussed.

It is becoming increasingly clear that the switch to renewables is ultimately dependent on political decision-making, and pressure from the general public can make all the difference. Citizen and community participation in energy production must in turn be facilitated by government policy and new business models.

> "One of, I think, the most important infrastructure projects that we need is a whole new electricity grid. Because if we're going to be serious about renewable energy, I want to be able to get wind power from North Dakota to population centers like Chicago. And we're going to have to have a smart grid if we want to use plug-in hybrids, then we want to be able to have ordinary consumers sell back the electricity that's generated from those car batteries, back into the grid. That can create 5 million new jobs, just in new energy."
>
> – President Barack Obama

Chapter 4 –
Towards Energy Equality

Ever since the Earth Summit in Rio de Janeiro in 1992, sustainable development has been a key concept for creating a viable future for humanity on a finite planet. But in reality not very much has happened. The simple reason for this is that industrial and urban development as we know is fossil-fuel dependent. So far only minimal efforts have been made to power such development by renewable energy systems instead.

Energy equality means a new balance between the energy consumption patterns of countries across the world, prioritizing supplies from renewable energy technologies. Ways must be found for developing countries to reach parity in the 'reasonable use' of energy, and even to leapfrog renewable energy development in the rich countries.

The Clean Development Mechanism (CDM) under the Kyoto Protocol was intended to offer developing countries the tools to overcome energy inequality. The CDM aims to promote RE through the exchange of technology, finance and knowledge for emissions reduction units. But so far, the reality has not matched the expectations. Good examples from different parts of the world are now urgently needed, showing how development can be powered by renewable energy. Simpler and more cost-effective solar technologies are being developed, and this could make a huge impact in developing countries.

Grameen Shakti in Bangladesh now supports deployment of many RE technologies, including PV, wind, biogas and cooking stoves. It enables rural people to improve their quality of life while also allowing them to take part in income-generating activities. These approaches are now being spread to other developing countries.

President Mohamed Nasheed of the Maldives announced in March 2009 that they aim to become the first nation in the world to become fully carbon neutral. As a low-lying island nation, the Maldives could be among the first to drown if sea levels rise as predicted. This threat has concentrated the President's mind, and he argues that the cost of powering his country with renewable energy would roughly equal the amount they spend on importing fossil fuels over ten years.

The road to energy equality between rich and poor countries may continue to be a long, arduous and contested one, but the establishment of the International Renewable Energy Agency headquarters in Abu Dhabi could signal a major acceleration in the journey.

Chapter 5 – Energy Sufficiency

Maximum energy efficiency is crucial in a world demanding ever-greater energy supplies. Efficient technologies and processes will deliver the same amount of services with a lower input of energy resources. Besides behavioural changes, increases in energy productivity can achieve such savings.

Increasing energy efficiency in buildings, in the transport sector and in production requires that efficiency standards, financial incentives and regulations are introduced for replacing inefficient practices. Government agencies should take the lead in this by adapting appropriate public procurement policies.

Assuring people's wellbeing across the world, whilst defining limits to the use of non-renewable energy, is one of the great challenges ahead of us. Whilst energy efficiency measures are necessary first steps, there also has to be an actual upper limit of global per capita fossil-fuel use. We argue that the concept of energy sufficiency needs to be applied across the world if we wish to prevent runaway climate change. A clear understanding of energy sufficiency is crucial for the long-term ecological viability of the global economy.

Limiting total energy use per person will be a critical goal in any future energy scenario. In Switzerland the idea of the 2000-Watt Society has been mooted. 2,000 watts corresponds to the average consumption of Swiss citizens in 1960 and is approximately the current world average. It compares to around 6,000 watts in Western Europe, 12,000 watts in the United States, 1,500 watts in China, 1,000 watts in India and only 300 watts in Bangladesh.

Energy Descent is a term that is used in this context – we will have to start reducing the number of 'energy slaves' working for us, which will require significant changes in our habits. But gains in quality of life may emerge from this energy descent – life will become less hectic, there can be more personal contacts, more walking, less driving, better air quality and less noise.

Chapter 6 – The Green-Collar Economy

'Green-collar jobs' are becoming a major plank of economic policy in many countries. These new jobs allow, society to focus equally on protecting the environment and future-proofing the economy. The transition to a low-carbon, 'circular' economy will deliver many employment opportunities, bringing environmental protection into the daily lives of many more people than at present. The greening of existing jobs and the creation of many new green jobs is already a multi-billion dollar global reality.

The green jobs agenda is one of the most important in the environmental and social justice movements. It unites people with responsibility and opportunity. Green-collar jobs can cover many sectors, from low to high skill levels. They are not necessarily brand new types of jobs, but can be 'greener' versions of existing job types, such as in research and development, or in manufacturing and agriculture, with associated support staff and service sector positions. These jobs are all directly associated with addressing the vast panoply of environmental issues around the world, including food, water, ecosystems, energy, manufacturing, transport, buildings and waste.

Over the past three decades, several European countries have been quietly moving ahead with a transition in their economies, mainly in renewables and energy efficiency. Studies come mostly from Germany, which has forged ahead in these areas, but countries such as Denmark and Sweden have excelled in introducing renewable energy generation, insulation, heating and more efficient building design, as well as reducing urban transport and increasing recycling rates.

Green-collar jobs have recently become a major issue in US politics, as the nation attempts to address its environmental, economic and financial crises. While they had been held back for many years, the focus on green jobs is increasing due to efforts by state and municipal governments, non-profit initiatives, trade unions and social partnerships. The fact that the US administration has identified the 'green-collar economy' as a key for restarting stalled industrial production, re-visioning failing industries, securing energy supplies and protecting the environment, is an important signal that is now being heard globally.

Chapter 7 – Renewing the City

In many towns and cities around the world a renewable energy revolution is underway. For many, the aim is a 100 percent renewable energy supply from within the city region.

The last 300 years have seen the growth of ever-larger cities – there are now 20 cities of over ten million people and hundreds over two million. Large modern cities are perhaps the primary products of fossil-fuel technologies. Such vast urban structures depend on a continuous supply of energy – for powering high-rise city centres and low-density sprawling suburbs, as centres of production, consumption, services, transportation and communication.

On just three to four percent of the world's land surface, and with half its population, cities consume around 80 percent of global energy supply and emit the bulk of greenhouse gases. What will it take for our existing modern cities to exist sustainably and to be powered by renewable energy systems instead?

City administrations across the 'developed world' are becoming increasingly aware that the cities in their charge are primary contributors to – and potentially primary victims of – global climate change, because many are located in costal regions vulnerable to rising sea levels, or in river valleys prone to flooding, or are vulnerable to loss of water supply. Therefore in an urbanizing world, sustainable development must, above all else, mean sustainable urban development. Most cities are here to stay, but they must fundamentally change their energy supply systems. The 'Solar City,' powered 100 percent by renewable energy, must be top of the agenda in an age increasingly defined by climate change.

Understanding cities as dynamic and ever-evolving eco-technical systems can help us formulate strategies for a sustainable urban future. For their long-term viability we would be well advised to model our cities on the functioning of nature's own highly complex ecosystems, such as forests or coral reefs, in which every output discharged by an organism becomes an input that renews and sustains the continuity of the whole.

Developing environmentally sustainable cities is one of humanity's greatest challenges for the new millennium. Across the world, a revolution in 'future-proofing' our urban systems has started, assuring high levels of energy efficiency and rapidly switching to renewable energy technology.

Sustainable City Principles

- **Compact urban development**
- **Renewables as primary energy supply**
- **Small ecological footprint**
- **'Circular urban metabolism'**
- **Biodiversity in landscape design**
- **A city embedded in farmland**

Chapter 8 – From Global to Local?

Industrialization and globalization have created many things, and increasing dependency on forces beyond our control is one of them. The view that local economic resilience is a desirable goal has been strengthened by the recent international financial upheavals. A profound sense of insecurity has come to affect many people. This new kind of 'insecuritization' has triggered a search for alternatives, including increased localization.

People involved in this burgeoning movement start by pointing out the social benefits. They speak of a better sense of community spirit, of empowerment, of meaningful relationships, of neighbourhood living. A great priority is the urge to reduce the daily, routine dependence on fossil fuels, but can this be achieved without having to 'give things up'? Options for 'energy descent', local resilience and richer community living are all on offer here, but not by creating hermetically sealed neighbourhoods cut off from the rest of the world.

The introduction of many regional currencies offers a pragmatic way of establishing an alternative form of globalization. As the world experiences financial and economic upheavals, peak oil and the dangers of climate change at the same time, smaller-scale solutions look increasingly plausible. The development of regions as economic units may present one of the most successful ways of moving toward another form of globalization, and the introduction of its own currencies can strengthen this development.

In the UK the rapidly growing 'Transition Movement' sees the move towards more localized approaches as being an inevitable change. It is not so much 'Small is Beautiful' but 'Small is Inevitable,' a transition from a time when economic success and personal prowess depended entirely on our degree of oil consumption, to one where our degree of dependency is also our degree of vulnerability. But it is a transition that will not be successful without an extraordinary level of co-ordination, community spirit, creativity and determination.

Chapter 9 – Problem Technologies

Any arguments for or against the nuclear question will be immediately and absolutely countered by the other side. Nuclear energy is now, above all else, being sold as a low-carbon technology. Decisions around replacement and/or expansion of existing nuclear facilities are likely to follow the traditional pattern of dominant interests seeking all avenues to advance their agenda, while an infinitely poorer, decentralized opposition will seek to stop it in its tracks.

In the UK and the US the links between government and the nuclear industry are very close. This "friends in high places" strategy by the nuclear industry is one of the most troubling aspects of the issue; it could be considered undemocratic and does nothing to develop trust in the industry. It also serves to underline that it is not necessarily a matter of what makes sense in terms of energy investment and planning for the future, but of who has the power to decisively influence government policy in their favour.

The future for nuclear energy has rarely looked rosy, but fast-changing circumstances and the financial and economic crisis could see it stranded by a lack of taxpayer's money to guarantee its development. The pro-renewables side would surely see this as the time to finally get serious about truly 'clean' energy.

Nuclear energy is not the only controversial technology. Biofuels were hailed as a vital option for the future until it became apparent that there is direct competition for land that is needed to produce food for a rapidly growing world population. Second generation biofuels, which depend on crop and forestry wastes, look more plausible, but the jury is still out on what role they will ultimately play. Algae biofuels, now the subject of enormous investment by the oil giant Exxon, appear to offer a more sustainable option yet.

Chapter 10 – Thinking Deeper, Going Further

Prevailing economic theory views the earth as an infinite resource which can be exploited and polluted at zero cost. But this view has become untenable. The global economy is unprecedented in scale, but the damage to the atmosphere or the loss of ecosystem services

Credit: Herbert Girardet. Children and future generations must be accounted for in national and international policy making.

may ultimately cost us more than its entire output.

Having grown up in a fossil-fuel dependent world, most of us understandably find it hard to imagine complex societies organized in very different ways. There is no doubt now that we need a revolution in the way we live and the way we invest. The global financial crisis offers a unique opportunity to transition to a low-carbon, resource-efficient and socially sustainable economy, incorporating sustainability and social responsibility measures into short-term economic recovery measures, and longer-term reform of the credit and investment markets.

Some commentators say that it is too late to 'turn the ship around', that we are inevitably headed for the rocks. It is true that we are currently living of the earth's natural capital and that we are, therefore, living on borrowed time. But the growing realization of this has also become a spur for action, imagination and the realization that we *can* create a renewable world, but that it is up to *all* of us to make this a reality.

To extend the way of life currently practised in the developed countries to the rest of the world would require three planets. Let us be clear: it is quite difficult to make new inhabitable planets, and transferring humans to them in large numbers is a misguided illusion. Even if a few daredevil astronauts might try a trip to Mars at some point, it will be no more than a fleeting visit.

There is now a great deal of evidence that a combination of feed-in tariffs, green taxes, local trade and exchange, green consumerism and conscious investing can redirect very large amounts of money towards creating a sustainable world. It will be a major contribution to the historic challenge of (re)directing adequate money flows towards:

- the regeneration of the world's ecosystems in the face of climate change, and
- the vigorous development of an efficient and sustainable energy system for the world.

International cooperation and connectedness is going to be vital, more than ever, in meeting these challenges. A local-only strategy has no hope of reforming the global energy, food, trade and financial systems. All sectors of society, all governments and all businesses will need to find ways of working together towards some clear common goals. There is simply too much at stake to leave it to purely market forces, or purely person action, or government regulation alone.

This book is seeking to show that we can renew our world, despite many of the grim developments of the last few centuries, and particularly of recent years. It is an essential part of the World Future Council's Climate and Energy Campaign, but it is equally relevant for all policymakers, organizations and individuals who want to influence real action on climate and energy, and biosphere restoration. If it achieves this aim it will make a useful contribution to the cause of sustainable development across the world.

Herbert Girardet and Miguel Mendonca,
July 2009

Credit: Herbert Girardet. Kayapo mother and baby. It is our duty to guard the future of this new child, and that of all children. This means assuring the continuous renewal of the biosphere, and our lifestyles within it, rather than the continuing devastation of the world's ecosystems.

Acronyms and abbreviations

1G	first generation
2G	second generation
3G	third generation
ANU	Australian National University
ASES	American Solar Energy Society
AusAID	Australian Agency for International Development
BRT	bus rapid transit
CCS	carbon capture and storage
CDM	clean development mechanism
CERT	carbon emission reduction target
CtL	coal-to-liquids
DFID	Department for International Development
DMF	2,5-dimethylfuran
DSO	Distribution System Operator
EDF	Électricité de France
EE	energy efficiency
EEG	Erneuerbare-Energien-Gesetz (Renewable Energy Sources Act)
ESCO	energy services company
EU	European Union
FIT	feed-in tariff
GDP	gross domestic product
GEF	Global Environment Facility
GM	General Motors
GNP	gross national product
GHG	greenhouse gas
GTC	Grameen Technology Centre
GTZ	Deutsche Gesellschaft fur Technische Zusammenarbeit GmbH
GW	gigawatt
HVDC	high voltage direct current
ICS	improved cook stove
IEA	International Energy Agency
IPCC	Intergovernmental Panel on Climate Change
IPP	independent power producers
JRC	The Joint Research Centre of the European Commission
km	kilometres
kWh	kilowatt hour
LPG	liquefied petroleum gas
MDG	millennium development goal
MIT	Massachusetts Institute of Technology
Mt	megatonnes

NASA	National Aeronautics and Space Administration
NGO	non-governmental organization
ODA	official development assistance
PPA	power purchase agreements
PV	photovoltaic
R&D	research and development
RE	renewable energy
REEEP	Renewable Energy and Energy Efficiency Partnership
REP	renewable energy payment
RESCO	rural energy service company
RMI	Rocky Mountain Institute
SCAD	Social Change and Development
SEFI	Sustainable Energy Finance Initiative
SHS	solar home system
SOC	soil organic carbon
TCW	The Converging World
UNCLOS	United Nations Convention on the Law of the Sea
UNDP	United Nations Development Programme
UNEP	United Nations Environment Programme
UNFCCC	United Nations Framework Convention on Climate Change
UNIDO	United Nations Industrial Development Organization
UK	United Kingdom
US	United States
USA	United States of America
USSR	Union of Soviet Socialist Republics
WFC	World Future Council
WHO	World Health Organization
WIREC	Washington International Renewable Energy Conference

Chapter One

Energy Change, Climate Change

" *Modern man does not experience himself as a part of nature but as an outside force destined to dominate and conquer it. He even talks of a battle with nature, forgetting that, if he won the battle, he would find himself on the losing side.* "
E.F. Schumacher

"Sea levels are rising twice as fast as predicted only two years ago by the United Nations." This was the startling message from a scientific conference in Copenhagen in March 2009, an overture to the global summit on climate change to be held in Copenhagen in December. "Rapidly melting ice sheets in Greenland and Antarctica are likely to raise sea levels by a metre or more by 2100, inundating coastal cities and obliterating the living space of 600 million people who live in deltas, low-lying areas and small island states. . . . Without significant, urgent and sustained emissions reductions, we will cross a threshold which will lead to continuing sea level rise of metres." [1]

This assessment is the consensus view of Professor Konrad Steffen from the University of Colorado, Dr. John Church of the Centre for Australian Weather and Climate Research in Tasmania, Dr. Eric Rignot of NASA's Jet Propulsion Laboratory in Pasadena, and Professor Stefan Rahmstorf from the Potsdam Institute for Climate Impact Research, who are all experts in sea-level rise. Their views now represent the mainstream opinion of researchers in this field, taking account of the most recent data available.

How did we get to where we are today? This first chapter is a concise overview of the processes that led to the massive increase in fossil-fuel combustion that emerged from the industrial revolution. Climate discussions often lack a historical perspective, and by exploring the qualitative and quantitative changes that occurred over the last 300 years we may get a better sense of the actions that are needed to create a sustainable world in the 21st century. The first half of this chapter deals mainly with the economic and ecological impacts of the industrial revolution, and the second half with policy responses to these impacts.

The fierce logic of the industrial revolution

Our current way of life had its origins in events which took place exactly 300 years ago. In 1709 the British entrepreneur Abraham Darby built the first blast furnace in Coalbrookdale, Shropshire, which could use coke, derived from coal, rather than charcoal, derived from wood, for smelting iron ore. His new coke-smelted iron proved to be superior as well as cheaper than iron smelted with charcoal. Crucially, Darby's inexpensive cast iron helped to trigger the start of the industrial revolution, a self-accelerating chain reaction of industrial and urban growth based on ever-greater refinements in fossil-fuel-based technologies. Only a few voices at the time challenged the wisdom of the ever-greater use of coal by pointing out its potentially catastrophic environmental consequences.

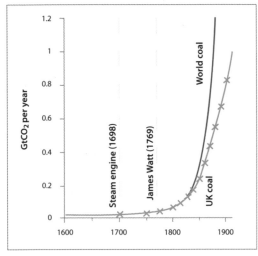

GtCO₂ per year. The growth in coal mining caused a massive increase in CO₂ emissions.

In 1711 the first steam engines, made with cast iron, started to pump water out of British mines that were up to 50 metres deep. These pumping engines, with the muscle power equivalent of some 500 horses, enabled miners to dig ever deeper to extract minerals from the earth's crust. Sixty years later, the firm of Boulton & Watt introduced the next generation of steam engines, and by 1800 over 500 were in use, first in mines and then to drive machinery in factories. In 1830 steam locomotives were used to pull passenger trains for the first time, and in 1845 the first steam-powered ship, the SS Great Britain, triggered a revolution in the mass transportation of goods and people across the oceans.

Until the early 18th century, muscles, firewood and charcoal were our main sources of energy, augmented by the limited use of water and windmills, with human lifestyles dependent on living within nature's productive capacity. As the industrial revolution unfolded, the dramatic increase in the use of coal, and then oil and gas, not only massively increased human productive power and mobility but was also a major contributor to the ten-fold growth in human numbers, from some 700 million in 1709 to nearly 7 billion today. Decayed and compressed plant and animal matter which had been transformed into fossil fuels, accumulated in the earth's crust over a period of some 300 million years. At the start of the 21st century we are burning one to two million years' worth of these fossil-fuel deposits every year. This routine use of stored hydrocarbons has truly changed the world.

Made in Britain

Britain enjoyed many advantages that helped it take the lead in the Industrial Revolution. It had plentiful iron and coal resources and a well developed canal-based transportation system. As a leading commercial and colonial power, it also had the capital to invest in new enterprises which turned out to be highly profitable.

Another reason why the industrial revolution started in Britain was that land available for fuel wood, charcoal and to feed horses had become scarce by the 18th century, and competed increasingly with the land needed to feed people. Small amounts of 'sea coal' had been used for centuries, mainly for heating buildings in cities like London, but from the early 18th century onwards its most significant use was for smelting metal ores and for powering steam engines. An astonishing transformation got underway: in 1700 coal had supplied fuel equivalent to a forest area covering about eight percent of Britain's land surface. By 1840 this had grown to the equivalent of a forest covering the whole of the UK, and today the use of fossil fuels is equivalent to a land surface ten times the size of the country. From 1800 to 1850 coal production in Britain increased sixfold, from 10 to 60 million tonnes. [2]

The industrial revolution transformed the human presence on earth. It gave humanity unprecedented powers to exploit the riches of nature – cutting down forests, clearing new farmland, expanding the world's fisheries, accelerating industrial production, extending transport systems, and building new cities or enlarging existing ones. But after three centuries of urban-industrial growth on a finite planet there are clear indications that we are reaching the limits of the earth's capacity to cater for our wants and to absorb the ever-increasing amount of the waste gases that we discharge.

> **THE 'COAL EXPLOSION'**
> *– David MacKay,*
> *Sustainable Energy without the Hot Air, 2009*
> *A very clear expression of the changes was the increase in coal mining: "In the 30 years from 1769 to 1800, Britain's annual coal production doubled. After another 30 years (1830), it had doubled again. The next doubling of production-rate happened within 20 years (1850), and another doubling within 20 years of*

Credit: Ruhrkohle AG. Coal-cutting machines were invented in the 1880s. Until then coal had been mined with a pick and shovel.

that (1870). . . . British coal production peaked in 1910, but meanwhile world coal production continued to double every 20 years. . . . From 1769 to 2006, world annual coal production increased 800-fold. Coal production is still increasing today. Other fossil fuels are being extracted too . . . but in terms of CO_2 emissions, coal is still king. "

Technology and people

In addition to the technological changes of the industrial revolution, major social changes also occurred. Capitalist entrepreneurs, many funded with Quaker money, built new factories in Britain's cities. Legions of industrial workers, many of them displaced from farms and villages, manned the new production centres, often located near coalfields. They supplied the spinning machines, power looms and other factory machinery with endless repetitive labour. The vast range of new manufactured products brought unprecedented riches for a few, new prosperity for many, and great misery for many more.

Steam technology was not static but continuously improved upon, sharply decreasing the consumption of fuel relative to the 'horsepower' produced. From 1700 to 1800 there was a 14-fold improvement in the energy efficiency of steam engines, and the increasing sophistication of the technology allowed an ever-wider range of applications. But if the efficiency of steam engines increased 14-fold, the numbers of steam engines used increased 1,000-fold, spreading from Britain across the world.

Terrestrial transport, in particular, changed beyond recognition. The first 'serious' passenger railway, the Liverpool and Manchester Line, opened in 1830. The Stephenson brothers who built the line and the locomotives were subsequently commissioned to engineer many other new railway lines. The railways challenged the canal network that had connected the towns of Britain and which had provided a steady but slow means of bulk transport, including the movement of coal. The speed and profitability of rail transport made its victory inevitable. Every town wanted a rail connection to increase its prosperity by increasing markets for its products and to allow its people to travel greater distances. As the demand grew inexorably, the length of rail tracks in Britain went up from 30 miles in 1830 to nearly 14,000 miles in 1870. [3]

An important change that was closely linked to the development of railways in Britain was the emergence of the concept of the limited liability company, which allowed investors to restrict the financial liability to their investment in a given company rather than to the total extent of their wealth. The resulting limited legal and financial liability of investors greatly encouraged risk-taking and led to a tremendous increase in profitable lending to new enterprises.[4] It also reduced the potential responsibility of companies for environmental externalities caused by activities such as fossil-fuel burning, which is one of the major factors in the climate problems we are experiencing today.

The rise of the modern city

The growth of industry and the easy availability of fossil fuels also contributed to unprecedented urbanization. For instance, Manchester grew 33-fold in 90 years, from 12,000 people in 1760 to 400,000 people in 1850; and Birmingham, Liverpool and Newcastle grew at a similar pace on the back of factory production and trade. The downside of

this astonishing growth was appalling air and water pollution, and housing conditions that are familiar today from Third World cities. In Bradford, another boom town, only 30 percent of children born to textile workers reached the age of fifteen, and the average life expectancy, at just over eighteen years, was the lowest in Britain.

The growth of Sheffield, another industrial centre, was largely due to Henry Bessemer, who patented his Bessemer Converter in the 1850s, a technology for turning molten pig-iron into steel by blasting air through it. His innovation dramatically reduced the cost of making steel, and was perfectly suited for bridges, steel girders and also for cannons. By 1879 Sheffield was producing 10,000 tons of Bessemer steel weekly, a quarter of Britain's total output. Bessemer's cheap and highly profitable steel also stimulated the construction of iron steamships for commerce and warfare, and the expansion of the railway network, which by 1885 extended to some 18,000 miles. [5]

London, Britain's economic and political powerhouse, was a great beneficiary of the industrial revolution. In 1800 London had a population of one million people. By 1850 it had reached four million, and had become the world's largest city. By 1939 it had grown to 8.6 million, with a suburban region accommodating a further four million. Of course, London's growth was not only driven by new technologies, but also because of its role as the centre of a global trading and financial empire. As steamships rendered distances increasingly irrelevant, London came to rule over a global hinterland 'on which the sun never set'.

In today's language, London could be described as both a magnificent city and a great pioneer in unsustainable development. Many of the processes of mega-urbanization that started in London subsequently spread across the world and are still unfolding today.

The farming revolution

The industrial revolution was closely linked to a revolution in farming methods. It provided an ever-increasing range of new agricultural machines which increased food production whilst reducing reliance on farm labour. In the 1730s the first iron ploughs came into use; in the 1780s the first threshing machines were introduced; and in the 1860s stationary steam engines were used for ploughing fields and for digging drainage channels for the first time. Redundant farm workers, first from the UK and the rest of Europe, swelled the numbers of migrants seeking a better life in the New World. The abolition of the corn laws in Britain in 1846 marked a significant step towards free trade in food. In the US and Canada ever more forests were cleared, prairies were ploughed up and soon steamships transported grain back to Europe. When refrigerated cargo ships became available in 1877, it became possible to import meat long-distance for the first time, from places such as Australia, New Zealand and Argentina.

A key aspect of modern farming is the way in which it decoupled itself from the use of local organic fertilizer as the main source of fertility supply. From the mid-18th century onwards the German chemist Justus von Liebig pioneered the science of plant nutrition, arguing for the importance of ammonia, phosphate and potash for increased food production. It took some time to turn the theory into practice – assuring that the new 'artificial fertilizers' could be properly absorbed by food crops. In England, Sir John Bennet Lawes developed new methods for producing superphosphate from phosphate rock in 1842. In Germany, Carl Bosch and Fritz Haber developed a new process by which

nitrogen, extracted from the atmosphere, could to be cheaply synthesized into ammonia for subsequent oxidation into nitrates and nitrites. From 1913 onwards a cheap supply of the new fertilizers became available, but it was and is dependent on massive use of fossil fuels. Today the Haber/Bosch process produces 100 million tons of nitrogen fertilizer per year. Up to 5 percent of world natural gas production, and as much as 2 percent of the world's annual energy supply, is consumed in the production of farm fertilizers.[6]

The industrial revolution spreads

After the 1850s the Industrial Revolution entered a new phase as Belgium, France and Germany started to industrialize. In Germany, the Ruhr region, where rich coal seams were discovered in the mid-19th century, went through a transformation similar to that Britain's Black Country. From 1852 to 1925 the region, centred around Essen, was transformed from a landscape of small farms, villages, towns and forests into an industrial landscape of mines, steelworks, slag heaps, tenement buildings and railway lines, increasing its population tenfold, to 3.8 million people. The industrial revolution in the Ruhr in turn contributed greatly to Germany's economic development and, ultimately, to the growth of Berlin, which became its capital city in 1871. From 1755 to 1933 its population grew tenfold, to 4.3 million people.[7]

The many technologies pioneered during the industrial revolution were eagerly adopted in the USA. Pittsburgh, Pennsylvania, in particular, had all the right ingredients for rapid industrial growth: it was located in a region rich in coal, had abundant forests, and its rivers provided good access to the Great Lakes and to new manufacturing centres such as Detroit. The industrialist Andrew Carnegie made a fortune licensing Bessemer's steel-making technology. Pittsburgh soon turned into the 'steel capital of the world'. It was also less excitingly known as 'Smoky City', or 'hell with the lid taken off'. Often the air was so sooty that streetlights had to be lit during the day and office workers had to change their shirts at noon.

New York City originated as an Indian settlement conveniently located at the mouth of the Hudson River. In the late 16th century it was becoming a centre for European immigration; then in the 19th century, with the increasing mechanization of European farms, a trickle of migrants turned into a flood, with waves of immigration from all over the world. From 1800 to 1950 New York's population grew 100-fold to 7.9 million.

By the 1890s, the United States had overtaken Great Britain as the world's leading industrial nation. Industrial revolution technologies profoundly influenced the country's urban development patterns. In 1870 Thomas Edison used a steam-fired power station to light up New York's streets with arc lights for the first time. Other landmark developments followed: the 1,600 feet Brooklyn suspension bridge became the longest; and its electricity-powered subway system, started in 1904, became the most extensive in the world, extending to 368 km, enabling New Yorkers to commute from newly developed suburbs. At the turn of the 20th century, New York no longer just grew outwards – it started growing upwards as well. Using steel girders and lift cables made in Pittsburgh, its first tall buildings had 'made-in-America' stamped all over them. In 1913 the revolutionary 241-metre Woolworth Building was hailed as a 'Cathedral of Commerce'. In 1930 the 320-metre Chrysler Building, with 77 floors, was briefly the world's tallest. But in 1931 the 443-metre Empire State building, with 102 floors, became the tallest of them all. The important point here is not just the size of these buildings but the fact that they rely on a permanent, uninterrupted supply of electricity. [8]

London and New York are only symbols of the fossil-fuel powered urbanization that has been spreading across the world ever since. From 1900 to 2000, whilst the global human population increased fourfold, from 1.5 to 6.2 billion, the global urban population grew 13-fold, from 225 million to 2.9 billion, or to about 47 percent of the world's population. In 2000 the more developed nations were about 76 percent urbanized, while the figure for developing countries was about 40 percent. By 2007 urban dwellers outnumbered rural dwellers for the first time. By 2030, 60 percent of the world population, or 4.9 billion people, are expected to live in urban areas, more than three times more than the world's entire population in 1900. In the coming decades, virtually all the world's population growth will occur in cities, and about 90 percent of this will take place in developing countries.

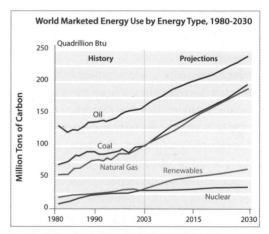

World Marketed Energy Use by Energy Type, 1980-2030

Sources: History: Energy information Administration (EIA). International Energy Annual 2003 (May-July 2005), website www.eia.doe.gov/iea/. Projections: EIA, System for the Analysis of Global Energy Markets (2006).

Only a few percent of people live in megacities with 10 million inhabitants or more,

Credit: English Russia. Moscow has one car for every 3 inhabitants. For much of the day the city is one gigantic traffic jam, and much of Russia's oil is burned in the engines of stationary vehicles.

yet the unprecedented growth of cities of this scale is still a very important trend. Their numbers rose from just one (New York) in 1950 to five in 1975, to 19 in 2000, with 16 of them in developing countries. By 2015, there will be some 23 megacities, of which 15 will be in Asia.[9] Urban landscapes such as Tokyo, São Paulo or Mexico City, which sprawl across hundreds of thousands of hectares, are unprecedented in human history, and are by far the largest structures ever created by humanity. Their emergence would have been impossible before the age of coal, oil, steel, industrial mass production and global trade.

Cars, wonderful cars

The chain reaction and proliferation of industrial production that started in Britain in 1709 further accelerated 150 years ago when, in 1859, America's first oil wells started gushing into the sky in Pennsylvania. It did not take long for new uses for oil to be found. In 1877 Nikolaus Otto

patented the internal combustion engine, and then in 1886 Karl Benz patented his first 'horseless carriage' in Germany, though France, which had Europe's best roads, took to the new mode of transport most quickly. But nowhere was the victory of the car to be as complete as in the USA.

It is the story of the Model T Ford that most vividly illustrates the transport revolution that got underway at the start of the 20th century. At that time cars cost around $5,000, and few Americans could afford them. Then in 1908 Henry Ford set out to mass-produce his Model T cars by using a moving assembly line. By 1925, Ford workers were able to complete a new car every ten seconds. As a result, the price of a Model T could be brought down to $260 and tens of millions of Americans could afford a car for the first time. City and state authorities were obliged to 'mass produce' roads to accommodate a proliferating car population. Companies such as Standard Oil had a booming new market, pumping oil as never before.[10]

The increase in oil extraction in the USA vividly illustrates the change that occurred: in 1859 2,000 barrels of oil were extracted in the USA. In 1879 that figure had risen to 20 million barrels, and in 1906 to over 120 million barrels. One hundred years later it is an astonishing 7.6 billion barrels a year, of which 70 percent is burned in transportation.[11]

After the horrors of the Second World War, more and more Americans started to realize the dream of owning a car and a house and garden in the suburbs. Soon the American dream also became the European dream. Low-density, automobile-dependent urban development became a favoured option, even though in densely populated Europe it was more difficult to implement than in the USA. But the proliferation of motorways – connecting cities right across the Europe – became a symbol of post-war progress.

Until the mid-1950s, coal was still the world's foremost fuel, but oil was quickly taking over. The horrendous scale of the Second World War itself had only been possible because of the unprecedented use of oil in warfare, and much of the grand strategy of the opposing nations was driven by a struggle to control oil fields. Since then, oil has been a key factor in several major military conflicts, including the Iran-Iraq War, Operation Desert Storm and the Iraq War.

The use of oil in transportation has transformed the world. Today visitors from outer space would be forgiven for believing that cars are the 'real' inhabitants of this planet, particularly in cities, given that they populate roads that are much wider than the pavements and sidewalks to which mere people are confined. Civilization has given way to 'mobilization'. Worldwide this trend is still accelerating, as more than 70 million new cars every year demand ever more road and motorway space.

Credit: Garve Scott-Lodge, www.oilrig-photos.com. Ever-more sophisticated technologies are needed to extract oil from ever-deeper offshore deposits. This semi-submersible drilling rig weighs 30,000 tons and can access oil deposits up to 3 km deep.

Oil and the Middle East

Another turning point in the history of energy use was the discovery of oil in the Middle East, first in Persia in 1908 and then in Saudi Arabia in 1938, followed by Iraq, Libya and Algeria. It soon became clear that the Middle East possessed the world's largest easily accessible crude oil reserves. Western oil companies pumped and exported most of the oil to fuel industrial development and the world's rapidly expanding automobile fleets. The Middle Eastern countries between them possess about two-thirds of the world's proven oil reserves, with 27 percent of these on Saudi Arabian territory. Not surprisingly, the control of all this oil has been hotly contested during the last few decades.

Until 1979, US policy in the oil-rich Gulf region concentrated on both Iran (Persia) and Saudi Arabia. With the victory of the Iranian Islamic Revolution that year, the US came to realize not only the great challenge of trying to protect its Gulf oil supplies, but also the huge cost of this protection in seeing the need to fight two Iraq wars. Even President Bush, not known for progressive policies on fossil-fuel burning, conceded that something had to be done about US oil addiction. As the new Obama administration has realized, completely new policies have to be developed to assure energy security, both in the context of climate change as well as the ever-increasing global competition for fossil fuels.

Industrialization goes global

Whilst there has been much talk about Europe and America having become post-industrial societies, the industrial revolution has continued to spread across the world. With Japan and Korea having made a start soon after World War II, Brazil, Mexico, Venezuela, China, India and South Africa – all with substantial indigenous energy resources – are on their way to becoming major industrial nations in their own right.

China, in particular, has been grabbing the headlines for the last decade or so, for its world record economic growth of 10 percent or more. China's export-led industrial boom is intimately linked to a rapid increase in domestic consumption. This is most vividly reflected in statistics on motor car ownership. In 2002 China had a fleet of 15.5 million cars, one car for every 84 people, compared with one car for every 1.3 people in the USA. China has since become the world's fastest growing car market, with production of 4.5 million cars in 2003, 5.15 million in 2004, and an astonishing 9.3 million in 2008, thus becoming the world's largest car manufacturer.[12] By 2020, demand for passenger cars in China is forecast to hit 20 million, with its car total fleet reaching 156 million vehicles, a tenfold increase in 18 years.[13]

The implications for China becoming a country of car users are astonishing. If China reached the USA's per capita level of car ownership it would have some 970 million cars,

50 percent more than the entire worldwide car fleet in 2003. Cars run on oil-based fuels: by 2010 China is expected to import half its oil, and as much as 75 percent by 2020.[14] Its oil consumption is expected to rise from 346.6 million tons in 2006 to 407 million tons in 2010 and 563 million tons in 2020, according to a recent Chinese Academy of Social Sciences forecast.[15] There is no question that global competition for oil will reach unprecedented levels.

Chinese coal consumption, mainly in power stations, is going up at a similar rate. At the end of 2005, China had an estimated 299 gigawatts of coal-fired capacity in operation. To meet the demand for electricity linked to its rapid economic and urban growth, an additional 735 gigawatts of coal-fired capacity is projected to be brought on line in China by 2030, along with very substantial investment in renewable energy.[16]

From 2005 to 2030 world energy consumption is projected to expand by 50 percent. In the same period energy consumption in the developing countries of Asia, including China and India is expected to increase by 100 percent. Most mainstream energy analysts assume that the bulk of this will be met by fossil fuels, though they don't explain whether the availability of supplies might become an issue, and what the ever-increasing global use of fossil fuels might mean for the global climate.[17]

Air pollution and the law

The last few pages described the historically unprecedented process of fossil-fuel powered industrial-urban growth that has come to define the modern world. It has profoundly changed the way we relate to the living world around us – it has literally turned humanity into a new species – the 'amplified man'. This one species has come to demand more resources than all

Credit: UNEP. Air pollution, a problem in all major cities, is particularly acute in Mexico City. The biggest health problems are ozone, dust, smoke and haze, causing thousands of premature deaths a year.

the other living species put together. But in our so-called victory over nature, will we find ourselves on the losing side?

In the next section of this chapter we look at the history of air pollution legislation, starting with measures to deal with local and regional air pollution and then moving on to discuss the global impacts of carbon emissions. Concern about the impacts of fossil-fuel burning and air pollution has a long history. In London the use of coal was temporarily prohibited as early as 1273 because it was deemed to be 'prejudicial to health', and in 1306 a Royal Proclamation prohibited craftsmen from using 'sea-coal' in their furnaces for much the same reason. [18]

Since the start of the Industrial Revolution, numerous laws have been passed which aimed to reduce air pollution in Britain. For instance, the Railway Clauses Consolidated Act of 1845 required 'that any engine should be so constructed as to consume its own smoke', though no indication was given as to how this might actually be done. The Improvement Clauses Act of 1847 was intended to reduce factory smoke pollution. The Sanitary Act of 1866 and the Public Health Act of 1875 empowered local authorities to take action against smoke nuisances. The Smoke Abatement Act of 1926 contains sections that are still current today.

GLOBAL WARMING IN HISTORY

In 1896 Svante Arrhenius publishes first calculation of global warming from human emissions of CO_2.

In 1957 Roger Revelle finds that CO_2 produced by humans will not be readily absorbed by the oceans.

In 1960 Charles Keeling accurately measures CO_2 in the Earth's atmosphere and detects an annual rise.

In 1977 Scientific opinion tends to converge on global warming as the biggest climate risk in the next century.

In 1982 Greenland ice cores reveal drastic temperature oscillations in the recent past. Global warming since the mid-1970s is reported, with 1981 the warmest year on record.

Following the Great London Smog in the winter of 1952, in which some 4,000 people literally choked to death, the UK government passed two Clean Air Acts in 1956 and 1968 which limited domestic sources of smoke pollution and which, controversially, assured the dispersal of emissions by power stations and industry by the use of tall chimneys. In the US, the Clean Air Acts of 1955 and 1963 were concerned primarily with impacts on human health: in 1970 and 1990 further Acts were passed which were concerned with countering the wider impacts of air pollution.

Since the start of the Industrial Revolution, with the ever-greater use of fossil fuels, sulphur dioxide and nitrogen oxide emissions have become an ever-growing concern. In 1852, Robert Angus Smith first coined the term 'acid rain', making the connection between the polluted skies of UK cities and the acidity of the rainfall in the region. But it was not until 120 years later that scientists started to quantify the damage to lakes and vegetation which could be attributed to acid emissions. As forests started to show new symptoms of distress in Europe and America, scientists began to identify smoke from power stations and factory chimneys, and exhaust fumes of motor cars, as the culprits. For the first time air pollution was no longer seen as a local problem, but one that affected larger areas.

Since the 1970s the European Union has introduced more and more legislation to control pollution discharged by power stations, industry and transport. It has passed numerous directives to set limits for air pollutants such as sulphur dioxide, particulate matter, lead and nitrogen dioxide. In the 1980s and 1990s European countries concluded various agreements to reduce acid emissions. In 1997, 27 countries signed the Convention on Long Range Transboundary Air Pollution Protocol which was designed to abate acidification, eutrophication and ground-level ozone by cutting emissions of four pollutants – sulphur dioxide, nitrogen oxides, volatile organic compounds and ammonia – by setting country-by-country emission ceilings to be achieved by 2010.[19]

Throughout the industrialized world, air pollution legislation has been directed largely at the by-products of fossil-fuel combustion, but not at carbon dioxide emissions. In fact, until recently CO_2 was not really regarded as a pollutant at all since it does not directly affect human health or cause damage to plant or animal life. This reality is reflected in the theoretical models underlying groundbreaking books such as Limits to Growth, first published in 1972, which does even feature CO_2 as a potentially dangerous pollutant.

Kyoto and beyond

Whilst the impact of other forms of air pollution is primarily local or regional, CO_2 emissions are, above all else, a global concern. This was recognized in the run-up to the Rio Earth Summit in 1992, when the international community decided that a global agreement on limiting greenhouse gases was urgently needed. At the Rio Summit the United Nations Framework Convention on Climate Change (UNFCCC) was agreed, with the aim of creating an international treaty to achieve "stabilization of greenhouse gas concentrations in the atmosphere at a level that would prevent dangerous anthropogenic interference with the climate system".

The subsequent Kyoto Protocol was signed off after lengthy international negotiations in December 1997 in Kyoto, Japan, and entered into force in February 2005. By November 2008, 183 countries had ratified the protocol, with the notable exception of the USA.

Whilst the limitations of the Kyoto Protocol are widely recognized, it is a clear signal that climate change needs to be acted upon by the international community. Solving the growing climate crisis requires us to cultivate a new, globally shared common sense of concern, but in a world of greatly varying interests, strong common commitment is difficult to achieve. In recent years it became increasingly clear that several major fossil-fuel producing and consuming countries had strong sectoral interests opposed to any limitation of CO_2 emissions. They are represented primarily by energy and car companies and major energy users that depend on the throughput of fossil fuels for their businesses. Also, industry and government have a shared interest in economic growth and increased fossil-fuel consumption because increased company turnover tends to result in increased tax revenues. So perhaps it is not surprising that decisive action on curtailing climate change has taken a long time to get underway.

In the last few decades, thousands of scientists across the world have been piecing together an increasingly irrefutable case that climate change is an immediate threat. The Intergovernmental Panel on Climate Change (IPCC) reports of 2007 asserted that there remained virtually no doubt that climate change is man-made. Burning fossil fuels was held up as the single largest source of man-made greenhouse gases. But whilst the combustion of oil, coal and gas continuously heats up the planet's environment, one-third of humanity still has no access to fossil-fuel energy. Efforts to end poverty will lead to a further rise in fossil-fuel consumption unless dependence on coal, oil and gas can be replaced by rapid increases in the deployment of renewable energy, as discussed in Chapters 3 and 4.

The evidence that the current scenario of fossil-fuel-based urban-industrial growth cannot continue is all around us. Recent climate news make sobering reading: for instance in Kenya in April 2009 nearly 10 million people are facing starvation due to a drought which has severely affected the country's east, south and coastal provinces.[20] According to Oxfam, as many as 400 million people – one in 17 of the world population – could be affected by climate change as soon as 2015 by a combination of floods, droughts and excessive temperatures. [21] These are just two of an ever-increasing number of news stories on the human impacts of climate change.

It is obvious that to contain climate change, major changes in the way we live and manage our societies are needed. Moreover, there is growing evidence that these changes have to take effect within a few years if we are to limit global temperature increase to 2°C or less. The required policies need to be rapid, global and just. "Unless we act now, with a sense of great urgency, there is an incalculable risk that the Earth's environmental systems will cross a tipping point beyond which costly, disruptive, and irreversible impacts will be inevitable," warns a recent report by the United Nations Foundation. [22]

Climate change is real

So far global temperatures have risen by 0.8 degrees centigrade since the start of the industrial revolution. Latest research suggests that the world has already burned half the fossil fuels necessary to bring about a 2°C rise in average global temperatures, which in itself is increasingly regarded as being potentially too high. The key implication of the research, climate scientists say, is that access to fossil fuels must somehow be rationed and eventually turned off altogether, if the 2°C target is to be met. [23]

Anthropogenic carbon emissions have increased atmospheric concentrations of CO_2 by about 35 percent during the past 300 years. Much of that carbon does not go on to affect the global climate because it is absorbed and re-emitted by the natural carbon cycle, from carbon sinks within vegetation, soils, the seas and by other natural processes. But the critical issue now is that these processes are now severely overloaded, so that overall carbon concentrations of the atmosphere are rising relentlessly. Current levels of 387 parts per million are higher than at any time in the last 650,000 years and probably in the last 20 million years. Projected future emissions will lead to a doubling of pre-industrial CO_2 concentrations to 550 ppm within the next 50 years, and this would lead towards global average temperature increases of 6 or more degrees centigrade. This would mean the end of life on earth as we know it.

The global climate is heating up far faster than scientists had predicted, as increases in greenhouse gas (GHG) emissions, including CO_2 and methane, from emerging countries like China and India are being added to those of the developed countries. In recent years, GHG emissions, as well as GHG concentrations, have increased far more rapidly than was expected even in worst-case scenarios drawn up by IPCC researchers. Meanwhile it is likely that positive feedback – new developments reinforcing each other – is now at work: for instance, Arctic summer ice is melting decades ahead of IPCC predictions as the colour of the Arctic Ocean changes from white to dark, thus increasing the amount of solar radiation that is absorbed by the sea. There is now growing concern that the melting of permafrost in Alaska will cause the discharge of vast quantities of methane, a greenhouse gas over 20 times more potent than CO_2, which in turn will further accelerate climate change. The same is happening in Siberia, and partly in response to this, Russian president Dimitry Medvedev stated in June 2008 that "parts of Russia will be uninhabitable within the next three decades if the country does not take better care of the environment". [24]

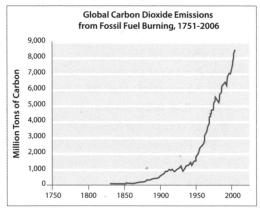

Source: CDIAC, BP.

Russia decided to sign the Kyoto treat in 2005, whereas the United States, under President Bush, refrained from doing so. But at last, with a new US government, change is on the way. The US is becoming actively involved in the negotiations for a new, comprehensive global climate treaty to succeed the Kyoto Protocol.

During his election campaign Barack Obama promised to classify CO_2 as a dangerous pollutant that needs to be regulated. He stated that he will instruct the Environmental Protection Agency to make the designation under the 1990 Clean Air Act to set emissions limits on power plants and manufacturers. When Obama was elected as president, he appointed as his Energy Secretary Steve Chu, director of the Lawrence Berkeley National Laboratory and a Nobel Prizewinner. In an interview before he was appointed, Chu demanded that the world wake up to the calamity that faces us if we continue to delay action to prevent irreversible climate change.

He argues that a shift away from fossil fuels is essential to combat global warming.

The Arctic problem

The situation in the Arctic is the most acute climate-related problem the world is facing:

- **In 2004 an international scientific panel forecast that the Arctic summer ice cover could vanish by 2100.**
- **Five years later some experts predicted that the summer ice could disappear in the next 10 to 20 years.**
- **The latest research suggests that within five to ten years the Arctic sea ice might disappear entirely during the summer months.**

The Arctic Ocean is a vast area of some 14 million square kilometres surrounded by continents. This is an area one and a half times bigger than the USA, and the Arctic Circle as a whole encompasses about six percent of the Earth's surface area.

The Arctic Sea is regarded as one of the most resource-rich regions in the world. In the recent past, the five Arctic coastal states – the US, Russia, Canada, Norway and Denmark (via Greenland) – have shown increasing interest in the recoverable oil and gas reserves on their doorstep. Using geology-based assessment techniques, US scientists have estimated the fossil-fuel resources north of the Arctic Circle to be around 90 billion barrels of oil, 44 billion barrels of liquid natural gas and 1,669 trillion cubic feet of natural gas. [25]

The implications of these figures are huge: the consumption of the entire Arctic oil and gas reserve could lead to emissions of between 130 and 150 Gt of CO_2, which corresponds to eight times the annual CO_2 emissions of the OECD and China put together, or 160 times Germany's current annual CO_2 emissions. If all this oil and gas were burned, it would bring about a rise of 17 to 20 parts per million of CO_2 volume in the atmosphere. [26] This is equivalent to the change in global greenhouse gas concentrations for the period from 1996 to 2005, causing an increase of the annual global mean temperature by around 0.3 degrees C.

ARCTIC SUMMER COULD BE ICE-FREE BY 2013

A new study on climate change says that the Arctic is warming up so quickly that the region's summer ice cover could vanish as early as 2013, decades earlier than some had predicted. The data "appears to be tracking the most pessimistic of the models", said Warwick Vincent, director of the Northern Studies Centre at Laval University in Quebec, adding that "each year we're finding that it's a little bit faster than expected".

The Arctic is warming at twice the rate of the rest of the world, with the sea ice cover shrinking to a record low in 2007 before regrowing slightly in 2008. Researchers fear that some of the changes will be permanent, and that the warming in the Arctic may be a sign of trouble ahead for the rest of the world. "We're in a train of events at the moment where there are changes taking place that we are unable to reverse – the loss of these ice shelves, for example," Vincent said. "But what we can do is slow down this process, and we have to slow down this process because we need to buy more time."

In 2008 the maximum summer temperature on the Arctic's Ward Hunt hit 20C compared with the usual 5C. Last summer the five ice shelves along Ellesmere Island in Canada's Far North, which are at least 4,000 years old, shrunk by 23 percent. "As the Arctic warms, so does the rest of the globe . . . as a result we may see some associated increase of sea level," Vincent said. "Right now

> *most of the shipping that goes between Asia and Europe must go around to the Panama canal or around the tip of South America. If the northern sea route does open up, that would make it the most efficient route for shipping between Asia and Europe. . . . That would be dramatic and have global implications."*
>
> **Reuters, 12-3-09**

Because the Arctic ice is melting as never before, shipping firms have already proposed using the North-West passage, which would be a short-cut for sea trade between Europe and Asia, connecting the Atlantic and Pacific Oceans.

But melting ice offers other options as well – including the extraction of oil and gas. Several onshore areas in Russia, Canada and Alaska have already been mapped in great detail. As a result, more than 400 oil and gas fields north of the Arctic Circle have been discovered.[27] Now the governments of some of the adjoining states are getting excited about the prospect for extracting oil and gas reserves from the Arctic Ocean floor. Russia in particular is getting vocal about its right to extract these resources. And yet it is evident that this would lead to further greenhouse gas emissions, and a further acceleration of climate change. The response to such proposal seems obvious: the oil and gas in the Arctic region should not be touched if we want to begin to counter climate change.

Until recently scientists have underestimated the pace by which temperatures might rise in the Arctic Circle. One of the factors was a lack of understanding of potential 'positive feedback loop'. It was insufficiently understood how summer ice losses will allow more solar energy to be absorbed by the ocean and thus increase water temperature.[28] In summer 2008, the Arctic sea ice dropped to the second lowest level since satellite measurements began in 1979. This confirmed the downward trend, observed in the last 30 years. In 2007, the surface temperature in the Arctic was the highest since measurements started 78 years ago.

All this points to an urgent need for a far-reaching international agreement on the protection of the Arctic, yet the applicable international law, the 1982 UN Convention on the Law of the Sea (UNCLOS), does not provide an adequate answer to this problem. The Arctic Council, an intergovernmental forum of the circumpolar states, has proposed environmental mitigation measures, but does not take a clear stance against drilling in the Arctic. But in the face of dangerous climate change and the potentially severe climate consequences of oil and gas extraction, the protection of the Arctic Ocean region should not be subject to a trade-off between regional economic interests and global environmental concerns.

The World Future Council is, therefore, calling for the creation of an internationally binding ban on the exploitation of fossil resources in the Arctic region.[29]

> **GREENLAND**
>
> *At the beginning of the chapter we cited the work of Konrad Steffen and his colleagues regarding sea level rises. Here is a summary of a Wikipedia text on Greenland:*
>
> *Positioned in the Arctic, the Greenland ice sheet is especially vulnerable to global warming. The Greenland Ice Sheet has experienced record melting in recent years and is likely to contribute substantially to sea level rise as well as to possible changes in ocean circulation in the future. The area of the sheet that experiences melting has increased about 16 percent from 1979 to 2002. The area of melting in 2002 broke all previous records. The number of glacial earthquakes at Helheim and the*

northwest Greenland glaciers increased substantially between 1993 and 2005. In 2006, estimated monthly changes in the mass of Greenland's ice sheet suggest that it is melting at a rate of about 239 cubic kilometres per year. A more recent study, based on reprocessed and improved data between 2003 and 2008, reports an average trend of 195 cubic kilometres per year. These measurements came from the US space agency's Grace satellite, launched in 2002. Using data from two ground-observing satellites, ICESAT and ASTER, a study published in September 2008 shows that nearly 75 percent of the loss of Greenland's ice can be traced back to small coastal glaciers.

If the entire 2.85 million km^3 of ice were to melt, global sea levels would rise 7.2 m. Recently, fears have grown that continued global warming will make the Greenland Ice Sheet cross a threshold where long-term melting of the entire ice sheet is inevitable. Climate models predict that local warming in Greenland will exceed 3 degrees Celsius during this century. The models project that such a warming would ultimately cause the inundation of almost every major coastal city in the world. But how fast the melt would occur is a still matter of discussion. According to the IPCC, the expected 3 degrees warming at the end of the 21st century would, if kep rising further, result in about 1 metre sea level rise over the millennium. Some scientists, however, have cautioned that the rates of melting assumed by the IPCC are overly optimistic as they assume a linear rather than an erratic progression. James Hansen has argued that multiple positive feedbacks could lead to nonlinear ice sheet disintegration much faster than claimed by the IPCC.

The melt zone, where summer warmth turns snow and ice into slush and ponds of meltwater, has been expanding at an accelerating rate in recent years. When the meltwater seeps down through cracks in the ice sheet, it accelerates the melting and, in some areas, allows the ice to slide more easily over the bedrock below, speeding its movement to the sea. Besides contributing to global sea level rise, the process adds fresh water to the ocean, which may disturb ocean circulation and thus regional climate change.

Credit: Greenpeace. New research suggests that meltwater pools on top of Greenland's ice sheets tend to drain down to the bedrock, lubricating the sheet and allowing it to more easily slip forward and off into the sea.

Source:
en.wikipedia.org/wiki/Greenland_ice_sheet

Carbon capture and storage

It is understandable that the world is desperately looking for ways to reduce CO_2 emissions. As Chapters 3 and 5 will show, rapid moves towards renewable energy and energy sufficiency are essential for dealing with climate change. New energy technologies that replace the combustion of fossil fuels are clearly the best solution, but meanwhile we have to deal with the continued discharge of greenhouse gases from across the world including those from newly built power stations. In this context Carbon Capture and Storage (CCS), also known as geo-sequestration, has become a favoured intermediate technical option. The idea is very simple: CO_2 from fossil-fuel burning should be captured and stored within the earth's crust. CCS is widely touted as the technology that can make a major contribution to reducing carbon emissions to achieve the cherished 2°C target.

The coal industry and power station companies, in particular, are singing the praises of this technology. They uses terms like 'clean coal' to describe CCS in glowing terms, yet the clean burning of coal is evidently a contradiction in terms: CO_2 is a 'dirty' waste gas unless ways can be found to make good use of it by storing it by biological means. This alternative approach is described in the next chapter under the heading of 'bio-sequestration'.

There is a major flaw in investing in CCS: whilst its large-scale application could help us deal with the climate problems we are facing, large-scale investment in the technology may absorb funds and delay the deployment of renewable sources that offer a more sustainable energy future. Nevertheless, deployment of CCS may be an intermediate step towards a clean energy future – if it can be made to work at the required scale. The European Union has decided to put substantial financial resources into CCS on the understanding that the development of the technology is an important 'learning by doing' experiment.

CO_2 capture is the most complex technical part of CCS. Various capture technologies are being tested: they include seemingly exotic options such as solvent-scrubbing with amine solutions, cryogenics, membranes and absorption technologies. All CO_2 capture is bound to be expensive, and there is no doubt that inevitable efficiency losses will significantly increase overall electricity generating costs.

Once CO_2 has been removed from flue gases it will need to be transferred through pipelines and injected into underground storage facilities. The injected CO_2 forms a pressurized plume

that displaces water which may be present in the chosen geological formation. The main option for storing CO_2 underground is in depleted oil and gas reservoirs, deep saline-water-bearing formations or un-mineable coal seams. The safest way to store the CO_2 is in a geological formation under dense low-permeable rock that acts as a tight seal through which CO_2 cannot escape. The most crucial issue is that the CO_2 is stored safely and permanently, i.e. for many thousands of years.

Depleted oil and gas fields are particularly good candidates for CO_2 storage because they have held oil and gas in place for very long time-frames. Their geological parameters are known, and the infrastructure (wells and drilling equipment) is in place. But old oil and gas fields also have disadvantages: the presence of wells can create potential CO_2 leakage pathways that may compromise the security of the storage site.

Of the various CO_2 storage options, deep saline formations have the largest storage potential. Such formations exist in many parts of the world, and they usually do not contain man-made disturbances such as oil wells. On the other hand, these structures are usually not well known and may also have competing uses for geothermal energy.[30]

At present, information about the potentially detrimental external environmental effects of carbon dioxide storage is far from complete. For instance, storing large amounts of CO_2 underground could result in unwelcome changes to underground geological formations. It may be possible for most of the gas can be stored safely for millennia, but some leakage can never be ruled out. The conclusion must be that storing CO_2 underground is a risky business, since permanent storage cannot be guaranteed one hundred percent. Whatever happens, storage sites need to be selected, managed and monitored very carefully indeed.

Around the world a number of programmes are underway to develop CCS technology. However, no single full-scale project is running to date. While small-scale pilot plants with capture technology have started recently, such as Vattenfalls' Schwarze Pumpe pilot plant in Germany, and larger plants for up to 300 MW capacity are in the planning stages, truly large-scale 1,000 MW plants are still a long way off. A McKinsey study estimates that if 23 to 27 demonstration projects were operational by 2015, the early commercial phase could be reached in the 2020s and a mature commercial stage could be achieved in the 2030s.[31]

Statoil's Sleipner project in the North Sea and BP's In-Salah project in Algeria are the most prominent small-scale examples for CO_2 storage currently in use. For more than ten years Statoil has been injecting one million tons of CO_2 annually into sandstone formations 1,000 metres below the North Sea bed in the Sleipner gas field. A million tons per year may seem like a lot, but it is nothing compared to the amount of storage ultimately be needed. No experience exists with handling tens of millions of tons of CO_2 – that may come from just one large coal power plant.

Worldwide, thousands of new coal power plants are currently under construction or at the planning stage. Many of those plants are claimed to be 'capture-ready', suggesting that they can be retrofitted with CCS. The IEA estimates that for CCS to deliver any meaningful climate-mitigation effects by 2050, 6,000 projects would be required, with each of them sequestering and storing a million tons of CO_2 per year.[32] However, even if this were to succeed, coal power plants can only lower their CO_2 gas emissions by 65 to 79 percent – they cannot sequester them from their flue gases completely.

The extent to which CCS might ultimately be used will depend on many factors, including future emission reduction targets, installation costs, safety of CO_2 storage, availability and costs of available fossil-fuel resources, environmental risks associated with CCS, as well as public acceptance. No other mitigation option has gained more attention than CCS (also known as geo-sequestration). However, in the next chapter we are outlining an alternative option that may have much greater benefit for people and planet: bio-sequestration.

Major international bodies such as the International Energy Agency (IEA), not known for their support for renewables, argue that CCS is a cost-effective way of reducing CO_2 emissions compared with other possible measures. But there is no doubt that CCS is expensive and could lead to a doubling of powers station plant costs, and to substantial increases in electricity prices. Part of the problem is that CCS technology will use between 10 and 40 percent of the energy produced by a power station, erasing power station efficiency gains that have been achieved in the last 50 years. Another concern, already mentioned, is that money spent on CCS will divert investments away from renewable energy and energy efficiency. In Chapter 3 we will argue that renewable energies promoted with the same effort as CCS can provide a rapid increase in the share of energy at a lower cost. [33]

A common argument used in the CCS debate is that fossil fuels, and especially coal, are abundant and available at relatively low cost. As a result, fossil fuels will continue to be the world's dominant energy source for some time and CCS will be a significant intermediate technology to help stabilize atmospheric concentrations at a viable level. But much of the rest of this book argues that the accelerated introduction of renewable energy technologies are the preferred option for developed as well as developing countries.

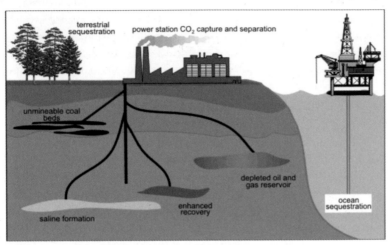

Credit: Martin Frost. Carbon capture and storage is the 'great white hope' of many policy-makers and yet it is unlikely to work on anything like the scale envisaged.

Prometheus Unbound?

In Greek mythology, Prometheus was a lowly challenger to the omnipotent god Zeus. His great misdeed was that he stole fire from the gods and gave it to humanity. This so enraged Zeus that he got his fellow god Vulcan to shackle Prometheus to a rock face in the Caucasus, where a vulture ate his liver by day, only for it to regrow again every night. After many years the Greek demi-god and hero Hercules killed the vulture and relieved Prometheus from his awful predicament by freeing him from his chains. But was it such a good idea for him to be let loose on the world again?

The myth of Prometheus has been used as a symbolic description of how humanity's ubiquitous use of fire has had serious consequences. Today it is evident that the ubiquitous use of fossil fuels has brought much convenience to those who have benefited from it. But it will be very difficult indeed to reverse many of the environmental impacts that resulted from the industrial revolution – the age of fire – and humanity's increased reliance on fossil fuels. The momentum of Prometheus's gift is still unfolding across the world.

Are our carbon emissions from fossil-fuel burning a crime against the future? It is certainly increasingly clear that humanity is on a collision course with its own future, and that it will take a tremendous effort to reverse the current trends of resource depletion and environmental destruction, and particularly climate change.

The systemic issue that needs to be addressed is that the industrial revolution was a new departure for the human presence on earth. It effectively reverses the transfer of carbon from the atmosphere into deposits within the earth's crust which has been occurring over hundreds of millions of years, and returns it back into the atmosphere. The question we need to answer now is how best we can undo the damage resulting from this, and what we can do to adapt to impacts that may have become unavoidable.

Some people will say that the earth and its inhabitants have always been exposed to changes, including, for instance, the actual lowering of sea levels that occurred during the last ice age when water levels were a hundred metres below current ones.

But the fact is that we have made our living arrangements at current sea levels and have built cities that accommodate some 30 percent of the world population close to the shores. If sea levels rise by a metre or more within a hundred years, as the first paragraph of this chapter suggests, billions of people will ultimately be affected.

The CO2 emission reductions now urgently required have in the past only been associated with major upheavals, e.g. the collapse of the USSR. The current recession will have slightly reduced global carbon emissions. A May 2009 report by the IEA states that the global use of electricity has gone down for the first time since 1945, by 2 percent since 2008. It remains to be seen whether this is a temporary blip or a long-term trend.[34]

Lord Stern's influential 2006 report on the Economics of Climate Change states that climate change represents "the greatest market failure the world has seen" because we have failed to include externalities in the cost of energy use. The report reached a very simple conclusion: the benefits of strong and early action to counter climate change far outweigh the economic costs of non-action: if we do not act swiftly, the overall costs and risks of climate change will be equivalent to losing at least 5 percent of global GDP each year, and the damage could rise to 20 percent of GDP or more. In contrast, Stern states that the actions required to avoid the worst impacts of climate change would only cost around 1 percent of global GDP per year, though more recently he has revised this figure upwards to 2 percent. The findings of the Stern report have since been echoed in many other reports.[35]

Our carbon emissions are inducing major changes in greenhouse gas concentrations, greater than those associated with the onset and termination of the last ice age.[36] What Lord Stern's work clearly indicates is that ultimately we can no longer avoid full cost accounting, particularly in the context of energy use. This is becoming apparent in the looming costs to future generations associated with fossil-fuel burning: sea level rises, increased droughts, and many other activities affecting natural ecosystems and human populations. A full cost-benefit analysis of our uses of fossil fuels will show almost certainly that renewable energy, despite its lower energy density, is the appropriate choice for the future. Therefore, it must be integrated into policy and decision-making without further delay.

Meanwhile there is a growing global consensus that for long-term climate security the developed countries have to reduce their greenhouse gas emissions by at least a factor of five by 2050 compared to 1990. In fact, several countries, including the UK and the USA, have already made this target official government policy.[37] But this still assumes that CO2 concentrations of some 450 ppm are an appropriate target for long-term climate

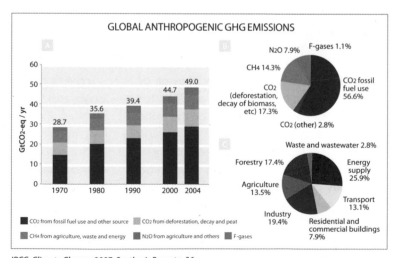

GLOBAL ANTHROPOGENIC GHG EMISSIONS

IPCC. Climate Change 2007: Synthesis Report p.36.
http://www.ipcc.ch/pdf/assessment-report/ar4/syr/ar4_syr.pdf

security. This figure is increasingly being challenged by climate researchers because it allows only for a reduction in GHG emissions rather than an actual reduction in GHG concentrations in the atmosphere. There is a growing minority scientific opinion that we need to actually reduce GHG concentrations to 350 ppm over the coming decades.[38]

There is little doubt about the enormous effort required to undo the effects of fossil-fuel burning and deforestation of the last 300 years. The next chapter proposes ways in which bio-carbon sequestration, together with the accelerated introduction of renewable energy and energy sufficiency strategies, may enable us to achieve targets that measure up to the changes that are now needed.

Acknowledgements

Axel Bree *WFC staff*
Stefan Schurig *WFC staff*

GREENLAND'S GLACIERS, MELTWATER AND CLIMATE CHANGE

Every summer, thousands of lakes now form on top of Greenland's glaciers, as sunlight and warm air melt ice on the surface. Past satellite observations have shown that these 'supraglacial lakes' can disappear in as little as a day, but scientists did not know where the water was going or how quickly.

Researchers have hypothesized that meltwater from the surface of Greenland's ice sheet might be lubricating its base to accelerate the flow of ice sheets into the sea, but did not know how the meltwater could penetrate through a kilometre of subfreezing ice.

In July 2007 Sarah Das from the Woods Hole Oceanographic Institution and Ian Joughin from the University of Washington were the first scientists to document the sudden and complete drainage of a meltwater lake from the top of the Greenland ice sheet to its base.

They observed the sudden, complete draining of a 5.6 square kilometres lake that held some 44 billion litres of water. Like a draining bathtub, the entire lake emptied in 24 hours with a maximum drainage rate faster than the average flow of the Niagara Falls.

As cracks and crevasses formed and become filled with water, the greater weight and density of the water forced the ice to crack open. The pressure of the water split open the ice sheet from top to bottom, and the meltwater drained through 980 metres to the bottom of the ice sheet. It subsequently accelerated the movement of the ice to twice its expected speed.

Scientists fear that temperature increases in the Arctic due to climate change will cause more and more of Greenland's ice sheets to be lubricated by meltwater and slide off into the sea.

Extracted from Woods Hole Research Institution news item.
www.whoi.edu/page.do?pid=7545&tid

Chapter Two

Carbon and the Biosphere

*" The Great Work, now . . . is to carry out the transition from
a period of human devastation of the Earth to a period when
humans would be present to the planet in a mutually beneficial
manner. . . . All human activities, professions, programs,
and institutions must henceforth be judged primarily
by the extent to which they inhibit, ignore, or foster
a mutually enhancing human/Earth relationship. "*

Thomas Berry

The previous chapter aimed to provide an overview of developments that led up to the climate problems we are facing today. There is growing scientific evidence that to avoid a climate catastrophe in the coming decades we need not just to reduce carbon emissions, but, beyond that, to reduce actual concentrations of CO_2 already present in the earth's atmosphere. This is an agenda that goes significantly beyond the targets currently being pursued by the world's 'climate guardians' such as the IPCC.

Jim Hansen, the eminent climate researcher and director of NASA's Goddard Institute for Space Studies, has recently stated that the IPCC has been much too cautious in its assessments and that we are rapidly reaching crucial tipping points which compel us to act very rapidly indeed to prevent runaway climate change. In an interview published in 2008, he said this:

"Recent greenhouse gas emissions place the Earth perilously close to dramatic climate change. . . . There is already enough carbon in the Earth's atmosphere for massive ice sheets such as West Antarctica to eventually melt away, and ensure that sea levels will rise metres in coming decades. Climate zones such as the tropics and temperate regions will continue to shift, and the oceans will become more acidic, endangering much marine life. We must begin to move rapidly to the post-fossil-fuel clean energy system. Moreover, we must remove some carbon that has collected in the atmosphere since the Industrial Revolution."[1]

Hansen's views have been reinforced by alarming news about melting mountain glaciers and by the unprecedented thinning of polar ice, with the prospect that summer ice in the Arctic may largely disappear in a matter of years. Far more solar energy will be absorbed into the arctic oceans as their colour turns from white to dark as ice dissolves during the summer months. This and other positive feedbacks are alarm signals of an unprecedented crisis that have led the Secretary General of the United Nations Ban Ki-Moon to refer to a global *climate emergency*.

So, where do we go from here? By 2009 global carbon dioxide (CO_2) concentrations have already reached 387 parts per million (ppm), up by 40 percent from 275 ppm in 1900. Until recently a doubling to 550 ppm was widely regarded as an acceptable target, but this has been revised downwards to some 450 ppm as new scientific evidence about a warming planet has emerged. Now a growing number of climatologists are questioning even this limited increase, and argue for an actual reduction of CO_2 concentrations to 350 ppm or below. This goes way beyond scenarios currently being proposed by governments in developed countries, whose policies are homing in on an 80 percent reduction of carbon emissions from 1990 figures by 2050.

The problem is that every year we are now discharging nearly 10 billion tonnes of carbon into the atmosphere. Of this, four to five billion tonnes are not being reabsorbed into the world's ecosystems, but are instead accumulating in the atmosphere above our heads. This chapter aims to explore options for absorbing surplus greenhouse gas emissions, and, beyond that, to find ways to actually reduce existing GHG concentrations.

The last chapter ended by looking at the potential for removing carbon by technical means through carbon capture and storage (geo-sequestration). Yet even if CCS were to succeed, it will not deal with existing carbon that is already in the atmosphere. This chapter discusses alternative approaches, and particularly bio-sequestration, which can deal with new emissions as well as existing CO_2 concentrations if done on a large-enough scale.

For global temperatures to stabilize, carbon

emissions must ultimately not exceed what can be absorbed by the biosphere, the Earth's vegetation, soils and oceans. So can we enhance the capacity of the biosphere to absorb CO_2?

There is no question that this is a controversial issue, particularly regarding the idea of using reforestation for carbon sequestration. For instance, in a joint statement in 2006, Friends of the Earth, Greenpeace and WWF-UK strongly argued against 'reforestation sink projects', mainly because "large-scale monoculture tree plantations often have negative impacts on the environment and forest communities". [2]

A number of other publications detail the perceived fallacy of carbon offsets. A report called *The Carbon Neutral Myth – Offset Indulgences for your Climate Sins* rails against the idea of people in the rich countries obtaining 'permission' to burn oil, gas and coal by paying for carbon offsets – more often than not through tree-planting projects somewhere in the global South where projects are being imposed on communities with little consultation.' [3]

These objections certainly have to be taken seriously. Nevertheless, we cannot ignore the need to find ways of enhancing the capacity of the earth's living environment to absorb carbon. Not only can this help to reduce atmospheric carbon concentrations – a critical necessity – but, if done right, it can also increase the options for sustainable food and timber production for a growing global population. In a world challenged by climate change and biodiversity loss as well as hunger, it is critically important to undertake new initiatives which can have such multiple benefits.

A key point to be considered is that whilst fossil-fuel burning has massively increased in the last 300 years, the capacity of the biosphere to absorb it has been significantly reduced at the same time. Dr. Rattan Lal, Professor of Soil Science at Ohio State University, has calculated that 476 billions of tonnes (Gt) of carbon has been emitted from farmland soils due to inappropriate farming and grazing practices, compared with 270 Gt emitted from over 150 years of burning of fossil fuels. [4] A more frequently quoted figure is that 200-250 Gt of carbon has been lost from the biosphere as a whole in the last 300 years. [5] Whatever the correct figure, these reductions of 'living carbon potential' have resulted from:

- **deforestation**
- **biodiversity loss**
- **accelerated soil erosion**
- **loss of soil organic matter**
- **salinization of soils**
- **costal water pollution, and**
- **acidification of the oceans**

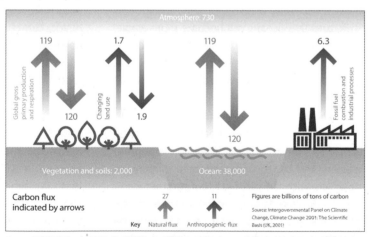

Source: Wilf Whitty. In 2001 the IPCC estimated annual carbon emissions as being around 6.3 billion tonnes. This figure has been revised upwards to around 10 billion tonnes. It is now estimated that about half of this carbon is being absorbed by forests, soils and oceans, with the other half accumulating in the atmosphere.

The main argument of this chapter is that carbon dioxide should be regarded not simply as a 'bad' that has to be stored in underground caverns out of harm's way, but that it can be turned into a good that can be used to enhance the wellbeing of the biosphere and humanity. Can the disruptive human impact on nature's carbon cycle, which is causing ever-worsening instabilities, be brought back into balance by deliberate action?

A matter of balance

A healthy balance sheet matches income and outgoings – in fact, on the balance sheet of a thriving company or household, income exceeds outgoings. But it is not so in the world's global carbon balance sheet: year after year we have been running up ever-greater deficits. For instance, WWF's annual Living Planet Reports indicate clearly that in our dealings with nature we have been creating ever-greater imbalances. The 2008 Living Planet Report tells us that we are consuming the resources that underpin the world's ecosystems services much faster than they are being replenished. Humanity's global ecological footprint now exceeds the world's capacity to regenerate by about 30 percent.[6] Indisputably, this state of affairs cannot continue.

The main constituent of life on earth is carbon, drawn from carbon dioxide in the earth's atmosphere. It is the chemical basis of all known life, and forms more compounds than any other element, with some ten million so far identified by science. Variations in carbon dioxide levels in the atmosphere have been known for some time to influence the impact of solar radiation on the earth, and with that, the earth's climate. Around 2,000 Gt of carbon are present in the world's soils and vegetation, and this has been fairly constant over the last few million years. The earth's remaining fossil-fuel reserves amount to approximately 1,200 Gt, or

1.2 trillion tonnes. Around 900 Gt of these are coal, and the remaining oil and gas reserves each amount to around 150 Gt.[7]

Over the course of some 300 million years, carbon was drawn down from the atmosphere by living organisms and 'relocated' in the earth's crust, ultimately becoming fossil fuels. These were formed out of biomass that was deposited on the ocean floor by sea organisms, by organic particles that were washed into the sea, and out of plant and animal matter on land which was then covered over by sediments and more decaying organic matter.

In the last 300 years we have reversed this process of biological carbon sequestration, and have transferred hundreds of billions of tonnes of carbon back into the atmosphere, with increasingly dire consequences. How can we balance the books? How can humanity re-establish a carbon cycle where income and outgoings are matched?

This matter is addressed in some detail by the IPCC reports published in recent years, and some mitigation measures have been agreed by the international community in the Kyoto Protocol. However, new thinking about how large amounts of carbon already present in the atmosphere can be sequestered is now urgently needed.

According to the Global Carbon Project, the land and ocean carbon sinks – such as forests, and plankton in the ocean – removed about 54 percent, or 4.8 billion tonnes a year, of the carbon that humans discharged into the atmosphere between 2000 and 2007. That leaves a carbon surplus of about 4 billion tonnes or so per year, which we need to find ways to reduce or absorb.[8]

We must take a new look at how better land-use and forest management can further enhance biological carbon sequestration. There has been much discussion about the feasibility of geo-sequestration of CO_2 from power stations, refineries, etc., as discussed in the last chapter. However, in this chapter we argue that we should give priority to biological carbon capture and storage (BCCS), or bio-sequestration, through deliberate measures of forest protection, reforestation, the improvement of soil by incorporation of compost and 'biochar', and by restoring ocean vegetation. The Kyoto Protocol's Clean Development Mechanism (CDM), as discussed in some detail in Chapter 4, should be expanded to incorporate bio-sequestration in all its various forms.

In this context it is important to realize that well-thought-out bio-sequestration has multiple benefits to nature and human society: in addition to absorbing surplus carbon, it also offers significant opportunities for biodiversity protection, soil erosion prevention and, potentially, enhanced food production and poverty reduction in rural areas. This could even help to enhance the economic viability of rural communities in an age in which billions of people have been and are being forced to move to cities to try and earn a better living.

Forests for life

Global forest cover extends to nearly 4 billion hectares, or 30 percent of the world's land surface.[9] The UN Food and Agriculture Organization (FAO) has recently done a Forest Resources Assessment which states that the world's forests contain 638 Gt of carbon – which is more than the total carbon contained in the atmosphere.[10]

Forest ecosystems are crucially important components of the global carbon cycle in several ways. They remove some 3 billion tonnes of carbon every year through net growth, absorbing nearly 30 percent of all CO_2 emissions from fossil-fuel burning and deforestation.[11]

Healthy forests play a crucial role as global ecological life-support systems. Reports such as UNEP's *Millennium Ecosystem Assessment* make it clear that the goods and services provided by forests are worth trillions of dollars to the global economy. In addition to carbon sequestration, they provide a wide range of 'ecosystem services' of benefit to all life: they are wildlife habitats, biodiversity centres, climate regulators and watershed protectors – not to mention medicine cabinets and cosmetics counters. By and large these services are regarded as free benefits – of no cost to human society – and they are absent from society's balance sheet. Thus their critical contributions to the viability of life on earth are largely overlooked in decision-making. This problem needs to be urgently addressed, for only if we recognize forests as important natural assets with economic and social value can we do what is necessary to promote their protection.[12]

FOREST AREA BY REGION, 2000						
Region	Land area (million ha)	Total forest (natural forests and forest plantations)			Natural forest (million ha)	Forest plantation (million ha)
		Area (million ha)	% of land area	% of world's forests		
Africa	2,978	650	22	17	642	8
Asia	3,085	548	18	14	432	116
Europe	2,260	1,039	46	27	1,007	32
North and Central America	2,137	549	26	14	532	18
Oceania	849	198	23	5	194	3
South America	1,755	886	51	23	875	10
World total	13,064	3,869	30	100	3,682	187

Source: UN (FAO) State of the World's Forests 2001.

Credit: Herbert Girardet. Tropical forests, which used to be net producers of oxygen, have become net producers of CO2 in recent years. This must be reversed if we are serious about enhancing the capacity of the biosphere to sequester large amounts of CO2.

As human populations and their economies grow, so do the resource demands imposed on ecosystems and the impacts of our global ecological footprint. But society is coming to realize that as ecosystem services are threatened across the world, there is an urgent need to evaluate both their immediate and their long-term benefits to humanity. Increasingly, researchers have been able to quantify the economic value associated with ecosystem services based on assessing the cost of replacing these with 'man-made' alternatives.[13]

Deforestation, a global problem

Deforestation, particularly in the tropics, has long been regarded as a major environmental problem. It is one of the biggest sources of greenhouse gas emissions and one of the primary contributors to climate change. The IPCC estimates that it is responsible for 18 to 20 percent of global carbon emissions. Deforestation today is concentrated in a few developing countries, primarily in the tropics, but countries all over the world will ultimately benefit from forest protection. So new international forest conservation efforts are urgently needed.

According to the FAO, between 2000 and 2005 the global annual net loss of forest area was 7.3 million hectares per year, mainly in the tropics.[14] This represents a loss of CO_2 sequestration capacity of 3.65 billion tonnes.[15] As well as being a major threat to the climate, deforestation also affects 1.6 billion of the world's poorest people who directly depend on forests for their survival.[16] Processes of deforestation vary from continent to continent. In South America it is driven primarily by logging and the expansion of large-scale farming, primarily to produce beef and soybeans; in South-East Asia, forests are being cleared primarily for timber production and for the expansion of oil palm and coffee for global markets.

The economic impacts of deforestation are immense. A 2008 study headed by Deutsche Bank economist Pavan Sukhdev, entitled *The Economics of Ecosystems and Biodiversity* (TEEB), estimates that the destruction of forests internationally is causing economic damage to the tune of $2 to $5 trillion, or up to seven percent of the global economy, annually. This calculation was done by placing value on the various services that healthy forests provide for free, such as carbon sequestration, food supply and water storage.[17] Sukhdev emphasizes that the cost of this decline dwarfs the recent losses on the financial markets. "It's not only greater but it's also continuous – it's been happening every year, year after year."

The Global Canopy Programme (GCP), an alliance of 37 scientific institutions in 19 countries, is a world leader in forest canopy research, education and conservation. The programme proposes realistic new ways of compensating countries and companies for protecting their forests, in their own interest as well as the interest of the world community.

Andrew Mitchell, director of GCP, says that tropical rainforests are the "elephant in the living room of climate change".[18] In other words, their presence may be overwhelmingly obvious, but few people know how to deal with it. His perspective is supported by the 2006 Stern Review, which states that deforestation from 2008-2012 will be responsible for more greenhouse gas emissions (GHG) than aviation since the invention of the aeroplane until at least 2025. It says that curbing deforestation should be regarded as a highly cost-effective way of reducing GHG emissions.[19]

A view from the Amazon

In its entirety the Amazon Basin covers some 7 million square kilometres. The lion's share, some 5 million square kilometres, is in Brazil, and the remainder stretches across eight other countries. At least 60 percent of the world's remaining tropical rainforests, with their unsurpassed biodiversity – including some 55,000 different plant species – are to be found in the Amazon. Moreover, the forests in the Amazon Basin contain at least the equivalent of one-fifth of all the carbon currently in the atmosphere, and recent studies show that intact Amazonian forests are also functioning as a globally significant carbon sink, even absorbing some of the carbon dioxide released into the atmosphere from industrial emissions.[20]

Deforestation for logging, cattle ranching, soybean production, mining and smallholder farming has so far affected about 20 percent of the Amazon forest, with the greatest impacts in the eastern and southern Amazon. Major concerns are not only carbon loss as a result of deforestation, but also changes in the moisture transfer across vast areas.

The Amazon basin is an enormous heat engine, taking heat from the sun, turning it into water vapour and powering tropical air circulation. It has been shown through modelling by two Russian climate scientists that the multi-layered canopy of rainforests is ideal for the transfer of water through cloud formation over long distances. For instance, the only way water will transfer from the Atlantic Ocean to the Andes is through the canopy of the Amazon rainforest.[21]

A recent report, Drought Sensitivity of the Amazon Rainforest, published by Science magazine in March 2009, presents evidence that the Amazon rainforest is very sensitive to drought – which is likely to intensify under global warming. The 25-year study, which involved some 68 scientists, has used the severe drought that struck the Amazon in September 2005 as a "unique opportunity to directly evaluate the large-scale sensitivity of tropical forest to water deficits". The study concluded that drought causes massive carbon loss in the forest – mainly through killing trees that are not able to tolerate the drier soil conditions.[22]

Credit: Maria Stenzel, National Geographic. The Amazon region stretches across an area the size of western Europe. Intact areas like this in Brazil's Amazonas State are increasingly rare as new roads open up the forest to loggers, cattle ranchers, farmers and miners.

The researchers found that the Amazon forest normally absorbs nearly 2 billion tonnes of carbon dioxide each year, but in 2005 the dry conditions caused it to lose more than 3 billion tonnes of living biomass. "The total impact of the drought – 5 billion extra tonnes of carbon dioxide in the atmosphere – exceeds the annual emissions of Europe and Japan combined", stated the press release from Leeds University, which led the research.

Covering the research in *The Independent* newspaper, Steve Connor wrote: "The Amazon has long been the lungs of the world. But now comes dramatic evidence that we cannot rely on it in the fight against climate change."[23]

Since the 2005 drought, the Brazilian government had some success in lowering the rate of deforestation caused by human activity. In 2006 deforestation was reduced by some 30 percent, but in 2007, with the growing interest in biofuels and rising food prices (which were also partly because of biofuels) deforestation rates shot up again and it was clear that the government did not have deforestation under control. It remains to be seen whether the current world recession has reduced deforestation rates once again.

While scientists and climatologists are hesitant about making predictions too far into the future, many believe that the forest system, particularly in the eastern Amazon, is dangerously close to collapse and that drought could occur regularly in the coming years, with dire consequences for areas beyond which depend on the Amazon for their rainfall. Brazilian hydrologists have shown that the Amazon basin evaporates some 20 billion tonnes of water daily, and that the standing forest helps to lower surface air temperatures through evaporation. This evaporative cooling and the resulting recycling of water is crucial for all the other services provided by the forests, including carbon storage.

Many scientists now think that we are approaching a critical point, certainly in the East Amazon. If the forest system were to collapse, this would disrupt huge energy and moisture flows which would have a 'shockwave' effect across the world's climate systems.[24]

New demands for forest products

Africa's Congo Basin Forest, the largest expanse of tropical forest outside the Amazon, is coming under huge pressure from international timber markets. This is epitomized by a story from the environment editor of *The Guardian* newspaper, John Vidal, who visited the region in 2007 to write about the logging operations there. In a saw mill he saw several huge trees being cut up, and when he asked where the timber was going to end up, the answer was: at the cycle track being built for the 2008 Beijing Olympics.

Rapidly growing economies such as China are scouring the world for timber and other forest products. China now buys 55 percent of the Republic of Congo's timber exports, which come almost entirely from virgin forests.[25]

Increasingly, not only timber but also palm oil and soybeans are being imported from ecologically vulnerable rainforest regions. Malaysia is supplying ever-growing amounts of palm oil from converted rainforests. In 2006 it exported some 14.4 million tonnes of palm oil, and of this China imported nearly 3.6 million tonnes.[26] In the last 20 years China has become the world's largest importer of whole soybeans as well as oil and meal by-products.[27] Brazilian soy exports to China, mainly from the Amazon and former savannah regions in Mato Grosso, increased from one million tons to four million tons between 1999 and 2003.[28]

"What if China reaches the US consumption level per person?" asks Lester Brown, CEO of the Earth Policy Institute. "If China's economy continues to expand at eight percent a year, its income per person will reach the current US level in 2031. If at that point China's per capita resource consumption were the same as in the United States today, then its projected 1.45 billion people would consume the equivalent of two-thirds of the current world grain harvest. China's paper consumption would be double the world's current production. There go the world's forests."[29]

It is, however, important to point out that China is only following in the footsteps of Europe, the US and Japan, whose demands have been the primary contributor to deforestation in the tropics until recently, and this continues today despite substantial efforts by environmental lobbies such as the Forest Stewardship Council to certify timber and other

Credit: Greenpeace/Oka Bhudi. Palm oil monocultures have replaced much of the diverse rainforests of Malaysia and Indonesia.

tropical forest products. New strategies to protect and renew forests around the world are urgently needed.

Ecosystem services and 'avoided deforestation'

The fact that the 1997 Kyoto agreement did not address the need to reduce CO_2 emissions from deforestation is a major problem. This was partly due to a lack of sufficient knowledge of the emissions involved. The negotiators initially had difficulties with measuring the emissions and setting suitable baselines, but this has since been rectified. In 1997 there was also a major concern that the sheer scale of carbon credits produced from 'avoided deforestation' would tend to undermine incentives to reduce emissions by other sectors. As a result of these factors, reforestation projects were included in the agreement, but 'avoided deforestation' was left out.

Today, technological advances such as satellite monitoring technology have given us accurate measures of both annual forest losses and carbon emissions from deforestation. The notion that avoided deforestation should be included within international carbon markets is now being hotly debated. Many experts feel that without schemes for compensating developing countries for avoided deforestation, any post-Kyoto climate deal will not be able to achieve the global emissions reductions necessary to combat climate change.

The Global Canopy Programme says that it is crucial to acknowledge that living forests provide valuable climatic services that deforested areas cannot provide, and the overall economic value we place on forests needs to reflect this. Thus the only way to curb further deforestation is to put a price on carbon contained in forests and so provide an incentive for developing countries to protect them.

New financial incentives are important because the efforts of NGOs to reduce deforestation by appealing to the environmental and social responsibility of producers and consumers have so far had only limited success. Philanthropy has also been on an inadequate scale to deal with such a huge task. The urgency of the climate challenge means we must develop more effective and innovative methods of international cooperation to curb deforestation.

There is a complex set of factors behind deforestation, and they have to be well understood for any policy framework to be successful. The primary reason is that presently the conversion of forest to other land uses such as farming, plantations and mining is usually more profitable, particularly if it is supported by government policies, subsidies and international trade. Poorly defined property rights, non-transparency, financial gain by elites and weak law enforcement are other causes of deforestation. Any alternative policies intended to counter deforestation must deal with this complex set of issues.

Experts agree that ecosystems – and especially rainforests – must be a central part of any post-Kyoto agreement – because it is the most immediate and cost-effective way to achieve real and significant reductions in GHG emissions. There is now growing consensus that financial compensation for avoided deforestation is the best way to reduce loss of forests, particularly in the tropics.

Reducing Emissions from Deforestation and Degradation (REDD)

Since 2005 the United Nations Framework Convention on Climate Change (UNFCCC) has been trying to create a new international policy framework to counter deforestation. REDD has

Credit: Herbert Girardet. The rainforest canopy is not only a habitat for a vast variety of life forms; it also has the most remarkable capacity for carbon sequestration.

centuries, to participate in designing REDD schemes and to benefit from them. REDD schemes will only work if it is clear who is to be compensated and how. For that reason it is important to strengthen the capacity of forest protection agencies to assure that the rewards for avoided deforestation reach the right people and do not just end up in the hands of corrupt officials, cattle ranchers, and palm oil and logging companies.

A pre-emptive scheme for compensating those who have never deforested will be rather difficult to measure, but would be fairer. The Global Canopy Programme has proposed Proactive Investment in Natural Capital (PINC) as a complementary framework to REDD. PINC would reward nations and landowners for the ecosystem services that protected forests provide. A critical issue is to work out the present value of the forests to be protected, and this needs much careful thought and monetary calculation.

The forest canopy as capital

For many years forest campaigners have drawn attention to the ecological dangers of deforestation, but little has been achieved because the underlying financial interests have not been sufficiently addressed. As greenhouse gas emissions rise, conservation is becoming increasingly important. As the world realizes the enormous value of ecosystem services, countries which preserve their rainforests will have assets worth billions. Investors are beginning to recognize this opportunity, and this is the rationale behind a recently established organization called Canopy Capital, a not-for-profit financial lobby for rainforests, initiated by former London investment banker Hylton Murray-Philipson.

He started Canopy Capital to harness the power of the markets and the profit motive in

been developed largely as a result of initiatives by developing countries, led by Costa Rica and Papua New Guinea. It is intended to enable these countries to earn credits for avoided deforestation. The idea is that developing countries which protect their forests, which can therefore continue to provide essential ecosystem services for the world, should be compensated for doing so. If REDD is to be part of a post-2012 climate deal, agreement must be reached in Copenhagen in December 2009.

If REDD is to work effectively it needs to address carbon emissions, biodiversity, ecosystem services and rural poverty alleviation all at the same time. Above all else, it must help assure sustainable livelihoods for forest-dependent communities.

A crucial issue is for local communities, who have lived with and depended on the forests for the cause of conservation. The main point of his initiative is to establish that whilst markets have valued products such as beef and soya, they have ignored the services of the intact rainforest. If these are not valued, we are likely to lose them. By recognizing and valuing the ecological services the forest provides – such as carbon storage, moisture transfer, climate moderation and biodiversity – Canopy Capital aims to generate investment in rainforests which will enable their preservation for the benefit of all of humanity, whilst providing economic and social benefits to local communities.

Canopy Capital's first partnership is with the administrators of the Iwokrama Reserve in Guyana: "Murray-Philipson's goal is to counter the pressures of globalization that are driving deforestation by developing a new capital market to value standing forests. Specifically, this will include the launch of an Ecosystem Service Certificate attached to an €80m, 10-year tradable bond, the interest from which will pay for the protection and maintenance of 350,000 hectares of the Guyana rainforest. The deal is being conducted through a partnership with the Iwokrama International Centre for Rainforest Conservation and Development in Guyana."

Using income from the ecosystem services of the intact forest, the plan is to make Iwokrama financially independent of donors by 2010. But Guyana is only the first port of call – Murray-Philipson is aiming for a global trading model for rainforest protection. He is working towards creating a Forest Index so that investors can treat forest as a legitimate asset class alongside other renewables such as wind, biomass and solar. "Fundamentally, this is about the global management of global carbon stocks, part of which must preserve biodiversity levels, indigenous cultures, and the monitoring and governance of the rainforest."[30]

A priority for Canopy Capital is to ensure that the scheme is of real benefit to indigenous people. 90 percent of the upside from the scheme will go to the people of Guyana for the sustainable management of the Iwokrama reserve and to provide livelihoods for the local forest communities.[31]

Credit: FrostFlowers. Natural forests have many layers of living matter, depending on the availability of light. From the forest floor to the top of the canopy, a huge variety of life forms interact for mutual benefit.

IN ECUADOR, NATURE NOW HAS RIGHTS
Gar Smith

After many years of environmental destruction, especially due to oil-extracting activities, Ecuador has approved a new constitution that is the first in the world to extend "inalienable rights to nature".

Not too long ago, Ecuador would have seemed an unlikely nation to become the birthplace of Earth's first green constitution. To service its massive debt to US creditors, the World Bank and the International Monetary Fund forced Ecuador to open its Amazon forests to foreign oil companies. Nearly 30 years of drilling enriched ChevronTexaco, desecrated the northern Amazon, and utterly failed to improve the lives of millions of poor Ecuadoreans.

In 1990, the Siona, Secoya, Achuar, Huaorani and other indigenous forest-dwellers won title to three million acres of traditional forestland, but the government retained rights to the minerals and oil. In November 1993, indigenous communities filed a $1 billion environmental lawsuit against Texaco, and subsequently demanded a 15-year moratorium on drilling, environmental reparations, corporate indemnification, and a share of oil profits.

In 1997, when Ecuador's then pro-US government announced plans to rev up oil exploitation by a third, all eyes turned to the Yasuni rainforest, which harbours the country's largest oil reserve, estimated at 1 billion barrels. The Yasuni is home to indigenous tribes whose territories have been protected by international treaty. It is also home to rare animal species, including jaguars, endangered white-bellied spider monkeys and spectacled bears.

In 2007, the new government of President Rafael Correa announced plans to halt oil exploration in the Yasuni, in an action Amazon Watch called "a giant first step toward breaking Ecuador's dependence on oil". Correa's proposal marked a shift to making renewable energy the basis for Ecuador's economic future. The language in the new constitution takes the new policy several steps further.

Ecuador's radical new constitution features a chapter on the "Rights for Nature" that begins by invoking the indigenous concept of sumak kawsay (good living) and the Andean Earth Goddess: "Nature, or Pachamama, where life is reproduced and exists, has the right to exist, persist, maintain and regenerate its vital cycles, structure, functions and its processes in evolution." The constitution contains a Nature's Bill of Rights that includes "the right to an integral restoration" and the right to be free from "exploitation" and "harmful environmental consequences".

This idea is gaining momentum. In the US, municipalities in Pennsylvania, California, New Hampshire and Virginia have adopted Right to Nature laws in recent years.

Shannon Biggs of Global Exchange notes: "Slaves were once also considered property under the law" until Americans understood that "we needed to write new laws in order to change . . . the cultural climate."

With parrot-flecked jungles containing more than 300 different tree species per hectare, cloud forests of amazing biodiversity and a border that extends to the Galapagos Islands, Ecuador is the perfect spot for the world's first eco-constitution. Ecuador has swung a hammer against the chains designed to keep nature in thrall to commerce. It's time for other nations to pick up the same hammer.

Earth Island Journal, Winter 2009

Reforestation benefits: carbon and timber

Currently the CDM under the Kyoto Treaty considers only afforestation and reforestation as acceptable carbon-sequestration activities. Whilst it is widely accepted that protecting existing forests is much more effective for carbon storage than reforestation and the afforestation of degraded land, major tree-planting initiatives are underway in different parts of the world. Reforestation certainly has an important additional role to play in countering the build-up of carbon in the atmosphere:

Carbon sequestration: New plantations can sequester carbon from the atmosphere at a rate of between 5 and 15 tonnes per hectare per year.[32]

Timber supplies: Although reforestation can provide no substitute for the ecosystem services provided by primary forests, the world needs timber, and this demand should be met from plantations, not from the standing forest, wherever possible.

It is important to point out that monoculture plantations of trees which are to be grown on former forest land for the purpose of carbon sequestration, should not be encouraged by international policy. Entrepreneurs are proposing all kinds of fancy solutions for coming to the aid of the planet: genetically engineered eucalyptus, pine trees and oil palms, the Super Kiri tree, the kenaf plant, and jatropha and other 'miracle crops' for carbon sequestration and alternatives to fossil fuels. But rarely is the question being addressed of where the water and plant nutrients needed for growing vast acreages of super-fast growing monocultures are likely to come from, and how such monocultures would affect the livelihoods of local communities on whose land they might be planted.

It seems important to restate that we must look beyond the role of forests as carbon sinks – they can provide many other important services, as we have seen above.

There are some interesting examples of tree-planting initiatives which set out to recreate natural forest ecosystems. 'Analogue Forestry', for instance, aims to reproduce the mixed multi-layered ecosystems that a diverse forest

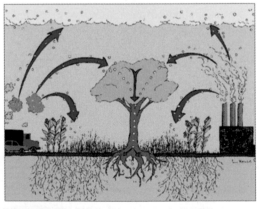

Source: ERS/USDA. Planning for a 'carbon neutral world' means assuring a global balance between carbon emissions and carbon sequestration capacity, with sustainable methods of bio-sequestration as the preferred option.

provides. And 'agroforestry', by which a variety of tree crops – including legumes – are produced on the same plot of land, is the most natural way of planting forests which can provide food, animal fodder and timber at the same time, whilst also capturing carbon from the air. Importantly, it can also help to restore the fertility of depleted soils for the benefit of local communities.

UNEP's Billion Tree Campaign

Reforestation, and the afforestation of degraded land, takes great effort and major investments, and the financial returns have to be counted in decades rather than years. Nevertheless, very substantial tree-planting efforts are now underway across the world.

The United Nations Environment Programme's (UNEP's) Billion Tree Campaign was launched in 2006, and is backed by Wangari Maathai, 2004 Nobel Peace Prize laureate and founder of Kenya's Green Belt Movement (which initiated the planting of some 40 million trees in Kenya.) The Billion Trees Campaign has encouraged people all over the world – from private individuals and community groups to businesses and governments – to plant anything from just a handful to several million trees. Initially the target was to plant one billion trees in 2007, but the success of the campaign has led to the much more ambitious goal of planting seven billion trees by the end of 2009. By December 2008 a total of 4.2 billion trees had been pledged and almost 2.6 billion planted.

Speaking in February 2009, Wangari Maathai appealed to Heads of State around the world: "Imagine soldiers marching for the planet. While the armies of the world are waiting to fight an enemy that comes with a gun, we have another enemy, an unseen enemy, an enemy that is destroying our environment. The enemy that takes away our top soil, takes away our waters, destroys our forests, destroys the air we breathe, clears the forest. This is the unseen enemy and it cannot be fought with a gun. This enemy can be fought with a tree. So you can imagine how wonderful it would be if every soldier on this planet started seeing himself and herself as a soldier for the planet, holding a gun on one side and a tree seedling on the other, to fight this unseen enemy which is actually more dangerous to us than the other enemy."

In Africa, Ethiopia has become a major tree-planting success story. In four decades Ethiopia's forest cover had dropped from 40 to just 2.7 percent. But spurred on by UNEP's Billion Tree Campaign, Ethiopia has planted more trees than any other nation – some 700 million in the last few years. Tewolde Egziabher, head of the country's Environmental Protection Authority and a member of the World Future Council, says that the combination of tree-planting and the development of organic farming has started to greatly improve the condition of rural communities in Ethiopia.

China, too, has undertaken very large-scale tree-planting schemes, talking of a 'Great Green Wall'. It has established 24 million hectares of new forests and natural forest regrowth – an area the size of the UK – to transform previously denuded landscapes, particularly in major watersheds, and has been able to offset some 21 percent of its fossil-fuel emissions in 2000.[33]

There are also major success stories from South America: Cuba has done much tree-planting. Before the Cuban revolution in 1959, just 13.4 percent of the country was covered by trees. In the last 50 years the government's planting programme has nearly doubled the national forest cover to some 25 percent. According to the FAO, Cuba, Uruguay, Chile and Costa Rica are the four Latin American countries that have implemented very successful reforestation efforts.[34]

These examples are heartening, but much, much more needs to be done. Balancing forest protection and renewal, and philanthropy and profit, new ways must be found to safeguard and enhance the condition of the biosphere, the most important climate regulation system we have at our disposal.

Expanding bio-carbon sequestration projects beyond a few pilot schemes requires key measures such as security of tenure, assured funding streams, political stability and institutional capacity. International carbon projects effectively represent an emerging market opportunity. Only those countries that are well prepared will be able to fully take advantage of this.[35]

Credit: Michael Halbert. Trees and their root systems are the most remarkable carbon sequestration organisms.

Farming carbon

The earth's major natural sinks of CO_2 are oceans, forests and, perhaps most importantly, soils. The global soil carbon pool is estimated to amount to 2,500 Gt, whereas the biotic (vegetation-based) pool is 560 Gt.[36] This section aims to provide a concise overview of the potential of soil renewal as a carbon sequestration option.

A new international climate treaty needs to cast its net much wider than the Kyoto Treaty as regards bio-carbon sequestration. In addition to the inclusion of reforestation and forest conservation, soil carbon storage should be included as an eligible carbon sink. In fact, the IPCC's Fourth Assessment Report (AR4) in 2007 indicated that carbon sequestration by improved soil management holds very significant mitigation potential. Whilst soils hold less carbon per hectare than forests, the carbon storage potential resulting from improved farming practices is very large indeed.

The world's total agricultural area is about 5 billion hectares, one billion more than for forests. Of this, about 1.5 billion ha (30 percent) is arable land and land under permanent crops, and the remaining 3.5 billion ha is permanent pasture. In addition, there are also up to 2.5 billion ha of rangelands.

Soils naturally contain large amounts of carbon, derived primarily from decayed vegetation. But the last few decades have seen a dramatic loss of top soil, soil carbon and inherent soil fertility due to the spread of unecological farming methods, and the one-way traffic of food supplies from rural areas to cities without the return of carbon back to the farmland where the food was grown. A recent report by the FAO states: "Most agricultural soils have lost anything between 30 and 75 percent of their antecedent soil organic carbon pool, or a total of 30 to 40 tC/ha. Carbon loss from soils is mainly associated with soil degradation . . . and has amounted to 78 +/- 12 Gt since 1850. Thus, the present organic carbon pool in agricultural soils is much lower than

their potential capacity.[37] . . . Considering all greenhouse gases, the global technical mitigation potential from agriculture is between 1.5 and 1.64 gigatonnes of carbon equivalent per year by 2030. Soil carbon sequestration is estimated to contribute about 89 percent to this mitigation potential".[38]

All over the world soil and soil carbon (humus) is disappearing through erosion and through harvesting crops that end up being consumed in distant cities. In recent years there has been much talk about the world approaching 'peak oil', but perhaps even more importantly we have actually passed the point of 'peak soil' decades ago. Says Professor David Pimentel of Cornell University: "Soil erosion is second only to population growth as the biggest environmental problem the world faces. Yet, the problem, which is growing ever more critical, is being ignored – because who gets excited about dirt?"[39]

We urgently need international policy measures to restore soils to their previous levels of fertility and water-holding capacity, and to stop the ongoing release of carbon stored in soils, the world's second largest carbon sink and potentially the world's most effective carbon capture and storage option.

The impacts of soil erosion and carbon loss on world food production have been masked to some extent by an ever-greater array of technologies used in farming which have produced higher yields – however unsustainably. But now we need to find ways to sequester much more carbon from the atmosphere by developing bold initiatives on renewing the world's living systems, including life in the soil. It is time to find ways of replacing the one-way linear systems of resource depletion, consumption and pollution that have prevailed in the recent past with circular systems which can replenish nature and assure a sustainable human existence on earth.

It is becoming apparent that the restoration of wastelands, degraded or desertified soils and ecosystems can dramatically enhance soil organic carbon content and soil quality. Such management practices include:

- **organic farming**
- **conservation tillage**
- **application of mulch, manure and compost**
- **use of cover crops**
- **agroforestry practices**
- **improved pasture management**

Farmers need support to alleviate agriculture's contribution to climate change by reducing tillage, increasing organic soil matter, improving grassland management, restoring degraded lands, planting trees and improving animal husbandry systems.[40] These sorts of practices not only enhance soil fertility but also the water storage capacity of soils, and thereby increase the productivity of farmland and grazing land. Restoration of soil organic matter can reverse land degradation, which is urgently needed in many parts of the world. Not only can this help increase food security, but its can also reduce the use of fossil fuels and associated GHG emissions.

The FAO states that soil carbon sequestration can take effect very quickly and is a cost-effective win-win approach which combines mitigation, adaptation, increased resilience and the promise of more reliable and increased crops yields.

"Soil carbon storage was hitherto left out of international negotiations because of envisaged difficulties of validation of amounts and duration/permanency of sequestration. However, in addition to the undisputable multiple benefits of soil carbon storage, soil sampling for verification purposes is less expensive and more accurate than the indirect estimation of carbon stored in living biomass.

The FAO has recently prepared a Global Carbon Gap Map that identifies land areas of high carbon sequestration potential, and is developing local land degradation assessment tools that include a simple field measurement of soil carbon. FAO is also working on tools to measure, monitor and verify soil carbon pools and fluxes of greenhouse gas emissions from agricultural soils, including cropland, degraded land and pastures."[41]

All in all, the potential for soil carbon sequestration is very large indeed and deserves to be incorporated into the post-Kyoto regime. With global population expected to grow to nine billion by 2050, and with increasingly uncertain oil and water supplies, well-thought-out new approaches to securing carbon-rich organic soils can help to secure the food supplies of future generations. We need policies to renew the world's soils in closed-loop, low-input farming systems based on a sustainable relationship between urban food consumers and rural farming communities.

"Millions of farmers around the globe could become agents of change, helping to reduce greenhouse gas emissions.... Agricultural land is able to store and sequester carbon. Farmers that live off the land, particularly in poor countries, should therefore be involved in carbon sequestration to mitigate the impact of climate change," said Alexander Mueller, FAO Assistant Director-General at a recent conference in Bonn.[42]

A potential major additional benefit of measures to support soil quality and carbon sequestration could be to halt or even reverse migration of people from rural areas to the cities. Funding for enhanced soil

Credit: Bruno Glaser. Terra Preta soils are deep and dark and far more fertile than nearby rainforests soils, which contain few nutrients and are not very suitable for agriculture.

carbon sequestration could thus have major environmental as well as economic and social benefits.

SEKEM – An Egyptian Initiative for Sustainable Development

SEKEM is an Egyptian development initiative founded by Dr. Ibrahim Abouleish in the Egyptian desert in 1977 which unites the ecological, social, cultural and economic dimensions of life. Dr. Abouleish, who is a member of the World Future Council, started cultivating desert areas near Cairo using sustainable agricultural practices. In 2009 SEKEM's work extends to 4,500 hectares and directly involves 2,000 people who work for SEKEM in all the different fields. Moreover, around 30,000 people from the surrounding community make use of SEKEM's cultural and social services that are offered by the SEKEM Development Foundation and other related NGOs.

Aware of the great demand for rural development, and of the negative side-effects of industrialized farming on humans and ecosystems, Dr. Abouleish and his collaborators decided to take a different path. Avoiding the use of chemical fertilizers and pesticides, they built up healthy soils by using organic materials. By combining various cultivation techniques, dynamic ecosystems were created in which natural methods are substituted for the input of chemicals and conventional fertilizer. Natural predators are used to fight parasites and sophisticated crop rotation practices sustain soil fertility and minerals. Today, the fruits, herbs and vegetables that are produced are processed into high quality foodstuffs, medicine and cotton textiles which are marketed nationally and internationally by the companies of the SEKEM Group. Each year 10 percent of their earnings are reinvested into the social and cultural activities of the SEKEM Development Foundation (SDF). The SDF runs a

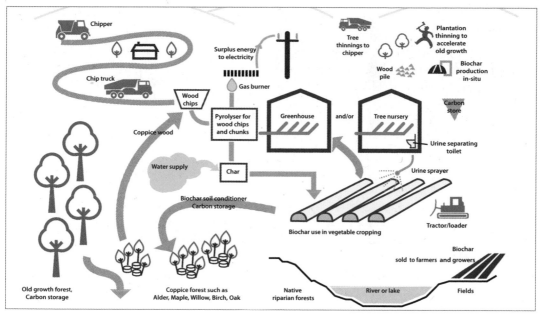

Credit: Rick Lawrence. Bio-char can be produced from many different organic materials.[45]

kindergarten, a school, a medical centre, a vocational training centre, programmes for disadvantaged children and a research academy embracing several research and adult training programmes.

Today, the organic farming methods SEKEM introduced into Egypt have been widely applied across the country. To spread the sustainable agricultural methods and secure raw material for the SEKEM companies, the Egyptian Biodynamic Association (EBDA) was established – a non-governmental, non-profit organization to provide training and consultancy to all farmers in Egypt, enabling them to apply organic and biodynamic agricultural methods and get the necessary certifications. To date EBDA has succeeded in facilitating the conversion of more than 800 farms with over 6,500 hectares to biodynamic farming. Through its research, in 1991 EBDA was the first organization in the world to supervise the cultivation and harvesting of

biodynamic cotton. One direct result was a landmark reduction in the use of synthetic pesticides in Egypt by over 90 percent, from over 35,000 tons per year. At the same time, the average yield of raw cotton was increased by almost 20 percent. Furthermore Libra, SEKEM's cultivation company, promotes and implements sustainable soil management and composting practices, including agricultural GHG emission reduction projects.

The important point here is that SEKEM's agricultural practices are helping to tackle climate change. Firstly they emit less greenhouse gases by avoiding the use of chemical fertilizers and due to lower needs for irrigation. Secondly, the healthy soils built up by the application of organic material store much higher levels of carbon than conventional agricultural soils that are cultivated using chemical fertilizers. Thirdly, SEKEM's farming practices also help farmers to adapt to effects of climate change such as droughts and heavy *rainfall. Today, scientists agree that enhancing the condition of global soils can play a crucial role in keeping atmospheric CO_2 concentration within acceptable limits. SEKEM's work shows that sustainable practices are not only cost-competitive but also address a range of urgent climatic, ecological, economic and social problems.*

The promise of biochar

In addition to measures for enriching farmland and pastures with 'conventional' organic matter, a very significant new option is becoming available under the heading of 'biochar'. This fairly new term is based on ancient farming practices that appear to have been used in the tropics.

In 1542, the Spanish explorer Francisco de Orellana was the first European to travel down the Amazon River near Ecuador. While he never found El Dorado, the city of gold he was looking for, he found densely populated regions along the river. He reported that the jungle area held a sedentary farming population, with many villages and towns, and even large, walled cities. The population levels he saw possibly exceeded even those found in the Amazon region today. Sadly, the arrival of Europeans also introduced new diseases which appear to have wiped out a large part of the Indian population within decades.

Because they used only wood as their construction material, the populations seen by Orellana and his companions did not create lasting monuments that visitors can see today, but they did leave behind dark, fertile soil in many riverside locations. The Amazonians of centuries ago appear to have produced charcoal by burning plant material in pits covered with earth. They then mixed this 'biochar' with organic wastes to create dark, fertile soil. This 'Terra Preta' can still be found across the Amazon basin – some 60 locations with deep rich, dark soil often containing pottery fragments have so far been identified.[43]

Amazonian Indians today still produce charcoal by burning areas of forest to turn them into gardens in a process called slash-burn agriculture. But the ash produced in this way is mainly left on top of the soil and not dug in, and neither is it mixed with organic wastes. The people from the riverside settlements seen by Orellana are long gone, but the dark, deep, fertile soil they cultivated over thousands of years remains.

Terra Preta soils contain far more charcoal than soils found elsewhere in the Amazon. Scientific research has shown that the porous quality of the biochar these soils contain allows them to harbour a vast variety and quantity of soil micro-organisms. The biochar particles can improve soil structure, and enhance the presence of micro-organisms and plant nutrients. Adding biochar to the soil not only enhances fertility and life in the soil, but also helps it to retain moisture – which is very important in an age of climate change.

Research into biochar started in Holland in the 1960s, and there are now hundreds of research programmes into various aspects of biochar across the world. A recent book, *Biochar for Environmental Management: Science and Technology*, edited by Prof. Johannes Lehmann, is a state of the art compilation, covering all aspects of biochar and written by some 50 researchers. Tim Flannery, the eminent Australian naturalist and a member of the World Future Council, states in his foreword: "This book, I believe, provides the basic information required to implement the single most important initiative for humanity's environmental future. The biochar approach provides a uniquely powerful solution: it allows us to address food security, the fuel crisis and the climate problem, and all in an immensely practical manner. Biochar is both an extremely ancient concept and one very new to our thinking. . . . Yet few farmers living today have heard about biochar."[44]

'Modern biochar' is produced by pyrolysis (low-oxygen combustion) of organic materials – forest thinnings, sawdust, agricultural wastes, urban organic wastes or sewage solids – and the resulting charcoal-like substance can be incorporated into farmland as a long-term carbon storage option. Importantly, biochar is also claimed to convert carbon from the atmosphere into stored carbon in soil. Unlike natural decay or the combustion of organic matter, the pyrolysis process releases only a fraction of the carbon content of the source material into the atmosphere.

By 'pyrolysing' one tonne of organic material which contains half a tonne of carbon, about half a tonne of CO_2 can be removed from the atmosphere and stored in the soil, whilst the other half can be used as a carbon-neutral fuel (this equals a quarter of the CO_2 absorbed by a plant during its growth). Biochar has the potential to lock the mineral carbon it contains safely away in the soil for centuries. In addition, the ancillary benefits – not just its soil-improving characteristics, but certain by-products of its manufacture – make it economically attractive as well.

Research has shown that biochar can last hundreds to thousands of years in the soil. It can change soil properties favourably, and help deliver nutrients to plants better than in soil that has not been treated. An ever-growing number of researchers now suggest that biochar-in-soil practices could be a most cost-effective means of reducing carbon in both the atmosphere and oceans.

Professor Johannes Lehmann of Cornell University and others have calculated that biochar applications to soil could remove several billion tonnes of carbon from the atmosphere per year.[46]

A major question that needs an urgent answer is how enough organic matter can be made available to produce significant amounts of biochar. Opponents argue that farming communities in developing countries may be forced to produce fast-growing tree monocultures on precious agricultural land to produce biochar to counter climate change for which they are not even responsible. It is certainly true that, unlike in Amazonia centuries ago, there is not likely to be much spare biomass available to produce the amounts of biochar that may be needed to make a significant difference.

Just how can large quantities of biochar be produced? To find an answer to this question it is worth having a look at the sewage works in Bingen, Germany. Here semi-dried sewage sludge is fed via a conveyor belt into a steel container where it is pyrolysed and turned into black granules: the sewage is turned into charcoal. This can then be buried in farm soil and the carbon it contains can thus be prevented from entering the atmosphere. At the Bingen University of Applied Sciences, Helmut Gerber, the engineer in charge of the project, is convinced of the enormous potential of sewage-derived biochar.[47] There is no doubt that the billions of tonnes of sewage that accumulate in cities every year, if turned into biochar and buried, could greatly benefit the world's soils soil as well as the atmosphere.

The potential of salt water crop irrigation

Another new option of great significance both for carbon storage and the production of food and timber is the use of saltwater-tolerant plants, such as mangroves and salicornia shrubs. Scientists estimate that saltwater-loving plants could open up half a million square miles of previously unusable territory for crops, whilst helping to settle the heated food-versus-fuel debate of recent years. By increasing the world's irrigated acreage by 50 percent, saltwater crops could provide a valuable additional source of biomass.

In a recent issue of *Science* magazine, two plant biologists, citing the work of Robert Glenn, a plant biologist at the University of Arizona, argued that "the increasing demand for agricultural products and the spread of salinity now make this concept worth serious consideration and investment." [48]

Glenn has been arguing for the value of saltwater farming for nearly thirty years, for both food and fuel production. His team estimates that salt-loving crops could be used to produce 1.5 billion barrels of ethanol annually on a swathe of new agricultural land almost five times the size of Texas.

Says Glenn: "I'm convinced that saltwater agriculture is going to open up a whole new expanse of land and water for crop production. Maybe the world hasn't needed a 50 percent expansion in irrigated agricultural land because we've had enough food, but now that biofuels are in the mix, I think it's the way crop production should go."

There is plenty of previously uncultivated land in the world's coastal deserts, and these could play an important role in crop and fuel production. Glenn estimates that 480,000 square miles of unused land around the world could be utilized to grow salt-tolerant plants, or halophytes. While salt damages most plants, these salt-loving plants actually use the saltwater to draw in fresh water. One particular plant, salicornia, produces 1.7 times more oil per acre than sunflowers, a common source of vegetable oil.

Halophytes could also be part of the solution to another environmental problem: heavily-salinated wastewater from large farms. Currently this is dumped into man-made wetlands. For example, in California, the Imperial Valley authorities dump their salty water into the Salton Sea. After absorbing 80 years of agricultural runoff, the Salton Sea is 25 percent saltier than the ocean and is facing serious ecological problems. Instead of pumping salinized water into these wetlands, the farms could capture that wastewater and use it to grow halophytes.

But even if halophytes can help solve some of the world's environmental problems, one has to be realistic about the difficulties of changing agricultural systems. Says Glenn: "I started in aquaculture back in the early 70s and we thought, golly, aquaculture is going to save the world. Looking back, it's been 35 years, but over half of the key fisheries products come from aquaculture, it just took longer than people thought. I think it's the same thing with saline crop production." [49]

In addition to salicornia, it would be possible to replant mangroves in estuaries and marine shorelines where they have been cut down, in areas affected by salinization, or in places that are deliberately flooded with saltwater or brackish water. Mangroves are found in tropical and sub-tropical tidal areas that have a high degree of salinity. There are about 110 species of mangrove, and apart from the benefit of their rapid growth they are also provide habitats for a great variety of living species and act as nurseries for fish and other marine species. Layers of soil and peat which make up the mangrove substrate have a high carbon content of 10 percent or more, and a hectare of mangrove forest can sequester about 1.5 tonnes of carbon per year. [50]

Carbon and the oceans

The oceans absorb about one-third of the CO_2 emitted into the atmosphere from the burning of fossil fuels – mainly through the growth of plankton. However, this valuable ecological service comes at a high price – the acidification of the oceans. When CO_2 dissolves in seawater, it forms carbonic acid and the pH of the water decreases as a result. Since the industrial revolution began, it is estimated that surface ocean pH has dropped by nearly 0.1 units, equating to approximately a 25 percent increase in acidity. This rate of change is a great cause for concern as there is no evidence that the world's oceans have ever acidified so rapidly. By the end of this century, pH could be three times lower and the change could be 100 times faster than that experienced during the transitions from glacial to interglacial periods.[51] The effects of ocean acidification are predicted to put maritime ecosystems at major risk, and there is an emerging scientific consensus that every effort possible must be made to prevent the pH of surface waters from dropping by more than 0.2 units below the pre-industrial value.[52]

The full ecological consequences of ocean acidification are still uncertain, but it appears likely that many calcifying species, such as corals and shellfish, will be affected. This could have adverse effects on climate change, both by reducing the bio-capacity of the oceans and by decreasing the earth's albedo via the effect of their bio-productivity on oceanic cloud cover. Global reductions of carbon emissions, with simultaneous efforts to enhance the earth's bio-sequestration capacity, are clearly urgently called for.

Meanwhile there are other aspects of what is happening to the oceans that have received much less attention from climate researchers. The massive growth of cities along rivers and in coastal regions all over the world has also led to a tremendous increase in the discharge of sewage into coastal waters. This represents a tremendous transfer of both carbon and plant nutrients from rural areas into the sea. All over the world polluted coastal waters cloud sea-bed vegetation, reducing its bio-productivity. At the same time, surplus nutrients produce algal blooms that remove oxygen from the water and further affect its productivity.

According to a new survey by the US National Academy of Sciences, seagrass meadows, an important habitat for marine life, have been in rapid decline due to coastal development and pollution. Up to 70 percent of all marine life is directly dependent on seagrass. From 1940 to 1990, the annual loss of seagrass meadows has accelerated from 1 to 7 percent and there are only 177,000 square kms left globally. The survey indicates that seagrass meadows are as badly affected as coral reefs and tropical rainforests. Says Professor James Fourqurean, professor at Florida International University: "Seagrasses are disappearing because they live in the same kind of environments that attract people ... in bays and around river mouths."

Seagrass meadows are presently under greatest pressure in the Pacific and the Indian Ocean due to rapid coastal development. In other places, such as in Florida, seagrass beds have rebounded due to improvements in the quality of water flowing into the sea and as the result of restoration efforts. Restoration was first undertaken on a large scale in 1973 in Florida's South Biscayne Bay by Prof. Anita Thorhaug of Yale University. Subsequently, seagrasses have been restored on all continental shelves. Much is now known about which species and techniques to utilize.

Says Thorhaug: "An evaluation of marine macro-plant sequestration potential by national and international carbon communities is urgently needed. The order of magnitude of carbon sequestered is potentially as great for marine macro-plant restoration as for forests. Unlike with forests there is little man-made competition for space for restoration."[53]

It seems evident that vigorous efforts to minimize sewage discharges into coastal waters and to enhance their bio-productivity need to be considered as an integral part of any strategy to enhance the bio-sequestration capacity of planet earth. Together with initiatives to reduce the acidification of the oceans, these are matters that need to be addressed urgently.

Credit: Herbert Girardet. This is the sewage plume of Rio de Janeiro. All over the world coastal water are polluted and clouded by sewage effluents. Capturing the nutrients and the carbon they contain is necessary for a sustainable world. Cleaning these sewage plumes is also crucially important for enhancing the productivity (and carbon sequestration capacity) of coastal waters.

Conclusion

In a recent article, NASA climatologist Jim Hansen and others stated that reforestation of degraded land and improved agricultural practices that retain soil carbon, between them, could lower atmospheric CO_2 by as much as 50 ppm.[54] If the carbon sequestration potential of restoring seagrass meadows and other types of aquatic vegetation to enhance the uptake of CO_2 is added, we can reach fairly optimistic conclusions. However, only joint initiatives on

bio-sequestration involving many different groups will ultimately achieve the desired goal of a climate-proof world.

It is a major challenge for the international community to come up with suitable funding mechanisms for level-headed bio-sequestration in all the various forms in a new Kyoto Treaty. Many carbon offset schemes are already available – both commercial and non-commercial. The successor to the Clean Development Mechanism under the Kyoto Agreement, which is intended to transfer funds from developed to developing countries for the benefit of climate protection, must incorporate proposals that benefit both local communities as well as the global human community. By initiating well-thought-out measures to improve the carbon sequestration potential of the biosphere we will also be investing in the sustainability and viability of rural communities in the face of rampant urbanization.

In the 1930s President Roosevelt created the Civilian Conservation Corps to "conserve our natural resources and create future natural wealth". Today an Earth Restoration Corps could be set up for a similar purpose and provide meaningful work for people who want to dedicate themselves to restoring the health of our planet for future generations.

These are the main challenges:

- **Quantifying the annual financial cost of damage to the world's natural environment**
- **Bringing together organizations involved in forest conservation, reforestation, soil restoration, biochar and aquatic ecosystems restoration into a joint international lobby**
- **Assuring that bio-sequestration is given international policy priority in countering climate change**
- **Using funds for bio-sequestration as a tool for reviving rural and coastal communities**

Acknowledgements

Andrew Mitchell *Global Canopy Programme*
Peter Bunyard *The Ecologist Magazine*
Hylton Murray-Philipson *Canopy Capital*
Nicola Wilks *WWF*
Johannes Lehmann *Cornell University*
Craig Sams *Carbon Gold*
Patrick Holden *Soil Association, UK*
Peter Segger *Soil Association, UK*
Helmy Abouleish *Sekem*
Anthony Simon *WFC advisor*
Josep Canadell *Global Carbon Project*
Anitra Thorhaug *Yale University*
Bruno Glaser *Bayreuth University*
Randy Hayes *WFC staff*
Bruno Glaser *Bayreuth University*

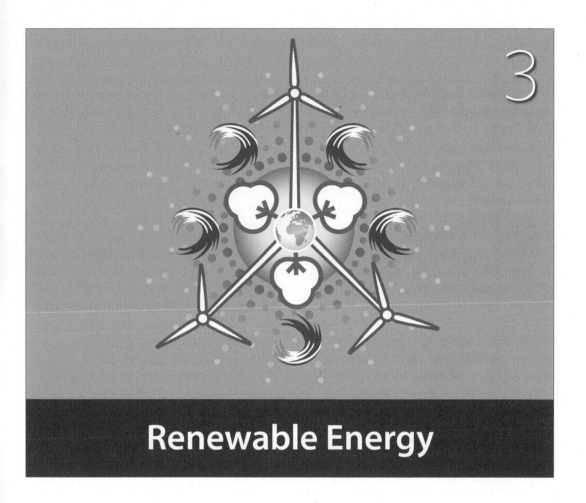

Chapter Three

Renewable Energy

" An invasion of armies can be resisted,
but not an idea whose time has come. "

Victor Hugo

" If there's a new way / I'll be the first in line /
it better work this time. "

Dave Mustaine

Humans are adept at side-stepping the fact of death. We treat it differently from culture to culture, but in the West it is especially suppressed. Like most limitations, we disregard it as much as possible, and even follow damaging and unhealthy pathways, knowing that death can follow. No matter what one's philosophy on an afterlife, the here and now is where the immediate action is, and where our ethics and values should guide our behaviour towards living good lives, taking care of others and considering the impacts we have on ourselves, our fellow living beings and the world in which we live. Does this not sound reasonable?

Consider then, the subject of energy, that which allows us to do work, to move, communicate, eat, drink – to live. Our lives have for 300 years been more or less dependent on long-dead matter we have extracted from its burial site in the earth. Coal, oil and gas have facilitated the most astonishing advances in technology, longevity and standards of living, for a large minority of the world's population. However it has also brought with it a host of all-too-human problems, driven chiefly by greed, selfishness, and a short-termism which we have come to regard as normal. Even though we know that catastrophic climate change becomes more likely every day we burn more fossil fuels, just as we know that terminal disease becomes more likely with every cigarette smoked, we ignore the facts and keep burning. Should we instead, employing every ounce of human ingenuity, cooperation and determination, try to prevent the worst-case scenarios from occurring? Everyone, and especially those with children, needs to think very carefully about what any answer other than "yes" means.

If we choose life, and a moral existence, we will choose an energy path that does not initiate chain reactions of every horror spelled out in a thousand books, reports, documentaries, websites and speeches. This is real, it is already happening, and we have only one chance to prevent the worst of it. It often seems impossible to imagine, yet every credible piece of evidence from the scientific world is gloomier than the one before.

Not only are fossil fuels the problem, but according to the IEA's *World Energy Outlook 2008*, we are likely to see an increase in world primary energy demand of 45 percent between 2006 and 2030. As set out in the Energy Equality chapter, developing countries and emerging economies are in great need of energy. Both need to fuel their growth, and the latter are beginning to converge with formerly dominant world powers, who are now seeing their economies contract.

The only logical and safe option is to channel all possible resources into a new world energy system, based on renewable energies which can provide millions of jobs, new industries and exports, energy security, and protection of the climate and environment. Any policymaker still voting for fossil fuels, and against renewable energy, on the basis of such pros and cons must be asked to give way to someone wiser and more caring. Our chapter on Problem Technologies details the many reasons why a new nuclear programme is not the answer either. The more one researches the subject, the firmer these conclusions become: renewable energy is the only reasonable and logical choice, with a huge variety of benefits; and the switch must be prioritized immediately.

But this is a highly complex matter – renewable energy and its applications are varied, and provide a unique energy endowment for each country. There is no one-size-fits-all approach on technology and policy which can be advocated. Ultimately, it will be up to each nation to determine how best to harness and protect investment in its renewable resources, and to decide how to share them.

There is no doubt that the renewables transition must happen, but those who currently gain most financially from the conventional energy industry will certainly put up a fight – keep in mind that 'turkeys don't vote for Christmas'. However, the multiple benefits of renewable energy are increasingly widely understood, and they are being embraced by a rapidly growing number of nations across the world. Change is coming, and not a moment too soon.

The diagram below gives an idea of the processes of social, industrial and technological development of renewable energy, with electricity generation in mind. There are further potentials for renewable heating and cooling. The examples on the right show the kinds of innovations that are emerging, and an indication of the scope of potential future development.

This gives an idea of the process and benefits of moving towards a renewables-based energy system, and the relationships between technological development, policy support, public buy-in and the expansion of commercial and technological possibilities which arise as the cycle accelerates and expands. The best policy support and potential for public buy-in comes from feed-in tariffs, a policy instrument now implemented in nearly 50 countries and regions across the world. By offering a preferential tariff for producers of renewable energy, as well as investment security, they have led to the most rapid deployment at the lowest costs of any policy.

Where are we now?

The diagram overleaf demonstrates that renewables have one major thing in their favour: rapidly falling costs. Economies of scale and

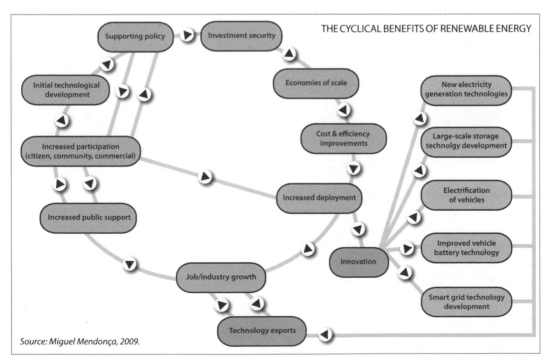

Source: Miguel Mendonça, 2009.

improvements in efficiency and manufacturing processes are enhancing the economics of production for renewables technologies, and incentives such as soft loans and other financing options, grants, and feed-in tariffs are improving the attractiveness of purchasing. Most renewable energy sources are by definition free – there will never be a cost curve for wind or solar 'fuels', only the technologies to exploit them. These technologies process wind, sun, water, geothermal and biomass energy. They are renewable because they cannot be exhausted, whereas finite fossil and nuclear fuels are running lower every day, and have the distinct disadvantage of being subject to volatile and disruptive short-term price shifts. Raw materials for renewables manufacture are a significant and variable cost factor, and securing supply chains for manufacturing is vital. The raw materials themselves are finite, and solar photovoltaic technologies in particular are challenged to innovate and make their products as cost-effective and efficient as possible.

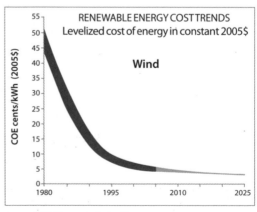

At the time of writing in May 2009, oversupply is driving down photovoltaic (PV) module cost. Planned capacity increases by silicon refiners have helped the price of photovoltaic-grade silicon drop dramatically, which will feed into reduced module prices. While cheaper panels

will be good for the end-user, many smaller companies will struggle with both oversupply and the impact of the recession on less than healthy balance sheets. Currently there are nearly 400 module/cell producers in the PV market, and buyouts by larger firms will be common.

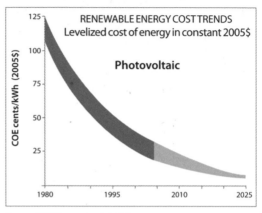

Source: NREL Energy Analysis Office.

In addition to the cost of the PV module itself there are a number of system costs, including wiring, an inverter, installation and structural support costs. Generally this accounts for half the price of a typical system, but this side of the business is far less efficient than the module industry and significant cost reductions could

Source: NREL Energy Analysis Office.

Credit: Nanosolar. Thin film technology is rapidly improving the economics of solar energy.

be expected in the near future. The improved economies of scale that will be presented by this market shake-out will further drive down the costs of solar, and the combination of all these factors could help bring prices down to grid parity in sunny regions comfortably by 2015, provided favourable government incentives continue. A trend report produced in April 2009 by Clean Edge suggests that the outlook is good. Between 2008 and 2018 they expect the following growth (in $US billions): wind from 51.4 to 139.1 and solar from 29.6 to 80.6.[1]

Deployment

Renewables are being deployed in numerous countries in ever-growing quantities. REN21's *Global Status Report: 2009 update* shows that the global generation capacity expanded to 280 GW by the end of 2008, up from 240 GW in 2007 and 75 percent more than in 2004.[2,3] This moves renewable energy closer to supplying a fifth of the world's final energy consumption, if one includes traditional biomass, large hydropower, and 'new' renewables (small hydro, modern biomass, wind, solar, geothermal and biofuels).

SELECTED INDICATORS

	2006	2007	2008
Investment in new renewable capacity (annual)	63	104	120 billion USD
Renewables power capacity (existing, excl. large hydro)	207	240	280 GW
Renewables power capacity (existing, incl. large hydro)	1,020	1,070	1, 140 GW
Wind power capacity (existing)	74	94	121 GW
Grid-connected solar PV capacity (existing)	5.1	7.5	13 GW
Solar PV production (annual)	2.5	3.7	6.9 GW
Solar hot water capacity (existing)	105	126	145 GWth
Ethanol production (annual)	39	50	67 billion litres
Biodiesel production (annual)	6	9	12 billion litres
Countries with policy targets		66	73
States/provinces/countries with feed-in policies		49	63
States/provinces/countries with RPS policies		44	49
States/provinces/countries with biofuel mandates		53	55

Source: REN21, Global Status Report: 2009 update. www.ren21.net

Wind power remains the largest component of renewables generation capacity, with more than 80 countries now deploying commercial wind installations. In 2008, wind power had revenues in excess of $50 billion, a first for renewable energy.[4] Capacity grew 29 percent to 121 GW, having grown by 28 percent in 2007.[5,6]

Credit: Abengoa. Powerful, efficient and cost-effective Concentrating Solar Power (CSP) systems work by concentrating sunlight with mirrors to create heat which may be used to raise steam to drive turbines and generators. Heat may be stored in melted salts or other substances so that that electricity may be generated at night or on cloudy days.

Grid-connected solar PV is the fastest-growing renewable energy sector, with a 70 percent increase in installed capacity in 2008, up to 13 GW.[7] This translates into over 3 million homes and other suppliers feeding solar energy into the grid worldwide. In 1999 global

installations stood at around 125 MW only, which represents a hundred-fold growth over ten years.[8]

Building-integrated PV (BIPV), thin film, solar hot water heating and utility-scale solar installations also grew significantly in 2008. Spanish solar giant Abengoa are, at the time of writing, close to the commissioning of their first molten salt energy storage facility for one of their CSP plants near Seville, and they have another in development in Arizona. This will extend the electricity-generating capacity of these plants through the night, removing one of the major limitations of solar energy.

Credit: Himin Solar Energy. China leads the world in the use of solar hot water systems.

Solar hot water heating systems are installed in around 50 million households worldwide, with capacity increasing 15 percent in 2008 to reach 145 gigawatts-thermal (GWth) globally.[9] In China alone 15 percent of households now have solar hot water systems.

Geothermal heat pumps now number more than 2 million worldwide, and are used in 30 countries for building heating and cooling,[10] producing a total of about 30 GWth.[11]

Production of ethanol grew by over a third in 2008 to 67 billion litres, and biodiesel production increased to 12 billion litres. For a discussion on the issues around biofuels, see Chapter 9.

Investment in renewable energy has been surging, and 2008 was another good year with $120 billion invested worldwide. Approximate figures suggest wind (42 percent), solar PV (32 percent) and biofuels (13 percent) attracted most of these funds, with biomass and geothermal power and heat, solar hot water and small hydro taking up around 6, 6 and 5 percent respectively. Manufacturing capacity has also benefited strongly from capital investment. The US ($24 billion), Germany, China and Spain ($15-19 billion range) and Brazil ($5 billion) were the biggest investors.[12] Renewables growth is also taking place through various means in developing and transition economies, as discussed in Chapter 4.

The economic and financial crises will impact growth in 2009, but as the Green-Collar Jobs chapter discusses in detail, with green technologies being pursued as part of the solution to the recession, as well as energy security and meeting carbon reduction targets, it will be very interesting to see how deployment develops over the next few years. Economic downturns will inevitably see some casualties: for example in 2009 FPL Group, the largest wind power operator in the US, announced within weeks of the first $700 billion bail-out of the US financial system in 2009, that due to the economic downturn it would reduce spending on wind power installations in the coming year by about 25 percent, to $5.3 billion for 1,100 MW.[13] Soon afterwards, in March 2009, the Spanish energy giant Iberdrola announced a cutback of £300 million in UK wind investments, citing poor economic conditions.[14] Vestas, the world's biggest wind manufacturer, cut 1,900 jobs, citing an oversupplied market,[15] and Royal Dutch Shell has dropped all support for renewable energy, choosing to pursue biofuels and CCS, stating that they are closer to its core business.[16]

Policies and targets

Policies and targets for renewables deployment are critical in terms of sending signals to the market and all those who wish to participate in it. The example of Germany shows what happens when the right policy signals are sent out to as many players as possible (see below). Around 73 countries worldwide now have targets for deployment. The United States and Canada do not as yet have national targets, but have many state- and provincial-level targets in place. The European Union has now finalized country-specific targets to be reached by 2020.

Targets do not add up to much unless policies and supporting conditions are established to reach them. The majority of countries that are seeking to rapidly increase their share of renewable energy employ the feed-in tariff (FIT) model. This system has brought about the deployment of more capacity than any other, and at lower cost. The Stern Review on the Economics of Climate Change confirmed this, through reviewing the literature comparing support schemes.[17] Our research has found the same.[18] Lord Stern reiterates the German case as a policy success story in his new book on addressing climate change, *A Blueprint for a Safer Planet*.

Until recently, many English-speaking countries, with a strong bias in favour of market-based mechanisms, had rejected feed-in tariffs on a wild variety of grounds, but mainly because they do not support 'price fixing'. This ideological barrier has begun to crumble under great pressure from various pro-renewables coalitions, with the growing realization that it is empirically the cheapest and fastest way to accelerate deployment, if well designed and implemented.

As noted in the public support section below, Danish and American experience shows that deployment is best facilitated by policies which allow the general public to invest and participate. Local people must have a stake in renewable energy deployment as they see the wind turbines or other installations in their area on a day-to-day basis.

As part of a wider strategy of public engagement it is crucial for citizens and communities to gain direct experience with climate and environment-protecting activities. This leads to awareness-raising and creates popular support for green policies. A more educated populace will also make it harder for governments to do nothing, or to implement badly thought-out measures. FITs offer this engagement in a simple way.

Feed-in tariffs are very straightforward and elegant. As a householder with PV panels you simply have an export meter for the energy you produce. In return for selling this energy to the local utility company, you get a monthly cheque in the post – just as you get a monthly bill for what your import meter says you have used. The right to connect to the grid and get paid is guaranteed in law. There are many different ways and means of designing FITs,[19] and they can be considered more or less 'market-oriented', although all such policies 'interfere' with the market, just as subsidies for conventional energy do.

Renewables policies called 'quota systems' (used in the UK and US, for example) are more suited to large, credit-worthy investors and utilities. They tend to seal off the market to new, smaller players, and are often significantly more costly. This system is fiercely defended by large energy companies and monopolies, partly because they receive high prices for renewable energy through certificate schemes, and they tend to fight feed-in tariffs hard. The same is true in the US with SRECs (Solar Renewable Energy Certificates). Ironically, opponents of feed-in

tariffs tend to accuse them of having the failings of the schemes they support, such as cost, complexity and preventing innovation. Policies should be analysed to see who really benefits from them, to avoid the potential for self-interested monopolies to prevent citizen and community participation in the energy market.[20] The importance of this cannot be overstated.

Good policy design is essential for increasing renewable energy deployment rates, through cost control, enhancement of participation and acceptance, economies of scale and improvement of the technologies themselves.[21] As noted extensively in the Green-Collar Jobs chapter, renewable energy is and will continue to be a key driver of new job creation and economic growth.

The case of Germany

Germany has become a world leader in renewables and renewables policy due to a combination of several key factors, including Chernobyl, green politics and new economic opportunities. The Chernobyl nuclear accident in 1986 highlighted the Green Party's concerns about nuclear power, and eventually a phase-out schedule was agreed for their nuclear power stations – which meant that new energy sources were needed. In the early 1990s, the Social Democrats and the Green Party formed a national government coalition. This helped bring green politics into the mainstream. The world market for renewable energy was wide open at that point. Although Japan had a market lead in photovoltaics, it did not have a plan for large-scale renewables use. The US and the UK had made no firm commitment to progress either, but Denmark was developing significant experience with wind power.

In Germany the first policies to support renewables were small programmes for wind

Credit: Phoenix Solar.
Solar farms are appearing in many parts of Germany due to the policy stimulus of Feed-in Tariffs.

and solar energy in the early 1980s and 1990s, and then came the establishment of the pivotal 1990 Electricity Feed-in Law or Stromeinspeisungsgesetz (StrEg). This crucially allowed people other than the large, traditional generators to sell electricity to the grid. It began as a simple law to help small hydro producers in southern Germany, but then other producers saw the potential benefit and got involved as well. They would receive a rate tied to the market price for electricity, but when Germany began to liberalize the electricity market, prices dropped, and so did the financial returns for renewables, until the law was replaced by the 2000 Renewable Energy Sources Act, or Erneuerbare-Energien-Gesetz (EEG). This was a more sophisticated law, which set fixed tariffs for fixed periods, differentiated by technology, size and location. It also had a digression rate built into the tariffs, which effectively meant that each year they waited to install, producers would receive less money for the electricity they sold.

The law also established a four-year revision process which looked at the state of technological development so that assessments could be made on tariff and degression rates. If prices were coming down as envisioned, or deployment rates needed a boost, tariffs could be adjusted as required. The total costs for renewable energy deployment were spread among all electricity customers in the country to equalize the burden, and an ever-greater number of producers were allowed to participate in the scheme, including municipal companies. The law was adjusted again in 2004, with much improved tariff rates for PV, and again in 2009, with higher rates for wind power. A new flexible degression rate was introduced in 2009 to further respond to price fluctuations in the PV market.

The German renewable energy industry now employs around 280,000 people, and has become a global market leader – selling equipment worth around €8.5 billion in 2007 – and has some of the highest deployment rates in the world. Many companies from around the world have to set up production facilities in Germany due to the stable political framework and the enormous experience and expertise concentrated there. They enjoy active government support and access to a huge domestic market and international distribution networks. Renewables use in Germany saved the emission of around 115 million tonnes of CO_2 in 2008 by displacing fossil fuels, and saved €4.3 billion in energy imports in 2007.[22] Germany now produces over 15 percent of its electricity from renewable energy sources, 7.3 percent of heat consumption, 5.9 percent of total fuel consumption and around 9.6 percent of total energy consumption.[23] All this has been delivered at the cost of a pint of beer – €3.10 – per household per month,[24] but even these costs are expected to fall by 2013. Along with Spain, and formerly Denmark, it is the most commonly cited example of successful renewable energy policy. As of 2008, Spain's employment figure is around 100,000, and they produce 7.5% of primary energy and 20% of electricity from renewables. They have similarly impressive figures on manufacturing, deployment, investment and market leadership.

Public acceptance

The issue of public acceptance has historically applied to wind power more than any other, although increasingly also with regard to CSP. The latter is currently receiving some criticism from environmentalists in the US over the impacts on desert ecosystems and microclimates, and on water requirements,[25] but these issues are certainly surmountable.[26] Large hydro has also been heavily criticized, especially in developing countries. This is addressed briefly in Chapter 4.

As noted above, in a 2009 study on Denmark and the US, public acceptance was shown to be clearly linked to the nature of the investment possibilities. From the 1970s onwards, Danish community wind partnerships became increasingly common, with local people pooling their financial resources to invest in a wind farm. When this model subsequently broke down due to less favourable policies, and was replaced by larger-scale, purely business investments, the public became less willing to entertain nearby wind turbines in which they had no stake.[27]

In Britain, where government policies favour large-scale investment in wind power with little benefit to local people, authorities or economies, onshore wind power has been off to a slow start, and seems to lead the world in NIMBYism. In Maine in the US, the 'Cape Wind' offshore development has been log-jammed due in part to the lack of local investment opportunities. It is likely that if the project had been pursued more along Danish cooperative ownership lines, or at least with real investment opportunities for local people, the passage of the project would have been smoother. This underlines the fact that due to its decentralized nature, and the fact that we must increase our use of it, renewable energy needs to win public hearts and minds. Shutting people out financially is the first wrong step to take.

Support or opposition for wind turbines is fairly staunch – most people are either for them or against them, but neutrals seem to drift more towards support than to opposition once they are installed.[28] The climate change docu-drama *The Age of Stupid* follows the story of a proposed windfarm in the UK, and illustrates the point that most opponents are concerned chiefly with their views of the local landscape, but tend to add specious arguments to reinforce their position. Protesters comment on the noise from the windfarm as the film cuts to Santa Pod Raceway, a nearby racetrack which is evidently one of the noisiest places in Britain. A memorable scene features a victorious anti-windfarm protester being interviewed outside the meeting in which the plans have been rejected. She seems to experience an on-camera logic meltdown as she celebrates the victory over wind while attempting to convey vocal support for renewable energy.

The German Wind Energy Association has produced a paper aimed at countering the various myths which have dogged the industry. These include the low popularity of wind power, dangers to wildlife, annoyance to local people, high subsidies and so on.[29] David MacKay gives some perspective on the argument that wind turbines kill too many birds:

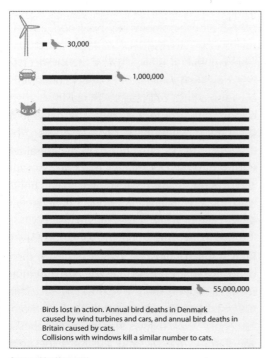

Birds lost in action. Annual bird deaths in Denmark caused by wind turbines and cars, and annual bird deaths in Britain caused by cats.
Collisions with windows kill a similar number to cats.

Source: MacKay, p.64.

Ed Miliband, the British climate and energy secretary, has said that opposing windfarms should be socially taboo – as unacceptable as not wearing a seatbelt.[30] By contrast, the Danish wind pioneer Preben Maegaard has said that wind farms should never be forced on people. As crucial as it is to get deployment accelerated (and he is a life-long advocate), he does not feel that democracy should be sacrificed. As illustrated below, wind turbines are becoming bigger, more powerful and more visible, yet fewer are required to produce the same amount of electricity.

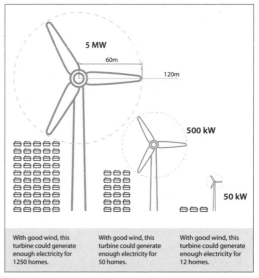

The increase in the size of wind turbines in recent years has been dramatic. Turbines today are typically rated at 1.5 megawatts (MW) capacity, with 6 MW machines in operation at the high end – capable of powering 6,000 households, and 10 MW designs are in development.

Political issues

Renewable energy should be much more advanced than it currently is. Lamentable political decisions, especially in the US and UK in the 1980s under the Reagan and Thatcher governments but still evident today, have picked conventional energy as the winner so far, and they continue to attract large subsidies from national governments. The UNEP report *Reforming Energy Subsidies: Opportunities to Contribute to the Climate Change Agenda*, gives a figure of around $300bn or 0.7 percent of GDP going to such subsidies each year.[31]

Due to politics, and therefore policies, the renewables industry has been generally divided – in some ways mirroring the dispersed and differentiated nature of renewables themselves. The lack of policies which support all viable technologies has created something of a technological battleground, with competing claims and counter-claims on what deserves support. Getting organized and speaking with one voice is going to be essential in future. For illustration, the UK's pro-feed-in tariff coalition has been very well organized, and successful in speaking with one voice and working together for mutual benefit in national policy.

The writings of German MP, renewable energy advocate and World Future Council member Hermann Scheer describe the politics of energy vividly – exploring the nature of the forces that have been, and continue to be, stacked against the use of renewable energy resources. His book *Energy Autonomy* challenges the arguments against the rapid expansion of the renewables industry, and illustrates why it is a much better bet than nuclear. For a look at the cons and pros [sic] of nuclear, see Chapter 9.

The lack of a renewable energy counterweight to the International Atomic Energy Agency (IAEA), and the lack of real support for renewables from the International Energy Agency (IEA) has been a major obstacle to high-level political engagement with, and support for, renewables. In fact, a group of experts from the Energy Watch Group produced a report showing that the IEA publishes 'misleading' data on renewables, and that it has consistently underestimated the amount of electricity generated by wind power in its advice to governments.[32] They say the IEA shows "ignorance and contempt" towards wind energy, while promoting oil, coal and nuclear as "irreplaceable" technologies.[33]

The establishment of the International Renewable Energy Agency (IRENA) in 2009 could help redress this, and ensure that renewable energy gets better representation when governments seek advice on energy strategy. Information provision, knowledge transfer, policy advice and capacity-building should all be part of IRENA's remit, drawing on the enormous wealth of expertise around the world. This crucial new international body could make a rapid and effective contribution to renewables expansion if its remit is not compromised. With only a handful of countries manufacturing renewables technologies at present, IRENA should be able to help many more to supply the growing global market. Although some notable large industrial nations have not joined yet, around 100 countries had already joined as of June 2009.

One must hope that the establishment of IRENA and President Obama's embracing of renewables will help to reshape views and activities on this energy path at the highest levels. Those who have power are generally very good at holding on to it, and those who produce energy are in a very influential position. The unionized jobs and massive sunk investments in conventional energy generation help those with related interests to influence government policies. However, the examples of the nations leading in renewable energy show that one can prise many more benefits from those sources than from conventional generation, and distribute them much more widely. It will be up to the many and varied supporters of renewable energy to work harder and smarter to overcome the political barriers, and keep political processes honest on this subject.

Technical issues

Getting renewable energy over the political, social and financial hurdles is just one part of making the transition. The business of getting this new energy physically generated and distributed is challenging to say the least, especially with a distribution system designed originally for conventional energy. This section looks at these infrastructure issues, and shows how new methods of storage, distribution, management and integration can be combined to create a self-reinforcing renewables revolution, which can cover all our energy needs. To begin the section, renowned energy analyst Walt Patterson provides a clear introduction.

INFRASTRUCTURE AND LOCAL ENERGY
Walt Patterson
What are the main infrastructure issues?

Three major categories of renewable energy application – electricity generation, heating and cooling, and liquid fuels for transport – give rise to infrastructure issues. Renewables technologies that convert ambient energy flows to electricity must be located in the flow – where the sun shines, the wind blows, the water currents run. The scale and distribution of these technologies differs markedly from those of traditional electricity generation. Traditional electricity networks, the 'legacy' networks now in place around the world, are essentially radial and one-way, delivering electricity from large generators in remote locations over long transmission lines operating at high voltages. Renewable electricity generators, however, usually come in units of less than 10MWe output, although they can be grouped, as for instance in wind farms or concentrating solar power arrays. A significant proportion may be located close to loads, generating at modest voltage. Optimum use of renewable generation requires meshed two-way networks that interact with both generators and loads to maintain system stability.

If we were starting from scratch to create an appropriate network for renewable electricity, all the necessary technology, including information and control technology, would already be available to set up autonomous, self-stabilizing networks. In much of the world, however, we rely on the legacy network to keep the lights on. The main issue for renewable electricity is therefore the challenge of driving the evolution of networks to accommodate and take advantage of the distinctive attributes of renewable generation. A corollary issue is the legacy institutional framework, regulation and business relationships, that takes for granted the century-old structure and function of traditional electricity. That too must change.

Renewable heating and cooling is best suited for local applications, in individual buildings or groups of buildings on a single site. Three options are of particular interest. A solar thermal collector can deliver hot water, central heating and – an especially attractive possibility – cooling, by absorption chiller. Biomass, either burnt or gasified, can do likewise. An air-source or ground-source heat pump can multiply severalfold the heating or cooling effect of electricity of whatever origin. All these technologies are best installed when a building or group of buildings is first erected; retrofits are inconvenient and more expensive. The main issues for renewable heating and cooling are the investment costs and the scarcity of suitably skilled fitters.

Liquid fuels from biomass are now intensely controversial, because of land-use impacts of producing ethanol and biodiesel, and of the interaction between fuels and food. If and when so-called 'second generation' biofuels become feasible, using for instance lignocellulose waste as feedstock, other issues will arise. The production and distribution of liquid biofuels will require physical arrangements significantly different from existing oil-based vehicle fuels, and major investment over entire countries, presumably by companies that now supply conventional petrol and diesel. Taxes and subsidies will have a crucial influence on the course of such developments.

What are the prospects for local generation?

The technical prospects are excellent, but the detailed preferences depend critically on the local context – everything from climate to population density. One factor is of overriding importance: you should first upgrade the local premises to optimum performance for thermal stability, natural light and natural air circulation, with fittings and appliances of similarly high performance. If you thus minimize the need for electricity, you can then get a substantial, indeed potentially dominant, proportion of it from local generation.

Depending on the location, local generation options will include gas-fired or biomass-fired microgeneration, microcogeneration and microtrigeneration, with gas engines, microturbines, Stirling engines or fuel cells; solar water heating and preheating; ground- or air-source heat pumps, possibly powered by on-site electricity generation; small wind turbines; microhydro where available; and several types of photovoltaics, especially when they can be integrated into buildings. The investment is usually significant, but may actually be only a modest increment for new buildings. In many cases the enhanced value of the premises, as well as the reduced running cost, will make the investment worthwhile. As such components of the building become mandatory, this will be automatically factored in, and not considered a burden, especially if carbon becomes rationed or priced.

Government financial incentives, direct and indirect, can help, including grants, low-interest loans, tax relief, accelerated depreciation and other instruments affecting investment, and feed-in tariffs, production tax credits and other instruments creating a revenue stream linked to output from local generation.

www.waltpatterson.org

Demand-side management (DSM)

As Walt says, energy efficiency is a vital part of the process, which we examine in Chapter 5. Another key element of trimming energy consumption is managing demand for it. The 'smart grid' approach is full of exciting possibilities in this regard, and the debate on it has been running very hot in Europe and the US in recent years. It is a concept still under development, as there is very little yet built that matches the description, although Boulder, Colorado has initiated one.[34]

'Smart grid' is an aggregate term, encompassing various technologies and properties. Smart grids can:

- **Reduce power consumption at peak hours**
- **Balance loads more effectively**
- **Allow bi-directional energy flows**
- **Incorporate energy storage technologies**
- **Coordinate production from small energy producers**
- **Encourage local/community generation**
- **Operate dynamic pricing**
- **Enable active participation by consumers in demand response**
- **Self-heal from power disturbance events**
- **Optimize assets and operate efficiently**
- **Operate resiliently against physical and cyber attack**

■ **Make the energy system safer and more reliable**

■ **Enable new products, services, and markets**

These properties result from the integrated use of information technology, microprocessors, and communication and monitoring systems. Smart grid technologies can smooth out peaks in consumption and feed electricity through the transmission and distribution systems in the most efficient way; for example, this could include decisions on whether to draw power for domestic lighting from the national grid or a local wind farm, depending on whichever is most efficient at the time. In short, it can respond to the needs and infrastructure possibilities of the 21st century, rather than those of the 19th century, when the conventional energy system was conceived.

'Demand response' is a key feature. It involves the voluntary reduction of electrical 'loads' (consumption) in response to grid instability or peak load. During times of peak demand sufficient electrical loads can be shed to prevent turning on a coal- or natural gas-fired plant and therefore save CO_2 emissions and potentially energy import costs.

Servicing the possibilities of DSM can create numerous opportunities for technological development. Load management devices can dynamically 'control' the switching of customer loads in order to enhance the efficient use of electricity, and have already been realized.

A DSM concept called 'Gridlights' has been developed by the Schumacher Institute in the UK. It actively engages the public in energy consumption decisions by providing them with simple, real-time information on grid demand through a small domestic visual display unit. Grid load is communicated by sending a signal which lights one of four small LED bulbs in the

Gridlights unit – white, green, amber or red (indicating low to high demand). People can then turn off energy consuming devices in response. A financial incentive could be provided by linking the lights to dynamic electricity tariffs.[35] The active consumer of power inevitably becomes more 'energy literate'. Using such an approach in conjunction with feed-in tariffs would create more energy literacy among the population, as well as driving job creation in these crucial modern markets.

The international renewable energy analyst Eric Martinot now provides an overview of the interconnected issues of grids, storage and electric vehicles.

RENEWABLE BENEFITS FROM CO-EVOLUTION OF POWER GRIDS, ENERGY STORAGE & ELECTRIC VEHICLES

Eric Martinot

In the coming decade, the rise of new power grid technologies, energy storage technologies, and electric vehicles will all make renewable energy more competitive and practical at increasing scales. Electric vehicles themselves, both plug-in hybrid and electric-only varieties, may facilitate a coming 'third wave' of renewable energy development, following the initial commercial wave in the 1990s and the recent wave of high-growth years.

There are five types of fundamental change at work:

(1) The emergence of new energy storage technologies that provide new technical opportunities (but may also require our existing institutions, policies and practices to adapt in new ways). Traditionally, our large-scale energy storage options have been very limited, primarily to pumped-hydropower and oil and gasoline tanks. New energy storage technologies are still costly, but prices are expected to decline with economies of scale

and technology improvement. And storage costs can be justified in some cases by the lower cost of renewable energy that results (it also depends on the policy framework). New storage options include:

■ **Grid-smoothing stationary storage such as vanadium redox-flow batteries, high-temperature sodium batteries, compressed air storage, supercapacitors and flywheels.**

■ **Mobile storage in electric vehicles, primarily lithium batteries now under development but possibly including compressed air or hydrogen/fuel cells. Storage needs are less for plug-in hybrids (PHEV) than for electric-only vehicles (EV).**

■ **Thermal heat storage, for building space heating and hot water, and even industrial process heat. This includes emerging development of seasonal storage reservoirs that can store heat during the summer for use in the winter.**

■ **Renewable-embedded storage, such as molten salt reservoirs, batteries, or compressed air systems integrated with solar thermal power plants or wind farms, can allow plants to operate as firm capacity (base load) with higher economic value.**

(2) The evolution of power systems, from centralized to distributed and from dumb to smart. So-called 'smart grids' represent a new paradigm in electric power networks, perhaps akin to the internet and distributed computing revolution that began in the 1990s. In a smart grid, electricity customers can also be micro-generators and/or provide system balancing and stability. Two-way communication and real-time demand and pricing signals can take place between interconnected elements of the power system. Distributed generators using renewables and energy storage, including vehicle batteries connected to the grid, can supply peaking power when the grid needs it most, at premium prices, and then soak up excess power at non-peak times, or just smooth short-term variations in grid supply-demand balance. (This is also known as 'vehicle to grid' or V2G.) Smart-grid operation, especially when combined with energy storage, can make the entire system more efficient, both technically and economically, and also increase the value of renewable energy connected to the system, thus making renewable energy generators more profitable than a conventional power system.

(3) The radical concept that 'load follows supply' on a power grid (i.e. the loads know about the supply situation and adjust themselves as supply changes). This contrasts with the conventional concept of 'supply follows load' that has dominated power systems for the past hundred years. Storage loads represent a variable-demand component of the power system that can adjust itself, automatically within pre-established parameters, according to prevailing supply conditions, for example from variable renewable power. With enough storage on a power system, for example from millions of electric vehicles all connected simultaneously, aggregate system demand can shift significantly in response to variable output from even large installations of renewables, such as centralized wind farms (this may not be intuitive until one realizes that the power output capacity, in equivalent gigawatts, of all existing vehicle engines in the US today is an order of magnitude larger than the power output capacity of the entire US electric power system; and that most vehicles are idle for most of the day.)

(4) The institutional and technical interconnection of the electric power and transport systems, really for the first time in history. Never before have the transport and electric power industries had any significant

common ground or reason to interact – they have been two entirely separate worlds, commercially and institutionally speaking. In the future, there will need to be new forms of interaction and possibly new operational and management structures. Without this integration, renewable energy opportunities can be lost. That is, if the power industry sees electric vehicles as simply another load on the system, and vehicle producers and those responsible for recharging infrastructure see the power system as simply a power plug, without recognition of the unique opportunities for renewables from this interconnection, then renewables can suffer.

(5) The changing institutional and managerial role of power distribution companies. Power distribution companies, whose historical role has been simply to ensure that customers are served with adequate capacity, may be transformed into power managers. Distribution companies will need to balance distributed generation and variable loads and sources, as well as foster end-use energy efficiency, while minimizing and smoothing utilization of bulk generation and transmission facilities. New regulation and business models are likely to be needed to ensure that all this happens efficiently, providing maximum incentives for both renewables and energy efficiency.

Recent analyses have shown significant energy savings and environmental benefits from smart grids and associated changes. And electric vehicles powered from renewable energy will certainly reduce oil consumption and greenhouse-gas emissions from transport. Public policies will need to anticipate and ensure that the economic benefits possible from the fundamental changes discussed here are realized and spread adequately among power producers and consumers, vehicle owners and grid operators, so that all players

have good incentives to make efficient investment and operational decisions. And public policies also need to recognize that institutional inertia and barriers may otherwise short-change the role of renewables in the rush to develop smart grids and electric vehicles.

www.martinot.info

To explore the storage issue further, Lynda O'Malley discusses the key area of financing renewable energy storage approaches.

FINANCING RENEWABLES STORAGE
Lynda O'Malley

Storage technologies present multiple benefits to grid administrators that improve the business case for storage systems, making it essential for storage system owners to be compensated properly for these benefits. These include the increased quantity and quality of renewable power entering the grid, frequency regulation (to protect equipment) and avoided power outages (with consequently avoided revenue losses).

These technologies also increase the capacity factor of a renewable energy system (the percentage of time the unit can deliver power), and therefore the revenues. They also lower the cost of grid connection, and can offset the need to upgrade the grid (reinforcements and extensions) and associated building and maintenance costs. In addition, storage can reduce grid losses and congestion, help provide higher revenue for off-peak renewable power, and lower time-of-use charges for customers.

There are a number of ways to finance storage systems that 'firm up' or improve quality and quantity of renewable power:

■ **Paying a higher rate or tariff for renewable systems connected with a storage system, either as a reward for dispatchability – the ability to provide power upon demand –**

and/or for guaranteeing supply at peak times

- *Paying a tariff for stand-alone storage options to pay for services to the whole system*
- *Allowing renewables to participate in day-ahead markets and be able to guarantee a specified amount of power*
- *Selling cheap off-peak renewable power at higher rates during peak times (termed energy 'arbitrage')*
- *Paying a price for carbon, where energy storage system owners would be paid for the carbon that is offset due to the elimination of, or reduction in, the need for back-up generators*

Daily, hourly, moment-to-moment, and seasonal storage options are available, and timescale differs depending on the technology in question. In considering a storage device, the desired services, timescale and energy versus power need to be considered, as well as how frequently or how full a 'draw down' on the device would be expected in the grid under consideration. For example, batteries which are being constantly topped up without running down will have a shorter life. In addition, climate and opportunity costs must be considered.

For power quality, technologies that operate on a smaller timescale are required, such as flywheels and supercapacitors. Power quality requires frequent moment-to-moment charges and discharges of varying power. Batteries are better suited to daily or periodic uses, such as alleviating grid congestion, in energy management and for frequency regulation. These three uses are also suited to the larger-scale technologies such as compressed air energy storage (CAES) and pumped hydro storage (PHS), as well as hydrogen technologies. CAES and PHS are particularly

well suited to energy management and energy arbitrage.

Investment costs remain high and must come down to enable storage technologies to be deployed on the scale necessary to reduce our carbon footprint. As the technologies advance, and experience and economies of scale increase, costs will continue to fall. In order to make a return on investment, as many services as possible need to be financially rewarded for the storage system owner. Profitability is directly connected to the selected use of the storage system, and the services the system can provide, which is in turn related to the use of full load hours in operation – in essence, the full life-cycle of the storage system.

The picture that emerges here shows new ways of thinking about and 'doing' energy. This is taken even further by the concept of the 'supergrid', another hot topic in current energy debates. In the final section, we look at concepts for covering all our needs with renewables.

Energy subsidiarity and supergrids

The discussions concerning the future of energy have reached a very interesting stage. The loudest voices tend to belong to those who support either centralized or decentralized solutions. The reasons are sometimes ideological, often financial, but all sides consider their advocacy to be based on practicality and a long-term view.

A concept that may be most useful in trying to clarify the relationships between local, national and international is that of 'energy subsidiarity'. As with subsidiarity in decision-making – bringing the process down to the lowest and most appropriate level – with energy this approach can mean, in short, sourcing as much renewable energy as possible

Credit: Marine Current Turbines.
Marine current turbines add another option for water bodies to generate electricity.

locally. This would mean measuring the renewable energy potential of an area, using appropriate technologies, and then looking at how this can be supplied given the various demand-side options, as well as addressing the 'energy sufficiency' question (see Chapter 5).

Human settlements range from small villages to megacities. As these settlements grow, they become ever more challenging to power. To generalize, a village will have more countryside to exploit, in terms of land for biomass production, or land and water for RE production and storage installations. Overall energy use will be relatively low. Megacities, on the other hand, have already swallowed up huge areas of land, and are supplied with resources from distant areas and often from distant nations. Large cities have many rooftop and façade options, but building ever higher, even with retrofitted efficiency measures, means more people using more power on a limited area of land. See Chapter 6 for more on cities and energy, and a look at some examples of where particular places have opted for a path towards power from 100 percent renewables.

It certainly seems possible to meet much of the demand for electricity, heating, cooling and transport by employing domestic renewable supplies, efficiency and demand management solutions. However, a variety of proposals for large-scale and interconnected systems have recently emerged, including options for international linkages of energy production and distribution. Britain already imports around 5 percent of its electricity from France via high voltage direct current (HVDC) cables. These cables can transmit energy more efficiently over long distances than traditional AC transmission lines.

Some energy planners in Europe are now looking at interconnecting renewables installations from across the continent, with the possible addition of solar and wind installations in North Africa; and in the US there is a debate about constructing such a network to distribute wind and solar power from high resource locations to the rest of the country. The idea is that large catchment areas and specialization in each region's best suited technology would compensate for variability of output, and allow renewable energy production to be efficiently transferred to any part of the network. A European supergrid would also use various kinds of storage for backup and grid balancing: Denmark, for example – a major wind energy producer – already has an agreement with Norway allowing it to 'bank' surplus wind-generated electricity in hydroelectric dams and then ship it back across the Skagerrak with a 250km HVDC line as demand increases.

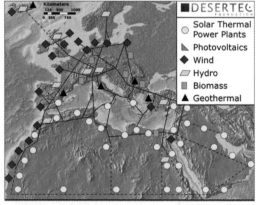

Source: Desertec Foundation.
The concept of a Supergrid, connecting Europe with North Africa and the Middle East, is being actively, and at times controversially, pursued by various interests.

With the European Directive on the promotion of the use of energy from renewable sources adopted in April 2009, various stakeholders in the EU arena have turned their attention to the further development of supergrid concepts. Whereas the basic characteristics of a supergrid idea remain the same, proposals from stakeholders such as Mainstream Renewable Power, the e-Parliament and Dr. Gregor Czisch vary in size, geographical scope and emphasis

on different types of RE integration. The European Climate Forum extended the supergrid idea to the SuperSmartGrid concept, which combines Supergrid and Smart Grid technologies into a single package. However, for implementation of a supergrid, many questions regarding legislative, political, financial and technical prerequisites still need to be addressed.

Plans for a supergrid are certainly feasible, and offer the potential for a transition to energy systems dominated by renewable energy. Supporters point to the need for a swift move away from fossil fuels, and huge opportunities for a rapidly expanded market in renewables and associated technologies. However, the idea is not without criticism, particularly from those who believe decentralization to be the optimum approach. Hermann Scheer sets out the case against:

> There are a number of technical and economic problems that stand against the super-grid concept – in addition to the even stronger political problems. These problems tend to be underestimated. It is correct that sun intensity is 2.7 times higher per square metre in the Sahara than in Europe. But that does not mean that 2.7 times more electricity could be produced in this region. The crucial point when looking at costs is not the relation between sun intensity and electricity production but between actual investment activity and power output. This relationship looks less favourable – installations and maintenance costs in the Saharan region are clearly more expensive. To this you must add recurring problems caused by sand dust and sandstorms.
>
> The structural problem is even more under-rated and is strongly related to the monopoly that results from the provision of solar power from the super-grid. No monopolist in the world's economic history asks only for prices

that cover production costs as long as he can dictate those prices. That is why analyses that aim at demonstrating the cost efficiency of the Sahara project are theoretical calculations that ignore socio-economic facts.

The countries in which these installations are located do not gain adequately from them. They need decentralized energy production and supply even more urgently than we do because their grid infrastructure is less developed than ours. The example of oil companies in the oil exporting countries can act as a warning example for the fact that those mega-investments hardly ever reach local populations – instead they often reinforce local disparities.

The socio-economic benefits of decentralized energy production and supply cannot be reaped with the super-grid. A simple comparison with much lauded offshore wind acts as a good example. Only until recently, offshore wind was being praised as a cost-effective means to produce wind power because the wind allegedly blows stronger and more constantly on the open sea than on land. But since investment expenses (for example submarine cables) and additional costs (caused for example by corrosion and maintenance costs) are considerably higher than with onshore, those that are experienced in this field know that onshore will always be cheaper.

Since we are aiming at a fast transition towards renewable energy, decentralized power production is the only option: its installation can happen considerably more quickly. It is not by coincidence that the number of power companies that prefer a super-grid solution to the feed-in-tariff concept which at its heart is a decentralized one, grows stronger every minute. They recognize it as a convenient way to circumvent the decentralization of the global power structures and to thus perpetuate

their monopolies. In doing so, they ignore all of the above-mentioned arguments. Solar power stations in the Sahara could make sense when supplying north-African capitals like Cairo, Tunis, Algiers and Marrakech with power. But the super-grid is no project for the transition to a renewable energy future for everybody.'

Gerry Wolff, Co-ordinator of DESERTEC UK, responds:

There is no evidence that "installations and maintenance costs in the Saharan region are ... more expensive". Land is much cheaper than in Europe and labour costs are likely to be lower. And sunshine is much more intense than in Europe. The TRANS-CSP report from the German Aerospace Centre (DLR) has calculated that CSP imports are likely to be one of the cheapest sources of electricity in Europe, including the cost of transmission. CSP plants have been operating successfully for more than 20 years in the Mojave Desert in California without significant problems from sandstorms or dust storms.

There is not a shred of evidence to support the idea that the provision of solar power via the supergrid will lead to some kind of monopoly. The supergrid is needed for the single market in electricity that is being promoted by the European Commission, to create competition amongst suppliers. The solar potential of North Africa and the Middle East is so large that there will be a buyer's market for solar power. And the variety of countries that have solar resources is much larger than with gas or oil. It would be extremely difficult to create any kind of solar cartel. Even if one was created, it is likely that it would be self-defeating because, unlike oil, solar power cannot be stored for long periods. If it is not used, it is simply wasted, with a corresponding loss of earnings.

There is no evidence that countries with CSP installations would not benefit from them. It obviously makes sense for solar electricity in desert regions to be supplied to people living nearby. And, since waste heat from CSP plants may be used for the desalination of water, local people can benefit from supplies of fresh water, something that is likely to be particularly welcome in arid regions. The shaded areas under the solar collectors have many potential uses, including the possibility of growing green plants, protected from the glare of direct tropical sunlight, and using fresh water from the desalination of sea water.

Even without CSP, it makes good sense to connect renewable sources together via the supergrid, and that includes 'decentralized' sources such as PV. If, for example, the sun is shining strongly in Germany, producing more PV power than local people can use, that excess power is simply wasted unless it can be transmitted to where it is needed. Conversely, if there is a peak in demand for electricity in Germany, it is useful if the shortfall can be met by hydropower from Norway or wind power from Scotland. In general, the supergrid helps to balance variable demands with variable supplies, ironing out peaks and troughs. The wind may be variable in any one spot but it is much less variable across a large area like Europe or, even better, Europe with the Middle East and North Africa.

The arguments against the supergrid are suggesting that the same monopolistic structures which hold back innovation in energy systems would be replicated here, and keep citizens and communities out of the process. However, there may be ways of guarding against monopolization, or countering other problems as argued above, but there is a long way to go to gain that kind of agreement,

and demonstrate the likelihood of an ethical, equitable, participatory supergrid. The matter of deploying renewable energy in developing countries and emerging economies is addressed in Chapter 4.

We will conclude with a discussion of some of the main issues around moving to a renewables-based energy system.

100% renewable energy supply

One of the key questions for the renewables community to answer, and one being asked very publicly by Al Gore's 'RePower America' campaign for example, is whether or not the world's energy needs can be met entirely from renewable energy. This is an inspiring vision – a future in which anyone, anywhere who switches on a light or drives a car is no longer inescapably complicit in warming the planet. No-one need watch the wholesale prices of fuels soaring and diving, or number-crunch what it will cost, in dollars and lives, to embark on an international conflict to secure energy supplies; no nuclear plants being studied by terrorists; air pollution levels dropping in every town and city; production costs staying lower, and future generations not being stranded with nuclear and coal plants which they cannot afford to fuel, decommission or store the waste from.

However, the picture is still far from clear. The 2009 book by Professor David MacKay *Sustainable Energy – without the hot air*, which analyses the production and consumption quantities involved in the UK energy system, suggests that although there are many options, in the end it comes down to priorities.[36] We can take this to mean: Who can influence government the most? Who can win the support of the public? Who has the organization, the funds and the strategies to prevail? Aside from the politics, what would be necessary for such a switch to renewables for not only electricity, but also transport, and heating and cooling? MacKay shows that many mixtures of technologies could power the UK in differing proportions (based on a variety of assumptions and preferences), but also highlights the challenges with public support for a mass expansion of renewable energy.

The potential for 100% renewables supply is evidently a highly politicized issue. But what are the conclusions of those crunching the numbers? The answers differ, depending on their methodology, what assumptions they used and when they produced the research – the number of variables is enormous. Energy is a highly complex, contested, dynamic field. A number of recent studies have attempted to answer the question,[37] but no precise consensus exists as to how much energy renewables can supply by a particular date in the future. It is complicated by the other emergent debates described above. For example, the fact that transport fuel replacement is still up for grabs – hydrogen, electricity or biofuels – means that we cannot calculate what energy needs may be required, as we don't know how many people will use what kind of fuel, at what consumption rate. Demand management is still a nascent approach, and we may see more or less application of it in the future. Energy-efficiency technologies and policies, global carbon agreements, carbon pricing, supergrids, not to mention nuclear and CCS – these and other possibilities, with their vociferous supporters and opponents, create a major headache for policymakers. How does one take a decision in the face of such complexity, and when so many vested interests are vying for control and profits?

The decisions that need to be taken on establishing renewables-based energy systems in every nation are not ones usually set out by international agreement. We live in a world shaped by vested interests, that will espouse any ideology which maintains or furthers their interests. To bring together disparate groups – commercial interests – for such an undertaking could be considered almost unprecedented in peacetime. But there is a great deal of global activity on renewables, and it is feasible to provide baseload and peak power requirements through a combination of diverse renewables production, energy efficiency, smart grids, storage, electric vehicles, demand management, time-of-use charges – in other words smart generation and smart use. How we make this happen fastest is up to policymakers and those who wish to influence them.

If we maintain our present approach to decision-making, however, the winners and losers may not always be what is best for the world at large, but a factor of public and political influence, of strategy, of making a convincing case and pushing it all the way. It is critical that in making the decisions, transparency, participation and a long-term, equitable view are central factors of the process. This approach can help construct an energy system with clear, equitable benefits for present and future generations, and demonstrate the overwhelming logic that acquiring the essential short- and long-term benefits of renewable energy for all must win out over short-term gains for private interests. Lord Nicholas Stern's advocacy of a "new internationalism" in addressing climate and energy issues must be based on energetic cooperation towards rapidly increased renewable energy capacity-building and use around the world. We have seen in this chapter that enough proven and emerging technical and policy options exist for us to make this vital energy switch, but as ever we must overcome vested interests in order to get where we need to go in time.

Renewable energy must underpin human existence in the 21st century. For maximum deployment, RE requires:

- Stable, transparent, participatory and long-term decision-making processes and policies, which allow anyone to produce renewable energy and sell it to the grid
- Well designed and implemented feed-in tariffs, with complementary measures such as streamlined planning procedures and adequate transmission lines
- Political commitment at local and national levels, and the removal of all barriers to deployment
- Policies ensuring public support and involvement

Acknowledgements

Walt Patterson *Chatham House*
Eric Martinot
Institute for Sustainable Energy Policy
Daphne Kourkounaki *The Schumacher Centre*
Lynda O'Malley *York University*
Gerry Wolff *DESERTEC UK*
Godfrey Boyle *Open University*
Peter Droege *Hochschule Liechtenstein*
Stefan Gsänger *World Wind Energy Association*
Frede Hvelplund *Aalborg University*
Stephen Lacey *Renewable Energy World.com*
David MacKay *Cambridge University*
Volker Oschmann *German Federal Environment Ministry (BMU)*
Dirk Hendricks *WFC staff*
Brook Riley *WFC staff*
Hugo Lucas Porta *Spanish Institute for the Diversification and Saving of Energy*
Lily Riahi *York University*
Martin Roscheisen *Nanosolar*
Janet Sawin *REN21* and *Worldwatch Institute*
Hermann Scheer *German Bundestag* and *WFC councillor*
Michael van Mark *German Federal Environment Ministry (BMU)*
Silvia Vazquez *Abengoa Solar*
Catherine Waugh *Pelamis Wave Power*
Undine Ziller *German Renewable Energy Agency*
Tony Colman *WFC councillor*

Pelamis Wave Power.

Wave power can provide a steady and predictable source of energy. The global potential is huge, with some estimates of up to 80,000 TWh/y – similar to world electricity consumption. In the 1970s research was conducted in countries such as the UK and US, until conservative governments in the 1980s switched the energy focus back to fossil and nuclear fuels. Today, sea trials are again taking place in these countries, and Portugal has been very active in the area. The units could feasibly be combined with desalination technology, and cabling could be combined with that from offshore wind turbines.

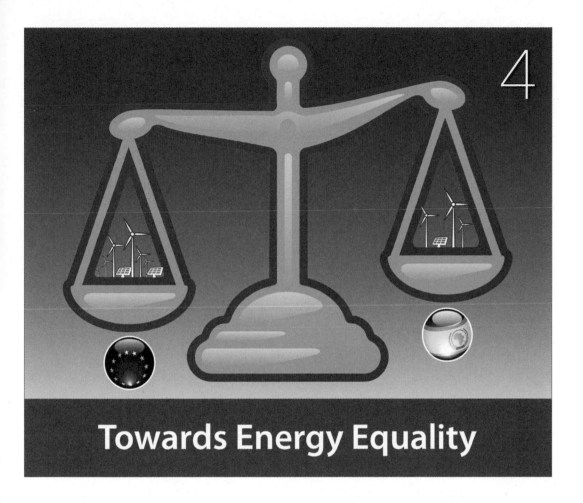

Chapter Four

Towards Energy Equality

" Although there is no specific Millennium Development Goal relating to energy, it will be impossible to achieve the MDGs without improving access to, as well as the quality and quantity of, energy services in the developing world. "

Shoji Nishimoto, Bureau for Development Policy, UNDP

" Inequality is a fact. Equality is a value. "

Mason Cooley

What does energy equality mean?

Ever since the Rio Earth Summit in 1992 sustainable development has been the core concept for creating a world that people can enjoy today and that assures sustainable livelihoods for future generations. But the reality is that there has been much talk and little action. A major reason for this is that development requires energy resources, but thus far, developing countries have predominantly been locked into fossil-fuel use, and hence energy dependency, economic risk and unsustainable development.

Renewable energy, therefore, is the most plausible energy source for underpinning sustainable economic development. Some countries are now pursuing this path. The President of the Maldives announced in March 2009 that they aim to become the first nation in the world to become carbon neutral. They say that the capital cost of powering themselves with renewable energy would be equivalent to the amount they would otherwise pay to import fossil fuels for a period of ten to twenty years.[1] As a low-lying nation of islands, they would be among the first to have to give up their home if sea levels rise as predicted. This is the kind of threat which concentrates minds very effectively.

Some 1.6 billion of the world's 6.7 billion people – more than one in four – currently live without access to electricity. Some 2.4 billion people – eight times the population of the United States – rely on fuels like dried dung, firewood, charcoal and crop residues to cook their daily meals. The daily gathering and use of these fuels leads to many problems including deforestation, risk of fires, lost education time for women and children in particular, and the threat of rape and murder for women, especially in refugee camps. As this process continues, less fuel means less food, so fuelwood gathering

ends up taking as much as seven hours a day, with people walking up to 20km to collect it. In addition, the World Health Organization (WHO) estimates that 1.6 million women and children die prematurely through breathing in wood smoke in poorly ventilated homes each year. This has been equated to smoking ten packets of cigarettes a day.

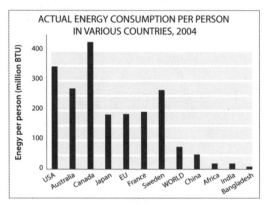

Source: US Energy Information Administration.

The extreme inequalities in energy use between rich and poor countries are well documented (see charts). Energy use and development are close relatives, are they not? A more correct statement would be that energy use and economic growth are close relatives because, as we know from the work of US ecological economist Hermann Daly, development for the benefit of all is what we should strive for, whereas economic growth often benefits only a minority of a country's population. The material comforts and economic potential of the developed world have become the aspiration of the developing world. Therefore, providing access to renewable energy as a prerequisite for development is critically important. This strategy can avoid fossil-fuel dependency and CO_2 emissions, and the 'resource curse' which countries such as Nigeria suffer. National oil wealth has not enriched the vast majority of citizens, and the country has been the subject of major health and environmental problems related to the industry.

Energy equality must mean that a new balance is found between the energy consumption patterns of countries across the world, and that those needs are supplied with sustainable, environmentally safe renewable energy.

The InterAcademy Council, representing 18 academies of science, in a 2008 report called *Lighting the Way: Towards a Sustainable Energy Future*, summarizes the issues:

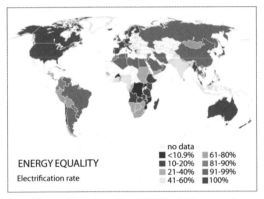

ENERGY EQUALITY
Electrification rate

no data
■ <10.9% ■ 61-80%
■ 10-20% ■ 81-90%
■ 21-40% ■ 91-99%
■ 41-60% ■ 100%

Source: Human Development Report 2007/8 UNDP. www.undp.org

Aggressive changes in policy are . . . needed to accelerate the deployment of superior technologies . . . With a combination of such policies at the local, national and international level, it should be possible – both technically and economically – to elevate the living conditions of most of humanity, while simultaneously addressing the risks posed by climate change and other forms of energy-related environmental degradation and reducing the geopolitical tensions and economic vulnerabilities generated by existing patterns of dependence on predominantly fossil-fuel resources.[2]

RENEWABLE ENERGY FOR RURAL DEVELOPMENT
Guido Glania, Alliance for Rural Electrification
Providing modern energy services to people in developing countries will be essential for the achievement of the Millennium Development Goals (MDGs). As this whole chapter shows, and the Grameen Bank exemplifies (see below), energy needs and development go hand in hand. A sustainable energy supply is a vital precondition for sustainable development. Cities are becoming the dominant living arrangement for humans, with, for the first time, over half the world's population now living in them. However, developing countries still have a great proportion of their citizens living in rural areas, and requiring energy.

The traditional focus in developing countries, as in the developed world, has been on centralized grids and power generation. Efforts to provide energy to rural areas have also maintained focus on grid expansion, even where decentralized systems are more suitable. Overall success in increasing access in rural areas has varied significantly between countries. Some innovative approaches that have utilized the private sector have been very successful in Latin American countries such as Chile and Argentina. But in sub-Saharan Africa in particular (with the exception of South Africa and Ghana), what progress has been achieved has been slow, and access rates remain critically low – 8 percent in rural areas.

Isolated systems based on renewable technologies are an appropriate and cost-effective choice for electrification, given the limited energy requirements of the rural population and the high per-household costs of grid-extension. Distributed generation also allows rural areas more energy autonomy and security in countries where power failures and load shedding are common. Isolated systems based on renewable or hybrid resources also avoid or decrease risks associated with fuel delivery and international price fluctuations.

Uptake of off-grid solar home systems (SHSs) has been embraced in rural areas of some parts of the world, with an estimated 1.9 million

Credit: IT Power. Rural school with PV system.

systems installed globally as of 2004. Particularly high uptake has been achieved in China, India, Mexico, South Africa, Kenya and Morocco, where the private sector has played a significant role. These systems can provide rural households with basic energy needs such as running lights, televisions and radios for a few hours each day. The development of mini-grid systems based on hybrid resources represents a further opportunity for rural communities to gain a reliable source of energy that can kick-start real economic progress.

Typical hybrid systems combine two or more energy technologies. These can be renewable, such as photovoltaic panels, wind or small hydro turbines, or can combine a renewable resource with a form of conventional energy such as diesel/LPG or biomass gensets as system backups. Hybrid systems have low fuel consumption and a high rate of efficiency within mini-grids. With a power range between one and several hundred kW they offer villages the opportunity to embark on economic activities that require a stable and reliable energy source. Major emerging productive uses of renewable energy have been for agriculture,

small industry and commercial services, as well as social services like drinking water, education and health care. Due to their efficiency, hybrid systems can also be integrated effectively into the national or regional grid when appropriate. More than 10,000 hybrid systems and 70,000 mini-grid systems utilizing mini-hydro technology have been set up in developing countries. China has been particularly successful with mini-grid systems, installing some 60,000. Some of these have been implemented by rural entrepreneurs through acquiring credit from agricultural banks, representing a promising course for project development where credit schemes can be mobilized.

Decentralized systems that make use of indigenous renewable supplies can be a competitive and even least-cost electrification option, depending on indigenous conditions. Recent reports point to the national benefits of exploiting such resources locally, producing a diversity of supply and avoiding the risks associated with international fuel prices and constructing very large power plants. By mapping out a strategy for which areas will be grid-electrified and which are better served by isolated grids, policy-makers can also give confidence to investors interested in mini-grids and electrification of remote areas. Thus remote areas that are traditionally viewed as only a future target for the grid, can be perceived as valuable consumers for companies, and electrification can proceed on a multi-dimensional pathway.

Access to energy is a key precondition for improving rural living conditions. Unfortunately in many countries, most pronounced in sub-Saharan Africa, there are insufficient efforts to advance rural electrification. This cannot be justified, since efficient, environmentally friendly and economical solutions are at hand. Renewable energy technology has made enormous progress in terms of efficiency and reliability in recent years. But we have more than technology. The vast project experience of the last decades has taught us how to put in place systems which really work in the long run. We know that the local community must fully embrace the new power supply system and assume responsibility. We know the crucial importance of trained local technicians and consumers, repairing parts, and appropriate 'financial engineering' to keep the system running. One solid financial solution is a combination of tariffs paid by consumers and additional funds guaranteed by state actors (or the development community). Hence, we have the technology and the experience on how to advance rural electrification with renewable energy in a sustainable way. So why don't we see electrification rates soaring everywhere in the world? What we still miss is the necessary political momentum to make it happen. Rural electrification should enjoy higher priority on the development agenda. The developed world can do a lot to facilitate this change.

www.ruralelec.org

Technologies for developing countries

As Guido has discussed above, there are many technologies available to developing countries which go from small to large scale, and cover cooking, lighting,

heating, process heat (heat used in industrial processes) and motive power. Over 25 million households use biogas for cooking and lighting (displacing kerosene and other cooking fuels), more than 3 million have solar PV for lighting, and an increasing number of small industries such as agricultural processors use small-scale biodigesters. As of 2007, developing countries accounted for over 40 percent of existing renewable power capacity, over 70 percent of solar hot water systems, and 45 percent of biofuels production.[3] The table below shows how renewables can displace conventional fuels in a variety of applications.

We now look at examples of technologies designed with developing country needs in mind.

As food is a basic requirement for human existence, and given all of the above issues with collecting and using fuelwood, it is no wonder that many different designs for efficient cooking

ENERGY SERVICES	RENEWABLE ENERGY APPLICATIONS	CONVENTIONAL FUELS
Cooking (homes, commercial stoves and ovens)	Biomass direct combustion (fuel wood, crop wastes, forest wastes, dung, charcoal and other forms) Biogas from household-scale digester Solar cookers	LPG, kerosene
Lighting and other small electric needs (homes, schools, street lighting, telecoms, hand tools, vaccine storage)	Hydropower (pico-scale, micro-scale, small-scale) Biogas from household-scale digester Small-scale biomass gasifier with gas engine Village-scale mini grids and solar/wind hybrid systems Solar home systems	Candles, kerosene, batteries, central battery recharging, diesel generators
Process motive power (small industry)	Small hydro with electric motor Biomass power generation and electric motor Biomass gasification with gas engine	Diesel engines and generators
Water pumping (agriculture and drinking)	Mechanical wind pumps Solar PV pumps	Diesel pumps
Heating and cooling (crop drying and other agricultural processing, hot water)	Biomass direct combustion Biogas from small and medium-scale digesters Solar crop dryers Solar water heaters Ice-making for food preservation	LPG, kerosene, diesel generators

Source: REN21, 2007

stoves have been produced around the world. In the UK the Ashden Awards for Sustainable Development have a case study database of award-winning examples of designs and projects. Most winners are producing cleaner, more fuel-efficient or alternative fuel designs. There is often an entrepreneurial aspect to the projects.

COOKING STOVES

Jane Howarth

There are many designs of improved stove, because people prefer existing cooking practices. Three generic types of improved stove can be identified. In Latin America people cook standing up, so the Lorena style or block stove was developed. In India, people squat, so the chula style is preferred. In Africa, many people cook outside, so use the jiko or bucket stove style.

The basic components of a stove are: (i) the combustion chamber, where wood or charcoal is burnt with air; (ii) a heat transfer area, where the hot gases heat the cooking pots; and (iii) often a chimney, which removes the combustion gases to the outside of the cooking area.

The Lorena stove and other subsequent improvements (such as 'Rocket' stoves) are made of a solid block of material, with chambers made into it so the cooking pots and/or the hotplate are at waist height. The hotplate, or 'plancha', is used to make tortillas. The chula is similar, but the cooking level is below knee height. Although chapattis are made in a similar way to tortillas, a chula seldom has a built-in hotplate.

Traditionally, jikos used charcoal, but some burn wood as well. The stove is portable, so does not have a chimney. The combustion chamber has a pot support, so the pot can be placed directly above the combustion gases. In Asia, similar stoves are called 'bucket' stoves. Indoor smoke pollution can be reduced with a hood connected to a chimney.

Credit: Herbert Girardet. Another approach is the solar cooker.

The basic improved stoves simply have a surround to reduce heat loss and the effect of wind. A grate or some other way of getting air to burn the fuel is a second improvement. The next step separates the combustion process from heat transfer to the cooking pots. The 'Rocket' stove concept uses a vertical combustion chamber, where the wood burns in air, with a horizontal air and fuel inlet at the bottom. At the top of the combustion chamber the hot gases are forced to flow through a narrow gap around the cooking pot, so that heat is transferred very efficiently to the pot.

The next improvement is to make sure that the hot gases are burned completely. This is achieved by enlarging the combustion chamber, and introducing a secondary supply of air to allow full combustion before the hot gases reach the cooking vessels. Several stove designs control the air flow with an electric fan, to achieve very efficient combustion. However, natural air-flow, driven by the chimney, can be very effective, provided that the shape of the stove is designed and manufactured very carefully.

www.ashdenawards.org

Green charcoal briquettes

Woody biomass consumption in developing countries, as discussed above, can be avoided by turning agricultural residues and savannah grasses into vegetable or 'green' charcoal briquettes. Pronatura International has developed a machine for this purpose called a Pyro-7 machine. By adding starch, clay or other local materials, the charcoal can be agglomerated into briquettes suitable for cooking fuel. By not going as far as the agglomeration process, the biochar itself can be used for soil improvement and natural carbon sequestration, as detailed in Chapter 2. The process as a whole avoids indoor pollution as well as greenhouse gas production.

Credit: Pronatura International.

Hybrid PV / solar thermal

The creation of hybrid solar systems which combine solar thermal and solar electric could provide a lower cost method of power generation, heating and cooling. These 'linear concentrator systems' are being pioneered by the Centre for Sustainable Energy Systems at the Australian National University (ANU) in cooperation with partners including the Californian company Chromasun Inc., Tianjin University in China and Anna University in India. Each partner provides research input, and the team will look to develop a market for what promises to be a versatile and cost-effective technology.[4]

Credit: Australian National University (ANU).
Prototype microconcentrator.

iJET solar cell

Another technology being developed in Australia is the iJET, an innovative solar cell created with nail polish, solvent, an inkjet printer and a pizza oven. It is the brainchild of Nicole Kuepper, a 23-year-old PhD student from the University of New South Wales' School of Photovoltaic and Renewable Energy Engineering. Cost and developing country conditions were in mind when approaching the design work, so low-grade, low-cost silicon and simple printing technology form the basis of the approach. The iJET production process itself requires far less energy than conventional PV manufacture and could make a huge impact in developing countries in terms of technical and financial accessibility.

Hydropower

Hydropower is an oft-promoted energy source in developing countries, but is an extremely contested subject, given the many pros and cons argued for and against it. In optimal conditions it can provide a reliable, efficient supply of energy, and is one of the longest-lasting energy installations, with a life expectancy of more than a century. However, over and above reported human rights abuses in the construction of dams in developing countries, their ecological impact is deeply concerning, as is their reliability in the increasingly drought-stricken tropics. Fertile valley land must be flooded to create the dams, thus sacrificing food for energy, destroying habitats, disrupting the flow of nutrients downstream and producing large amounts of greenhouse gases from plant decay. The Aswan dam in Egypt stopped the Nile from flooding, denying nutrient replenishment to farmed flood plains. Salinization arose from attempts to artificially irrigate, leading to deteriorating harvests. Increased soil erosion has also occurred in the area of the estuary.[5] The deployment of large hydropower therefore requires a case-by-case basis approach, and the most ethical of decision-making and construction processes.

Credit: Miguel Mendonça. The Three Gorges Dam in China will eventually produce over 20,000 MW.

Small hydropower, by contrast, has many things to recommend it, with few clear disadvantages. It is less intrusive in and damaging to the landscape, and creates power close to the point of use, whereas large schemes generally export the energy over large distances. Especially when using good technology, it is reliable, predictable and cost-effective.

Energy and mobility

The solutions to mobility issues in poorer nations are particularly challenging. One cannot simply tell the local populace that from Monday they must all drive Toyota Priuses. For developing countries, particularly those dependent on imported oil, fuelling vehicles is a problem with few immediate solutions. Brazilian sugarcane ethanol has taken the country a long way from oil dependency, but this cannot be replicated by other nations since most have far smaller territories per head of population on which to grow ethanol crops. Electric transport would require major infrastructural adjustment and investment, and would in any case be too expensive for low-income countries. Stimulus packages could help developing countries with retrofitting and retraining schemes for making electric vehicles, but could they be afforded by the world's poor?

In countries such as India, Ghana and Cuba, a common approach to personal mobility is to endlessly repair ageing vehicles. Havana's famed fleet of 1950s American cars is not a gimmick, but a product of the longstanding trade blockade which made new cars unaffordable and hard to import. While this repair-based approach cuts down the energy used in new build, new vehicles have much higher fuel economy and emissions standards.[6]

As China motorizes at a rate of knots, cars have been outsold by electric scooters – which are more than 20 times as efficient as the smallest car. It is suggested that in a hydrogen economy, the Three Gorges Dam, with its output of more than that of 12 nuclear power stations, could produce enough hydrogen to power fuel cells for the vast majority of China's car fleet – 56 million cars by 2020.[7] To combat air pollution and fuel costs, China has already implemented fuel economy standards greater than those of the US – meaning that American cars cannot be sold in China. In the Philippines, pilot projects suggest that retrofits to the highly polluting two-stroke engines used in many two- and three-wheeled vehicles could cut fuel consumption by 35–50 percent and emissions of air pollutants by as much as 90 percent. Installing and servicing the kits would create many new jobs.[8]

Tata motors in India have launched the world's cheapest car, the 624cc, 100,000 rupee (<$2,000) 'Nano'. Their aim is to get tens of millions of Indians into these 3-metre long, 5-seater vehicles. Global markets are also in sight for the carmaker, which could reduce emissions in large markets if more polluting vehicles are displaced. But if the net result is that significant numbers of people now using buses switch to daily commuting by car, road congestion and emissions will increase dramatically.

This is an interesting example of where the stated needs of people in the emerging economies come into apparent conflict with environmentalists. The reaction of the latter tends to be that they should avoid copying western development models; and besides which, the world cannot afford the emerging economies to suddenly explode in fossil-fuelled growth. The common response from those concerned is that poverty is the greatest evil, and that the West cut down its forests and built a car-based society, so what right do they have to tell others to do otherwise? Lord Nicholas Stern sees

no such contradiction: "It is neither economically necessary nor ethically responsible to stop or drastically slow growth to manage climate change."[9]

It is ironic, if we accept the view that those of the global South are seeking to copy those of the North, that as Indians and the Chinese are ditching bicycles, motorcycles and public transport for cars, 'Northerners' are increasingly doing the opposite. Fuel prices and other motoring costs, congestion and health issues are beginning to get people out of their cars. The increasing facilitation of cycling in cities breeds greater choice, and there are some government financial incentives to reduce the cost of purchase, such as the UK's 'Cycle to Work' tax-based initiative.[10]

Public transport can provide sustainable and affordable travel within cities. A sustainable transport programme set out by the Global Environment Facility (GEF) in 2000 contained a combination of approaches, including one focusing on cost-effective technologies and practices that were under-utilized, and another on technologies that were not yet fully developed. The table below shows the transport programmes the GEF has supported in developing countries:

TRANSPORT TECHNOLOGY	COUNTRIES SUPPORTED
Bicycle paths, non-motorized transit	Botswana, Chile, Nicaragua, Peru, Philippines, Poland, Vietnam
Bus Rapid Transit (BRT) systems	Argentina, Brazil, Ghana, Senegal, South Africa, Tanzania
Dedicated bus lanes	Argentina, Brazil, Chile, Ghana, India, Indonesia, Iran, Mexico, Peru, South Africa
Electric three-wheelers	India
Hybrid buses	Egypt
Hydrogen-based fuel-cell buses	Brazil, China
Traffic demand management	Argentina, Brazil, Ghana, Mexico

Source: GEF, 2008

Credit: National Bus Rapid Transit Institute. BRT platform.

BRT, or Bus Rapid Transit systems, have been implemented in several countries. They are a cheap and effective method of addressing mass transit with generally pre-existing infrastructure. It is essentially an 'overground underground' or metro. Overground bus routes are created instead of underground train systems, and buses move rapidly up and down the centre of main road routes through the city. People buy prepaid tickets and wait on raised platforms for quicker boarding and exiting. Notable examples include Curitiba in Brazil and Bogotá in Colombia.

On mobility, a 2008 UNEP report on green jobs concluded:

> *Hundreds of millions of people in developing countries suffer from insufficient mobility. They may never be able to afford an automobile, and may not even have access to public transit. Yet, bicycles and modern bicycle rickshaws offer a sustainable alternative and create employment in manufacturing and transportation services. Nevertheless, their growing essential mobility needs must be met, and this will require the*

> *development of innovative approaches that should also generate new employment opportunities.[11]*

What these innovative approaches might be is yet to be determined it seems. Balancing environmental, economic, cultural, geographical and infrastructural factors is a conundrum that requires a great deal of planning and a participatory process to solve. The Swiss brought together their various transport providers to improve the transport system. Just by synchronizing the timetables of the different modes of transport they managed to improve mobility significantly. Combined approaches such as Transportation Demand Management (TDM), a toolbox of policies and strategies, can cut congestion, improve transport flows and reduce emissions.[12] Many more options are covered in Chapter 7 on cities and transport.

To be truly sustainable, electrification of transport, or hydrogen use, means using renewable energy rather than fossil fuels as a source. With such a variety of good reasons to bring renewable energy to developing countries, how is it done? Who needs to be involved? And importantly, what has been achieved so far?

Development finance and technology transfer

In the Special Report of the IPCC Working Group III, Methodological and Technical Issues in Technology Transfer, the definition of the term technology transfer is discussed:

> Technology transfer is a broad set of processes covering the flows of know-how, experience and equipment for mitigating and adapting to climate change amongst different stakeholders such as governments, private sector entities, financial institutions, NGOs and research/ education institutions. Therefore, the treatment of technology transfer in this Report is much broader than that in the UNFCCC or of any particular Article of that Convention. The broad and inclusive term 'transfer' encompasses diffusion of technologies and technology cooperation across and within countries. It covers technology transfer processes between developed countries, developing countries and countries with economies in transition, amongst developed countries, amongst developing countries, and amongst countries with economies in transition. It comprises the process of learning to understand, utilize and replicate the technology, including the capacity to choose and adapt to local conditions and integrate it with indigenous technologies.

According to the GEF, this definition "includes a wide range of activities, extends to a broad range of institutions, and provides the basis for much of the current understanding of technology transfer. The IPCC describes three major dimensions necessary for effective technology transfer: capacity building, enabling environments, and transfer mechanisms. Barriers to the smooth working of the market for a specific technology, such as limited capacity, an unsuitable policy environment, or a lack of financing mechanism, will limit its diffusion."[13] These lessons are expanded upon below, in a more detailed look at the GEF's work in this area.

In terms of financing technology transfer, there are several existing routes, including development organizations, donors and dedicated programmes, and international technology transfer instruments. Development assistance for renewables investment has grown markedly in recent years, reaching almost $2 billion in 2008, up from $500 million in 2004.[14] The largest funders are The World Bank Group, GEF, and the German Development Finance Group (KfW). In 2008, KfW committed €405 million ($530 million), including renewables funding from its Special Facility for Renewable Energies and Energy Efficiency. The World Bank Group allotted $280 million (not including GEF funds and carbon finance), plus $1 billion for large hydropower. Around $200 million was pledged by The Asian Development Bank and the Inter-American Development Bank, and the GEF committed $10 million in 2008 (a fraction of the $100 million it has been committing annually in recent years). The top two bilateral donors in 2008 were Germany (€225 million expected, or $300 million) and the Netherlands (€166 million, or $230 million). In addition to these sources, other official development assistance (ODA) figures from a variety of bilateral and multilateral development agencies suggest additional funding for renewables in the range of $50-70 billion per year.[15]

Around US$500 million in development assistance grants is targeted at developing countries annually for renewable energy projects, and for training and market support.

This funds policy analysis work, economic assessment, market and business development, project feasibility studies, financing mechanisms, technology improvements and capacity building, and sometimes covers partial incremental costs of renewable energy projects.[16]

Several foundations and NGOs such as the UN Foundation and the Energy Foundation provide funds and manage programmes promoting renewable energy. Bilateral development banks and agencies also contribute, such as the European Union and the European Investment Bank, and national development institutions such as the Australian Agency for International Development (AusAID) and the Deutsche Gesellschaft fur Technische Zusammenarbeit GmbH, better known as GTZ.

As an example of where some of these agencies put their money, the UK's Department for International Development (DFID) is one of the many funders of the Renewable Energy and Energy Efficiency Partnership (REEEP) a global initiative concerned with reducing the policy, regulatory and financial barriers to renewable energy and energy efficiency technologies and projects. The partnership has funded more than eighty 'high quality' projects in forty developing countries. These projects are beginning to deliver new business models, policy recommendations, risk mitigation instruments and regulatory measures. REEEP also engages in international, national and regional policy dialogues.

Several United Nations organizations actively promote renewable energy. The United Nations Development Programme (UNDP) has an 'Energy and Environment Practice' which promotes access to sustainable energy services as an essential development strategy. UNEP's (United Nations Environment Programme) renewable energy activities focus on the needs of developing and transition economies in

various areas of renewable energy technology research, development and commercialization. UNEP's Sustainable Energy Finance Initiative (SEFI) is a platform providing financiers with the tools, support and global network needed to conceive and manage investments in the "complex and rapidly changing marketplace" for clean energy technologies. UNIDO (the United Nations Industrial Development Organization) focuses on rural energy for productive use. Other UN bodies work to spread renewable energy technology information, and to engage stakeholders in accelerating RE development.

The GEF was established in 1991 under the United Nations Framework Convention on Climate Change (UNFCCC), as a mechanism to help developing countries fund projects and programmes that protect the global environment while still supporting national sustainable development initiatives. They have become one of the largest public-sector technology transfer mechanisms in the world – a partnership between 178 countries, international institutions, NGOs and the private sector, providing $7.6 billion in grants and leveraging $30.6 billion in co-financing for more than 2,000 projects in more than 165 countries to date. Nearly a billion dollars has gone to around 150 renewable energy projects in developing countries.[17] Some of their experiences are related in the report 'Transfer of Environmentally Sound Technologies: The GEF Experience', in which they share many practical experiences, such as this:

The Transformation of the Rural Photovoltaic Market in Tanzania project was designed to incorporate the lessons learned from earlier rural PV projects. Reports indicate that this project has contributed to the removal of taxes and VAT on all PV components. Standards and a code of practice have been approved and are now in place. . . . PV awareness among key government decision-makers at district level has been raised through a series of seminars. . . . Technicians have been trained in sizing, installing, repairing and maintaining the systems, 60 percent of which are operational. Financial models for supply-chain and consumer financing are being developed to increase the number of consumers and companies that request financing for their PV investments.[18]

To conclude, let us look at the GEF's conclusions on technology transfer, drawn from their years of intensive work on the subject:

- **technology is transferred primarily through markets: barriers to the efficient operation of those markets must be removed systematically;**

- **technology transfer is not a single event or activity but a long-term engagement, during which partnerships and cooperation, often requiring time to develop and mature, are mandatory for the successful development, transfer, and dissemination of technologies; and**

- **technology transfer requires a comprehensive approach, incorporating capacity-building at all relevant levels.**

The work done by so many actors to get renewable energy technology and knowledge moving to developing countries, despite looking very generous in terms of the figures quoted above, is still a relatively small contribution. Internationally coordinated efforts to boost renewables deployment have arisen as part of the UNFCCC Kyoto protocol, and produced the much-maligned Clean Development Mechanism (CDM).

The Clean Development Mechanism (CDM)

"The purpose of the clean development mechanism (CDM) shall be to assist parties, not included in Annex 1, in achieving sustainable development and in contributing to the ultimate objective of the convention, and to assist Parties included in Annex 1 in achieving compliance with their [Kyoto] commitments"
Article 12 of the Kyoto Protocol

The Kyoto Protocol is a legally binding mechanism that requires signatories to make reductions in GHG emissions, and it authorizes the CDM. This allows GHG-reduction projects in developing countries to qualify for emissions-reduction credits that can then be sold to industrialized countries that have binding reduction targets to meet.

The ideal is that this would not only control CO_2 emissions, but help to facilitate a sustainable equilibrium of people living free from poverty, powered by a constant supply of renewable energy. Offered as a policy to assist developing countries to become free from energy inequality, the CDM aims to promote RE through the exchange of technology, finance and knowledge for emissions-reduction units. Despite the CDM being incorporated into key policy for the UNFCCC, it has received much criticism in the extensive literature on the topic. This is mainly for its failure to provide small-scale communities in rural areas with an energy supply, as well as many developers of CDM failing to recognize the importance of the need for sustainable development in poorer countries, not just large-scale projects which generate large numbers of carbon credits, irrespective of the social implications. The box overleaf lists some of the key pros and cons from studies.

CDM – PROS AND CONS

Pros

Encourages imports of equipment that have more capacity than local technologies [1]

Projects often incorporate the transfer of knowledge – passing on skills, not just technology that people do not know how to use; this allows project coordinators to implement the technology and not rely on the global North once up and running [1]

The market has been very successful in finding efficient mitigation options [3]

The CDM since its launch has been partially able to assist some Annex 1 countries in meeting their commitment under Kyoto through mitigating emissions in developing countries. On the other hand it has not been equally successful in achieving the sustainable development aim of CDM [2]

Cons

The system of carbon credits and trading allows governments to subsidize fossil fuels under the guise of development [2]

It remains that PDD (Project Document Design) editors have an incentive to overstate the existence of technology transfer as it helps with project registration [1]

It is claimed by many opponents that 'donor' countries are merely subsidizing their own technologies. [1] There is plentiful evidence that the 'additionality' requirement – that a project would not otherwise have taken place without the availability of money earned from the sale of carbon credits – has too often been fudged [4]

Technology transfers are limited in certain renewables – hydro power and biomass already used in Brazil, China and India [1]

Technology transfers are only likely if the amount of emissions reduced is large-scale – therefore shuts out small community-based technologies. [1] This has been linked to high transaction costs, making the CDM market favour projects with bigger returns [2]

Only a very small minority of projects can be verified as having contributed significantly to clean, low-carbon economic development

The CDM initiative is yet to adequately reflect its two aims: it has not shown that it can bring developmental benefits to the rural poor. It is also falling behind its aims for the industrialized countries' targets

The distribution of existing and developing CDM projects is concentrated in China, Brazil and India – countries with existing infrastructure. It has missed out Africa, where small-scale energy projects are needed by rural populations [2]

The enormous number of very low-cost emissions offset opportunities, created opportunistically with simple and proven technologies, at prices far lower than would be incurred if achieved through investments in new low carbon technologies, have created an economic disincentive to such investment [4]

The certificate price on the international carbon markets is rather volatile, making investment security rather low [5]

The CDM scheme is based on the logic that least-cost options for carbon reduction should be implemented first. This 'step by step' approach is no longer viable due to the urgency humankind is facing in the fight against climate change. Technology-specific, price-based instruments have proven to be more effective in promoting a large number of sustainable technologies instead of a 'one-size-fits-all' approach [5].

Policy Implications

In the next commitment period (2012 – 2016), policy needs to encourage small-scale community RE projects, rather than looking to maximize emissions reductions and minimize sustainable development [2]

CDM is currently flawed as it is built on same principles that have caused inequality in markets, has high transaction costs – so needs restructuring [2]

Should the programme continue to attempt to bring sustainable development benefits, or should it be streamlined to be simply a market mechanism? [3]

More research is needed on how sustainable development projects can be achieved through CDM – especially on what factors contribute to local social benefits [3]

In order to benefit the economies of rural communities, the RE initiative needs to be linked with a larger development project that is local – such as fishing, agriculture or local handicrafts – rather than expecting the implementation of RE to kick-start such economies. [5]

1: Dechezleptretre et al [19] 2: Lloyd and Subbarao [20] 3: Tyndall Centre [21]
4: Crawford, W [22] 5: Additional comments by Jacobs, D [23]

An alternative use of the CDM: The Converging World

The Converging World (TCW) is a UK-based charity that seeks to address the economic, social and environmental issues created by climate change, fossil-fuel depletion and energy security.

They promote and implement an alternative approach to reducing carbon emissions that they believe is both practical and fair. TCW invites donations that are used to invest in large-scale renewable energy projects in the developing world. This creates revenue streams; 75% of the profits are used to invest in more renewable energy and the remaining 25% are used to fund community-based sustainable development, with also a growing emphasis on supporting communities to adapt to climate change. The renewable energy projects generate carbon credits, and the donor can nominate that these be sold or retired. If sold, the profit associated with the sale of the carbon credit is again invested in more renewable energy and environmental projects. This approach multiplies the original value of donations.

Every £1,000 given to TCW is projected to result in total investments of up to £5,000 over a twenty-year period (£3,000 in net present values), funding renewable and clean energy, sustainable development projects, and establishing long-term initiatives that will help people in emerging economies to develop in ways that minimize carbon dioxide emissions now and in the future. A focus on local investment in turn creates quantifiable social returns, estimated as producing additional economic benefits at least equal in value to the sums expended. They also aim to provide much needed adaptation funds to communities impacted by climate change already and those most vulnerable in the future.

Their first project is a share in a wind farm in Tamil Nadu in south India, where they own and

Credit: The Converging World.

operate two 1.5MW wind turbines. Part of the income generated from these turbines then provides funds for a local development charity

called Social Change and Development (SCAD).[24] The Converging World seeks to address a key criticism of the CDM by ensuring that a fair share of the value arising from the creation and selling of carbon credits is used directly to support well defined local sustainable development and adaptation initiatives that make a real difference.

Adapting feed-in tariffs for developing countries

The benefits of FITs (see Chapter 3) can be transferred to developing countries if suitably adapted to local conditions in terms of funding and deployment details. David Jacobs has described the possibilities and issues in detail in *Powering the Green Economy: The Feed-in Tariff Handbook*. There are three main suggestions made: use CDM; establish a national fund; create village mini-grids.

Although the CDM mechanism might in theory be used to fund RE deployment, as above, it has several problems which militate against it, which are costs and returns, and investment security. Compared with typical CDM projects such as energy-efficiency projects, renewables projects could have relatively high costs and small size. This is less attractive to investors who are compelled to pursue projects based on the total amount of greenhouse gas emissions that can be avoided and the implied transaction costs. Projects with large emissions reduction potential therefore have a clear advantage over small-scale renewables projects. The natural volatility of the certificate price on the international carbon market would also go against the basic principle of investment security provided by a FIT. It is possible that these three issues can be overcome, but the case as it stands does not appear strong.

A national FIT fund could be supported by the

Credit: Alliance for Rural Electrification. Village mini-grid concept.

national budget and international donors. For the latter, payments to the fund can facilitate the promotion of hundreds of small-scale renewable energy projects. However, keeping government monies separate from FITs is considered a fundamental factor in stability, by protecting the payments from any government interference, or economic or political upheaval. Therefore feed-in tariff schemes are usually financed via a small increase of the electricity prices paid by all final consumers, and not via funds. The fund would also have to be of considerable size to ensure the typical 20-year payments guaranteed by a FIT, which might look larger when accumulated up-front than when spread over the full period.

To serve rural populations, village mini-grids could supply power without the need for expensive centralized production and long-distance transmission and distribution. The Joint Research Centre of the European Commission has examined the potential for feed-in tariffs to be applied to mini-grids.[25] Mini-grids are amalgamations of independent generation sources, such as wind and PV, and can be backed up by weather-independent sources such as biomass or small hydro, or by battery storage, or diesel or biofuel generators. Linking these resources can provide communities with reliable electricity supplies, as well as creating jobs in areas such as maintenance and installation.

Given the specific economic context of mini-grids of this kind, some work must be done on developing appropriate funding and payment systems; we explore a few of these here. Mini-grids will either exist within a nationally regulated, monopolistic ownership structure, or a liberalized market. The actors involved are independent power producers (IPPs), rural energy service companies (RESCOs) and co-operatives.

IPPs can generate electricity in liberalized markets. Unlike utilities, they are not legally or economically linked to transmission or distribution activities. They generally supply the grid via long-term Power Purchase Agreements (PPAs) which are negotiated with utilities or grid operators. RESCOs usually have a partial monopoly for energy services and other public services in a given area, and are quasi-governmental organizations. If operating renewable energy installations, they are usually responsible for the full chain of services, including operation, maintenance, and repair.[26] Co-operatives are usually non-profit and locally-based, such as so-called 'solar communities' and the well-known 'wind cooperatives' of Denmark.

To account for the different actor types and local conditions, the JRC has elaborated FIT financing schemes for three different scenarios of actor constellations: regulated service concessions, for IPPs, and for power producers which are at the same time electricity consumers.

Under regulated service concessions, the government offers a service concession to a certain company for a given period of time (usually selected via competitive bidding). This company has the right to supply energy exclusively, which in rural areas can be done via the technologies described above. The RESCO usually charges a fixed and affordable price (usually below the actual generation costs). To compensate the RESCO for the difference, additional monies from the local Energy Development Agency are granted, which is generally financed by local government. If funds for this are low, money from international donors may be necessary. In combination, all funds received should ensure reasonable profitability.

IPPs can provide renewable energy to mini-grids by twin financial flows: one from a FIT payment – paid by the national electricity regulator – and one from a regulated tariff from the local Distribution System Operator (DSO) which manages the mini-grid. The regional DSO usually sells the electricity at a predefined rate to final consumers. The total should, as above, provide a reasonable profit for the IPP.

Those with a solar home system or other small-scale renewables installation can become both an electricity producer and consumer. Micro credit schemes (see below) can help fund the initial purchase. The DSO purchases the electricity at a preferential rate, effectively a feed-in tariff set by the national regulator. So, in a similar way to IPPs, private producers of renewable electricity can sell the power to the grid at a preferential tariff. The private producer receives electricity at a lower price from the grid operator, as do all consumers within the mini-grid. The difference is paid by contributions from the national regulator. The consumer/producer can use the combined revenue to pay off the initial investment cost of the installation. After the system is paid off, all future income will be straight profit, an incentive which is likely to be taken into consideration at the outset.

Feed-in tariffs for mini-grids are a promising approach for linking off-grid and grid-connected renewable energy support. Funding the mechanisms through the transfer of money from state level to local level – in order to compensate for the additional costs of renewable energies – is the most challenging issue.[27]

Micro-credit finance: the Grameen Shakti model

It would be remiss to discuss this subject without looking at one of the most celebrated success stories in the area of access to rural energy: Grameen Shakti. This is the branch of the Grameen Bank dealing with renewable energies, and their work centres on empowering rural people through access to green energy and income. It was initiated in

1996 by the co-builders of Grameen Bank. The vision comes from Professor Muhammad Yunus, a Bangladeshi banker and economist, who developed the micro-credit concept, and in 2006 received the Nobel Peace Prize for his work, in conjunction with the bank itself. This low-interest loan system was melded with rural energy needs, and has grown enormously; it now acts as a replicable model for other countries. According to their own information, as of July 2007 Grameen Bank had issued US$6.38 billion to 7.4 million borrowers, 97 percent of whom are women, and the repayment rate is over 98 percent.[28] To ensure repayment, the bank uses a system of small informal 'solidarity groups' which apply jointly for loans. The members act as co-guarantors of repayment, and provide mutual support in efforts towards improving their economic circumstances.

Grameen Shakti now has programmes supporting deployment of many technologies, including PV, wind, biogas and cooking stoves, and is offering training and capacity-building, as well as entrepreneurship courses for women through the Grameen Technology Centres (GTCs). As of March 2009 they had installed 220,000 solar home systems, 35,000 Improved Cook Stoves (ICS), and listed more than 2 million beneficiaries in 40,000 villages. The list of impressive statistics goes on and on.[29]

The efforts of Grameen Shakti give the rural people a chance to improve their quality of life and also take part in income-generating activities. Their unique programme helps to break the social and economical divide between those who have energy and those who do not. It could be argued that this approach, as with so many others, arose to fill a void. The same could be said of the CDM in some respects, although that approach has yet to win any prizes.

What does it all add up to?

The picture which emerges from this brief survey is of scattered and more or less successful efforts at getting renewable energy deployed in developing countries and emerging economies. It seems to take charity, philanthropy, compassion and thorough, on-the-ground understanding to achieve real change, as demonstrated by the Grameen Bank. Having said that, one cannot discount the enormous funds pledged by so many donor nations and other sources, regardless of their motivations and values.

What is important is that key lessons are taken into consideration in future, particularly on capacity-building, taking a long-term view, and especially governance issues. Investment flows through corrupt political systems are like water flows through leaking pipes. Grasping the nettle on that issue will require joined-up thinking and doing – and perhaps a level of bravery.

The technological leapfrogging which has occurred in telecommunications in Africa is an excellent precedent for energy, and both are required as basics for an aspirational life which seeks opportunities in education and business. In Gambia, around 80 percent of telephones are mobiles, and two-thirds of the world's 4.1 billion mobiles are used in developing countries.[30] Renewable energy can see similar success if the will is there and the right deployment mechanisms are employed.

It may even be possible to create a new mechanism based on 'debt for nature' swaps. Some countries have 'sold' their foreign debt to charities and other groups, who then protect areas of rainforest, for example. The debt is forgiven in exchange for a promise of environmental protection, although enforcement is notoriously difficult to ensure. This has taken place in countries such as Bolivia, Costa Rica, Ecuador, the Philippines and Madagascar. A 'debt for renewables' project has been proposed by the Global Energy Network Institute (GENI), as part of their work towards creating access to ecologically sustainable energy for all.

Some of the technologies listed above show that local conditions can be accounted for very effectively, but it takes a great deal of understanding and local knowledge – the CDM is a broad-brush approach that does not seem able to work in the same way, and perhaps was never meant to. Whatever emerges from Copenhagen in 2009 will be challenged to improve its applicability to local conditions, and to achieve truly effective results in transitioning to a renewables-based energy system.

The 'shotgun marriage' of sustainability and development has yet to become guided by norms which produce development rooted in ethical sustainability. All in all, the road to energy equality between rich and poor countries continues to be a long and arduous one, with few worthwhile shortcuts having been discovered so far. Those that are established on the map, and those which have great promise, such as the adaptation of feed-in tariffs and the Converging World model, should be explored energetically – and soon. For the countries in need, renewable energy is the gift that keeps on giving.

To assure renewable energy deployment in developing countries, key measures are needed:

- Renewable energy deployment is the only route to securing sustainable development
- Depending on specific circumstances, Grameen Shakti, north-south community cooperation or feed-in tariffs are suitable for rapid RE development
- Major international mechanisms such as the CDM need to be reformed, particularly to enhance living conditions of the rural poor
- Capacity building is crucial at all levels
- Technological leapfrogging regarding RE deployment can provide both long-term energy security and protection from volatile fossil-fuel prices

Acknowledgements

Minoru Takada
United Nations Development Programme
David Jacobs
Environmental Policy Research Center
Guido Glania *Alliance for Rural Electrification*
Stephanie Harris *Bristol University*
Simon Manley and **Ward Crawford**
The Converging World
Brando Crespi and **Guy Renaud**
Pronatura International
Nicole Kuepper *University of New South Wales*
Igor Skryabin *Australian National University*
Nicola Wilks *Worldwide Fund for Nature*
Justin Bishop *Cambridge University*
Ansgar Kiene *WFC staff*
Jane Howarth *The Ashden Awards*
Eric Britton *The New Mobility*
Riane Eisler *WFC councillor*
Tony Colman *WFC adviser*

Chapter Five

Energy Sufficiency

" *You don't have to change – survival is not mandatory.* "
W. Edwards Deming

If we are serious about keeping the global temperature increase to no more than 2°C, we can only burn a quarter of the its oil, gas and coal reserves. This is the startling conclusion of two studies, by Myles Allen of the University of Oxford and Malte Meinshausen of the Potsdam Institute for Climate Impact Research. These are probably the most comprehensive efforts yet to define climatic limits to fossil-fuel combustion.

Since the industrial revolution, humanity has burned about 500 billion tonnes of carbon fuels. Says Myles Allen: "We can afford to burn only 250 billion tonnes more – or perhaps 500 billion tonnes if we are willing to run the higher risk. . . . It took 250 years to burn the first 500 billion tonnes. On current trends we'll burn the next 500 billion in less than 40 years."[1]

The 'safe' goal of a temperature increase of 2°C at the most, means that global emissions must start falling after 2015. Given that at present we are increasing emissions by up to 3 percent each year this is no small feat. The two studies suggest that the G8 countries' target of cutting global emissions to 50 percent of their 1990 levels by 2050 may not be enough – the cutbacks will have to be closer to 70 percent!

These are dramatic challenges: even the most ambitious climate stabilization plans tabled so far are totally insufficient. In Chapter 2 we suggested that to deal with increasing GHG concentrations in the atmosphere it is crucial to find every possible way to enhance the carbon sequestration capacity of the biosphere. In Chapter 3 we described the policies which can dramatically accelerate the introduction of renewable energy technologies. But none of this will be enough to assure climate stability.

In this chapter we argue that we need to get to grips with the concept of *energy sufficiency* across the developed world if we wish to prevent runaway climate change. Whilst *energy efficiency* measures are necessary first steps, we need to go beyond that: there has to be an actual upper limit of global per capita fossil-fuel use.

This chapter is trying to set the scene, but ultimately the world community has to agree the steps that are needed. There is no doubt that a clear understanding of energy sufficiency is crucial for the long-term ecological viability of the global economy. Assuring people's wellbeing across the world, whilst defining limits to the use of non-renewable energy, is one of the great challenges of the 21st century.

ENERGY SLAVES

How can the prolific use of energy use in the rich countries be illustrated vividly? It was US designer and futurist Buckminster Fuller who invented the concept of personal 'energy slaves' who make our comfortable lifestyles possible. This concept has been updated by World Future Council member Prof. Hans Peter Dürr, the former director of the Max Planck Institute in Munich. He divides our energy use into manpower equivalents – the muscle energy of a strong man (equivalent to a quarter horse-power) working six days a week, ten hours a day. By this reckoning, Americans have 110 energy slaves per person, Europeans have 60, Chinese have eight and Bangladeshis have one. If one looks at the global average, every person would only be entitled to 15 energy slaves. So energy supply is very unfairly distributed, whilst energy is also produced and used in a highly unsustainable way.

Dürr, like many other scientists, is convinced that increasing global energy consumption will soon threaten the integrity of the planet. He adds an additional perspective: "The question we must ask is not how many people the earth could sustain, but how many energy slaves it could sustain. My calculations indicate that the limit we have to observe so as not to destroy the world's bio-system is about 90 billion energy slaves. Yet the world is presently home to about 130 billion energy slaves – 40 billion more than the Earth can sustain. Europeans are using four times and Americans nearly seven times the amount of energy per person that the earth could sustain. So you have really to get birth control of energy slaves." [2]

Each European has about 60 energy slaves, each American about 110 energy slaves. That is the energy equivalent of a strong man working 10 hours a day six days a week represented by the energy output of the motors and engines, powered by fossil fuel energy, working on our behalf. In a sustainable world this figure would have to come down to a quarter or less.

Credit: Rick Lawrence.

Forecasting energy use

Energy is used for specific purposes – for cooking and heating, for cooling and powering buildings, for pumping water, for manufacture and food production, for transporting people and goods, and for providing us with information and entertainment.

Despite growing concerns about climate change and long-term energy security, the use of fossil-fuel energy is continuing to rise steadily, most recently driven by the economic boom in countries such as China, India and the UAE. Worldwide, energy use per unit of gross domestic product (GDP) is in decline, but it is widely believed that overall global energy demand will continue to grow steadily over the coming decades. According to a UN Foundation report, "demand for global energy services to support economic growth has grown by 50 percent since 1980 and is expected to grow another 50 percent by 2030". The International Energy Agency (IEA), in its 2008 report, estimates an increase in demand of some 45 percent by 2030[3] compared to 2005 if there are no major policy shifts.[4]

Efforts at energy forecasting by bodies like the IEA seem increasingly confused: it predicts ever-greater global energy use

1. whilst worrying about potential energy shortages unless there is massive continued investment in fossil-fuel extraction,

2. whilst also painting an apocalyptic picture of the future state of the world if fossil-fuel burning is not drastically curtailed.

The World Bank has similar perspectives. Researcher Heike Mainhardt-Gibbs, consultant to the Washington-based Bank Information Center, has found that during its 2008 fiscal year the World Bank and the International Finance Corporation increased funding for fossil-fuel development by 102 percent. This compared with just 11 percent for new renewable energy. The Bank has put twice as much into fossil-fuel financing compared with both renewable energy and energy-efficiency projects, and five times as much as into new renewable sources taken alone. From 2005 to 2008, the Bank spent 19 percent more on coal than on new renewable energy. Says Mainhardt-Gibbs: "The World Bank has the responsibility to assess each project's full contribution to climate change as its impacts . . . negatively affect developing countries and the poor of the world disproportionately – the very countries (its) programs are trying to benefit."[5]

These concerns are compounded by MIT's Center for Global Change Science in a

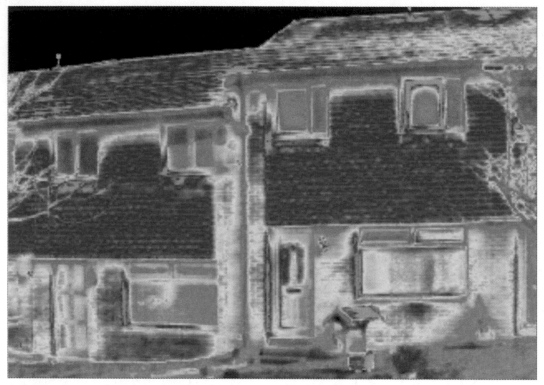

Credit: Thermal Survey. Infrared photography is a very effective tool for discovering the energy leakage of our houses. Retrofitting with high-efficiency insulation materials and energy management systems has huge implications for their energy performance.

comprehensive computer simulation of global economic activity and climate processes which it has developed over the last 20 years. 400 runs of the computer model, with each run using slightly different input parameters, indicate "a median probability of surface warming of 5.2 degrees Celsius by 2100, with a 90% probability range of 3.5 to 7.4 degrees" if current trends are not drastically altered. Ronald Prinn, co-director of the MIT Centre concludes: "The least-cost option to lower the risk is to start now and steadily transform the global energy system over the coming decades to low or zero greenhouse gas-emitting technologies." [6]

Where do we go from here? Large-scale investments in bio-sequestration and renewable energy, as suggested in Chapters 2 and 3, are crucial for a climate-proof world. This chapter argues that, in addition, large-scale energy savings are both necessary and possible. For instance, according to a 2007 study by the German Aerospace Centre, a 47 percent reduction in worldwide final energy demand can be achieved by 2050. This scenario is based, firstly, on current best practice, and secondly, on the assumption that continuous innovation will take place in the field of energy efficiency in the years to come. [7]

In the light of the findings by Allen and Meinshausen, cited above, even more ambitious energy savings now have to be envisaged.

The efficiency option

Renewable energy itself is a major contributor to energy efficiency since it can increase local supply for local demand by reducing the need for long distance energy supply. But, in addition, measures to enhance energy efficiency in buildings, industrial processes, transportation and food supply must play a major role in addressing the problems of climate change, energy dependency, fossil-fuel depletion and high energy prices.

Maximum energy efficiency is crucial in a world demanding ever-greater energy supplies. Energy efficiency is also termed energy productivity: it is usually defined as the provision of energy services per unit of energy input. Efficient technologies and processes will deliver the same amount of services with a lower input of energy resources. An increase in energy productivity is – besides behavioural changes – one way to achieve energy savings.

Like labour or capital productivity, energy productivity measures the output of goods and services generated with a given set of inputs. Energy productivity improvements result either from reducing the energy inputs needed to produce a given level of services, or from increasing the quantity of economic output. By being clear about the relative importance of each, measuring energy productivity is useful for enhancing efficient energy use.[8]

The productivity of energy use will always tend to grow over time as technologies are first developed and then improved upon. In Chapter 1 we described how the energy productivity of steam engines increased 14-fold over a period of 100 years. Continuous improvements in designs, processes and supporting policies are needed to achieve this kind of outcome.

Reducing energy demand by a rapid increase in energy efficiency (and renewables) is widely regarded as crucial for assuring global energy security and minimizing climate change. Throughout the developed world a wide spectrum of initiatives is underway – to improve the efficiency of power generation, to phase in energy-efficient light bulbs, to improve energy management systems, and to increase the energy performance of vehicles, household machinery, and most importantly, buildings.

New modelling by the World Business Council for Sustainable Development (WBCSD) shows how energy use in buildings can be cut by 60 percent by 2050 by a variety of measures – better building materials, new approaches to building design, better energy management. The central message of the WBCSD's four-year, $15 million Efficiency in Buildings research project, the most rigorous study ever conducted on the subject, is that immediate action is required to transform the way the building sector prioritizes energy.[9]

In the area of electricity supply and demand in particular, interesting new perspectives have emerged in recent years. In a speech in 1989 Amory Lovins, the founder of the Rocky Mountain Institute (RMI), coined the term 'negawatt power'. By this he proposed that significant investments in energy efficiency measures could reduce the need to produce additional megawatts in the United States.[10] He explained how this could be achieved:

"An electricity supplier that has a requirement for additional supply capacity can invite suppliers to quote for the supply of that electricity and can equally invite its customers to quote to reduce their demand. The electricity supplier can then compare these quotations to establish the most economic alternative. This comparison can refer to peak load management – how much per additional kW to get the power company through the peak load due to air conditioning on an unusually hot day – or may refer to longer-term investments – comparing the cost of building a new power station with the cost of, for instance, providing customers with low-energy light bulbs."[11]

Such approaches to energy efficiency are now widely regarded as the most cost-effective, 'low-hanging fruit' of climate-change mitigation. It is the "largest, least expensive, most benign, most quickly deployable, least visible, least understood, and most neglected way to provide energy services".

For many years RMI has played a key role as an influential global leader in energy-efficiency research and advocacy, particularly in the commercial sector. Lovins points out: "There are abundant opportunities to save 70% to 90% of the energy and cost for lighting, fan, and pump systems; 50% for electric motors; and 60% in areas such as heating, cooling, office equipment and appliances. In the US, 70% to 90% of the energy and cost for lighting, fan, and pump systems . . . up to 75% of the electricity currently used could be saved with efficiency measures that cost less than the electricity itself."[12]

The trick is to decouple a utility's profits from how much energy it sells. This means that it is no longer rewarded for selling more or, indeed, penalized for selling less. Consumers are encouraged to use more efficient appliances, by allowing suppliers to keep a small proportion of the savings as extra profits so that the incentives of energy producers and consumers are entirely aligned. This can have a dramatic effect on utility behaviour.[13]

There is no doubt that avoided electricity generating capacity is a hugely important step in an energy-hungry world. Enlightened self-interest has encouraged some US and European utility companies to help customers make more efficient use of energy, whilst reducing the need for making costly investments in additional electricity generating capacity. Providing efficient energy services rather than simply supplying megawatts of electricity according to 'unchallenged' demand has become part of the business vocabulary of utility companies.

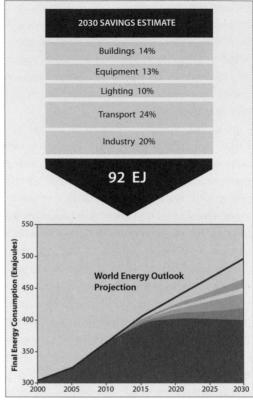

Source: IEA 2008; In support of the G8 Action Plan, Energy Efficiency Policy Recommendations.
http://www.iea.org/G8/2008/G8_EE_recommendations.pdf

FACTOR FOUR TO FACTOR FIVE

When first published in 1997, 'Factor Four: Doubling Wealth, Halving Resource Use' by efficiency pioneers Ernst Ulrich von Weizsäcker, Amory Lovins and L. Hunter Lovins, transformed the way economists, policy-makers, engineers, entrepreneurs and business leaders thought about innovation and wealth creation. Through examples from a wide range of sectors, the authors demonstrated how technical innovation could cut resource use in half while doubling wealth. Weizsäcker's new book, 'Factor Five', to be published in 2009, will examine the past 15 years of innovation in industry, technical innovation and policy. It aims to show how and where factor four gains have been made and how we can achieve greater factor five or 80 percent improvements in resource and energy productivity; and how to roll them out on a global scale to retool our economic system, massively boost wealth for billions of people around the world and help solve the climate change crisis.

The self-interest of energy producers and consumers certainly has to be further encouraged by public policy. Both energy efficiency improvements and emissions reductions can be achieved when effective policies are implemented to decouple energy consumption from profits made by utility companies. The idea that the latter can only make money by selling ever-larger amounts of energy must be discredited. Instead, companies must be allowed to benefit from offering demand-management services instead.

California Dreamin'

The negawatt approach has been particularly influential in California. Over the past 36 years, following the 1973 oil crisis, California has pursued an increasingly effective energy efficiency policy regime. A variety of regulatory programmes have been used to improve energy efficiency in domestic energy use, in building standards, and by utility providers and electrical appliance manufacturers. As a result, California has de-coupled from national trends of electricity demand, reducing its per capita energy requirements to 40 percent below the US average. This has brought considerable economic benefits. California has grown more prosperous even as its citizens have cut the amount of energy they use and the greenhouse gases they produce.

Household energy savings of $56 billion from 1972-2006 have enabled Californian households to redirect their expenditures toward other goods and services, creating about 1.5 million jobs with a total payroll of $45 billion. A report by Ceres, a US network of investors, environmental organizations and public interest groups, found that the economic benefits of energy-efficiency innovation had a compounding effect. For instance, it estimates that the first 1.4 percent of annual efficiency gains produced no less than 181,000 new jobs in California.[14]

More recent policy measures have seen the introduction of the Global Warming Solutions Act which became law in California in 2006. This is America's first comprehensive global warming legislation with an enforceable cap on GHG emissions. As well as a long-term goal of reducing emissions by 80 percent below 1990 levels by 2050, it sets out requirements for delivering further energy efficiency improvements. Through this legislation it is estimated California will gain more than 400,000 new jobs, a large proportion relating to energy-efficiency programmes.[15]

Now a new Long-term Energy Efficiency Strategic Plan is becoming a comprehensive roadmap for achieving even more energy savings in California. The Plan was developed by a stakeholder-driven process in 40 public meetings and workshops with some 500 organizations. It covers government, utility and private sector initiatives. The plan emphasizes a variety of practical 'negawatt' measures: for instance, utilities that help customers reduce energy demand can avoid the cost of investing in new power plants; manufacturers that conduct life-cycle assessments on their products can reduce energy and raw material costs.

It advances a detailed framework that incorporates energy-efficiency measures for utilities and businesses as well as consumers. It includes four 'Big Bold Strategies' for significant energy-savings across California:

- **All eligible low-income homes will be energy-efficient by 2020**
- **All new residential construction will be zero net energy by 2020**
- **All new commercial construction will be zero net energy by 2030**
- **The building services industry will be regulated to ensure optimal equipment performance** [16]

"If California had not moved as forcefully to decrease energy consumption over the last three decades, we would be in a much more precarious économic position right now. Imagine where the country could be if it were as efficient as California", says F. Noel Perry, venture capitalist and founder of the Next 10 project, an online, interactive, educational tool. [17]

Such findings provide much ammunition to those who want President Obama to launch a green energy revolution, encouraging renewable power and energy efficiency as a way of generating large numbers of jobs during the current recession. The American Council for an Energy-Efficient Economy is set to encourage other US states to replicate California's energy efficiency measures, and to get Washington to implement relevant nationwide policies.

Barriers to efficiency

It would be nice if caps on fossil-fuel burning were universally applied in developed countries. The reality is that only a small share of the energy-efficiency potential has so far been realized, because of various barriers. Identifying these barriers is a first step to overcoming them.

A major problem in the commercial building sector is split incentives: these exist where building owners are responsible for investment decisions, but tenants pay the energy bills. Owners have little interest in commissioning energy-efficient buildings. This reluctance can only be overcome by strong public policy directives regulating for high levels of energy efficiency in all commercial buildings.

Market barriers towards energy-efficiency investment also exist due to too low energy prices or the adverse effects of fiscal incentives. For instance, the office space market in London is a clear example why energy efficiency has not gone mainstream: energy costs there are equivalent to just 1 to 2 percent of total business running costs – a very limited incentive to save energy.

In addition, ignorance about energy matters among owners, end-users and energy providers all along the value chain can result in barriers to greater energy efficiency. This has to be addressed by better provision of information about the benefits of energy efficiency.

In the United States, another barrier to efficient energy use is in evidence: capital investments in commercial buildings must be depreciated over 30 years or so, while energy purchases can be fully deducted from taxable income in the year in which they occur.

Likewise, householders often find it difficult to evaluate information on energy use, for instance verifying savings and calculating the payback period for buying more efficient appliances. Energy-efficient equipment is often more expensive than the less efficient alternative. Even though efficient appliances often have a longer lifetime, end-users still tend to purchase the less efficient products because of their lower cost, and this applies particularly to low-income households and small businesses.

But probably the most important barrier to greater efficiency in energy use is the 'rebound factor', which refers to the fact that people tend to use more energy and buy additional appliances as soon as they see that they have reduced their energy bills. There is more about this at the end of the chapter.

The case for Combined Heat and Power (CHP)

The concept of energy efficiency relates not only to energy use, but also to production. With large centralized power stations, typical for much of the electricity that is produced, only about one-third of the energy contained in the fuel source is actually used, while two-thirds get lost during transmission. Therefore, a switch to decentralized and localized production of energy in CHP systems has great potential to minimize losses while maximizing energy efficiency. So called cogeneration or tri-generation plants can achieve up to 90 percent efficiency by providing electricity as well as heating (and cooling in tri-generation) for industrial and building sectors. Since CHP accounts for only 7 percent of world power generation today, a lot of energy and financial savings are yet to be made.

The Danish experience

The country with the most extensive use of cogeneration in Europe is Denmark. In the following paragraphs we describe some of the steps taken to switch the country to ever-greater energy efficiency.

In 1979, after the two major oil crises in the 1970s, the Danish government passed the first legislation on efficient energy supply, aiming to connect more than half the country's 2.5 million homes to a district heating system (DH), using gas or biomass boilers and CHP systems.

With the coming of the 1986 Agreement on CHP, decentralized cogenerated heat and electricity became a major policy priority. In 1988, the installation of electric heaters in new buildings was banned and this ban was extended to electric boilers in buildings with water-based central heating systems. Fuel taxes were levied, with biomass and biogas exempted. The legislation was complemented by energy savings initiatives, such as improved building insulation.

In 1981 the Danish Renewable Energy Development Programme was introduced, which enabled households or enterprises to apply for subsidies for installing biofuel boilers, solar hot water panels, wind turbines and heat pumps. In 1990 the law on heat supply was amended to support the use of cogeneration and environmentally friendly fuels.

The conversion of district heating boilers to CHP systems took place in three phases and was more or less completed in 1998. But a problem arose: electricity production increased so much that surpluses had to be sold to neighbouring countries below production costs. As of 2003, CHP plants were therefore exempted from the obligation to cogenerate heat and electricity at all times.[18]

Energy performance contracting

An energy performance contract is a partnership between a building owner or a long-term tenant and Energy Services Company (ESCO), whereby the ESCO provides the up-front capital for energy upgrade projects, which is then paid back over time with the energy savings those upgrades yield. This methodology is widely used to improve the energy performance of buildings because it is both simple and effective.

The building owner or long-term tenant enters into an agreement with an ESCO, which does a building survey by which opportunities for energy savings are identified. It then recommends a package of improvements on the understanding that they will be paid for through energy savings. The ESCO guarantees that savings meet or exceed annual payments to cover all project costs – usually over a contract term of seven to ten years. If savings don't materialize, the ESCO – not the owner or tenant – agrees to pay the difference. To ensure that savings are realized, the ESCO also offers staff training and long-term maintenance services. [19]

Funding for energy performance contracting is usually supplied by banks, but sometimes backed up by government-backed Energy Saving Funds. Their purpose is to support end-users in their energy-efficiency investment decisions. State programmes to finance energy efficiency measures exist in many countries. Funds can be supplied through:

- **treasury funds**
- **charges on energy prices**
- **emissions trading schemes**
- **taxes on inefficient products**
- **abolished subsidies for conventional energy sources**

Vacuum insulation panels

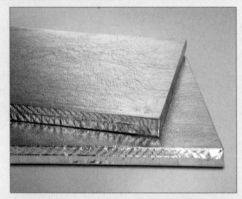

Source: RTF Manufacturing. This new insulation technology is highly efficient – a 3 cm layer has the same insulation capacity as a 30 cm layer of rockwool or fibreglass. It can be used on the inside of buildings without much loss of interior space.

Passive house design

The 160 million buildings in the European Union account for over 40 percent of its primary energy consumption. Energy use in buildings therefore represents a major contributor to fossil-fuel use and carbon dioxide emissions. The passive house concept has become increasingly influential in recent years, and more and more countries are passing legislation for ultra-low energy buildings to become standard in the coming years.

The term 'passive house' (Passivhaus in German) refers to a rigorous voluntary standard for ultra-low-energy buildings that require little energy for space heating or cooling. A similar standard, Minergy-P, is used in Switzerland. These standards can refer not only to residential properties but also to office buildings, schools and shops. The passive integrated design concepts are applied mostly to new buildings, but are increasingly used also for building refurbishment.

Beyond passive houses, 'energy-plus' houses are starting to be built as well – these are buildings that don't just supply their own energy needs from PV roofs and other renewable energy devices but are actually capable of supplying a surplus of electricity. An example of this is the Solarsiedlung in Freiburg, Germany, discussed in Chapter 8.

WARM ZONE KIRKLEES

In the UK the city of Kirklees is pioneering a comprehensive approach to urban energy efficiency. 'Kirklees Warm Zone' is Britain's biggest and most comprehensive programme to tackle domestic energy efficiency, fuel poverty and climate change, providing practical energy efficiency support to householders. The Warm Zone brand was established by the UK government in 2000 and has since helped over 500,000 homes across the country.

In Kirklees an estimated 45,000 householders are in fuel poverty, unable to adequately heat their homes. The Warm Zone can offer help to every household to its improve energy efficiency whilst also offering other support services. The main aim is to provide warm, energy-efficient homes. Installation of all energy-efficiency measures is made dependent on an initial technical survey of the home.

Warm Zone offers:

- *Free cavity wall and loft insulation for all households*
- *Free low-energy light bulbs to all*
- *Free improvements to heating systems for needy households*
- *Competitive prices for replacement boilers for households that can afford to pay*
- *Reduced prices for renewable technologies*

Warm Zone works on a ward by ward, street by street approach so no home is missed. Funding is being provided by Kirklees Council, Scottish Power, National Grid, the Regional Housing Board, Scottish Power Energy People Trust and British Gas Energy Trust.

www.kirklees.gov.uk/community/environment/ energyconservation/warmzone/warmzonefaq.shtml

Energy and transport

The evolution of transport technologies from the 18th century onwards has extended the distances which we travel and across which goods are transported further and further. In 2004, the transportation sector accounted for 26 percent of global energy use, 70 percent of which was caused by road transport (passenger cars and trucks). Roughly two-thirds of the global transport energy is used for passenger mobility, while one-third is used to ship freight. With many of the world's economies expected to grow in the decades ahead, the share of energy used for transportation could increase dramatically. Rapid moves towards more energy-efficient

transportation systems are therefore critically important.

Efforts towards energy efficiency in the transport sector involve improvements not only in vehicle fuel economy but also in transportation infrastructure, as well as limitations to the unnecessary use of carbon-based forms of transport. To make the vehicle fleet more fuel-efficient, standards to reduce carbon emissions have to be established, financial incentives have to be provided for the purchase and use of low-emission vehicles, and regulations introduced for replacing inefficient vehicles. Government agencies should take the lead in all this by adapting appropriate public procurement policies.

The following diagram by Canadian transport researcher James Strickland gives a concise impression of the energy efficiency (or the lack of it) of various modes of transport.

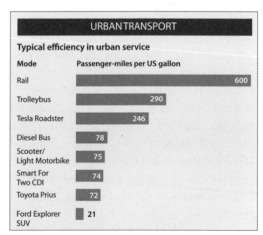

Source: IEA 2008; In support of the G8 Action Plan, Energy Efficiency Policy Recommendations.
http://www.iea.org/G8/2008/G8_EE_recommendations.pdf

The vehicle mileage in this graph assumes full utilization of vehicle seating capacity. Evidence from the work of many urban transport planners indicates the much greater efficiency of electric transportation. Of course, wherever possible the need for urban transportation should be minimized, by planning policies aiming to the reintegrate work, schools, shopping and residential land use in close proximity.[20]

Transport specialist Prof. Jeffrey Kenworthy ranks cities across the world according to their per capita transport energy use. There is a direct correlation between urban density and car use in the wealthy cities. Cities with the most sustainable transport produce about five times less CO_2 per person than cities with the least sustainable transport system. Kenworthy has been able to show clearly that cities must strategically raise their densities to develop more sustainable mobility patterns. High public transport usage is a key feature of cities with more sustainable transport. Integrated development around public transport stops, especially railway stations, is fundamental to achieving this. Improved conditions for pedestrians and cyclists are essential to sustainable urban transport development.

It has been known for decades that building more freeways pushes cities towards higher automobile dependence. Cities need to minimize, stop or even reverse their supply of freeways. Reserved routes are essential to ensure the speed-competitiveness of public transport. The most sustainable cities offer a high level of provision of rail systems and dedicated bus facilities. Reserved rights-of-way are critical for transit. The evidence shows that public transport, walking and cycling can compete successfully with cars when given priority.

In eco-cities a nexus between transport and urban form is the core framework around which many other factors must operate. Creating sustainable urban form and transport depends upon:

1. Compact, mixed use development;
2. Human-oriented city centres and sub-centres with high density levels;
3. Priority given to high-quality public transport and non-motorized mobility;
4. Protected natural areas and spaces for food production in and around cities.[21]

RIVERSIMPLE URBAN HYDROGEN CAR

Credit: Hugo Spowers.

Its creator, Hugo Spowers, said this at the car's launch in London in June 2009: "This is a car for the future. Travel powered by fossil fuels is a major contributor to climate change. We want to demonstrate that clean and efficient hydrogen fuel cell vehicles are within our grasp. Our car emits only 30g/km of CO_2, well to wheel, in the urban cycle, even with hydrogen from natural gas. This is a quarter of the emissions of the lowest emitting car on the market today.

But our concept is also about the ownership, or non-ownership, of the cars; they will only ever be leased, not sold. This business model rewards longevity and low running costs. We will persuade people to keep their cars as long as possible rather than change them as frequently as possible.

We are also creating a manufacturing model that generates high-quality jobs in human-scale plants. There will be a large number of small plants to build our cars from advanced composite materials. This allows much greater resilience in fluctuating economic circumstances and much greater flexibility to produce what *different regions and niches need.*

We have further created an open intellectual property model, based on that used in open source software but not yet implemented in manufacturing. This will encourage the adoption of efficient vehicle technology as widely and quickly as possible.

Finally, we have developed a partnership corporate structure that balances the interests of all stakeholders. We can never achieve a sustainable system whilst the interests of one stakeholder group, such as shareholders, trumps the interests of society or the environment. Our partnership is bound by its constitution to pursue our purpose above the interests of any one group.

Our purpose is to systematically work towards the elimination of the environmental impact of personal transport. There are many fine initiatives that focus on the particular, but everything is connected and we need to look at the whole system in order to develop truly sustainable solutions."

www.riversimple.com

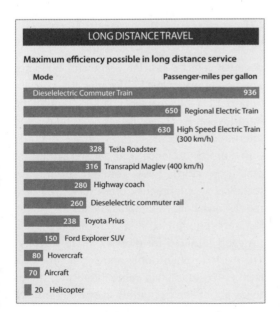

LONG DISTANCE TRAVEL	
Maximum efficiency possible in long distance service	
Mode	Passenger-miles per gallon
Dieselelectric Commuter Train	936
Regional Electric Train	650
High Speed Electric Train (300 km/h)	630
Tesla Roadster	328
Transrapid Maglev (400 km/h)	316
Highway coach	280
Dieselelectric commuter rail	260
Toyota Prius	238
Ford Explorer SUV	150
Hovercraft	80
Aircraft	70
Helicopter	20

The obvious conclusion from this graph is that passenger transportation rail vehicles are more efficient than road vehicles, except trolleybuses and the electric Tesla Roadster, and far more efficient than aircraft. Magnetic levitation (Maglev) trains, often proposed as a primary option for future long-distant transport, are about half as efficient as high-speed trains.

Road vehicles are, in general, more efficient than aircraft, but tend to cover much shorter distances. However, on some routes aircraft can be more efficient, as they can travel in a straight line whilst surface transport must often travel on winding roads. Generally road vehicles are less efficient than rail, though trolleybuses come quite close in similar service.

Goods transportation is a different matter, as bulk cargo is much more compact than 'people cargo'. Ships transporting goods are more energy-efficient than rail which, in turn, is more efficient than trucks.[22]

A more general point that needs to be raised here is that our insatiable appetite for mobility threatens to render all efforts to improve the efficiency of our transport systems wholly inadequate. Only a concerted effort to limit our desire for and dependence on mobility can ultimately deliver sustainable outcomes.

Image and patented 'solarsails' courtesy of Solar Sailor www.solarsailor.com.au. New approaches to reducing energy use and emissions in shipping include the use of kites, sails (some integrating PV), and blowing bubbles under the hull.

The rebound effect

Under the right circumstances, moves towards greater energy efficiency can become a useful tool for dealing with energy shortages or, indeed, climate change. But since reductions in CO_2 emissions by a factor of four or five over the coming decades are necessary in the developed world if catastrophic climate change is to be avoided, positive and very deliberate limitations on energy use may be required.

But the snag is that whilst encouraging efficiency helps consumers save energy, it does not necessarily stop them from buying an ever-greater variety of gadgets that require additional energy. Whilst energy-efficient light bulbs and fridges may reduce the consumption in this segment of energy use, additional computers or ever-larger plasma TV screens may add to overall energy consumption. While the consumer gets more service for the same amount of energy, they also increase overall consumption. So, all in all, greater energy efficiency per se does not necessarily result in reduced energy use.

Today's typical refrigerators, which account for 20 percent of a household's utility costs, use about one-fourth the energy of 1972 models. But, on the other hand, they are also likely to be twice or three times the size of 1970s models. Similarly, the thermal efficiency of car engines improved substantially in recent decades as design improvements were made. But this does not necessarily translate into better fuel economy of cars overall, as people in developed countries have tended to buy bigger and heavier cars with ever more powerful engines.

The relative simplicity of the benefits of demand management was being questioned as long ago as 1865 when the British economist W. Stanley Jevons published his book *The Coal Question*. The 'Jevons Paradox' states that conservation of fuel paradoxically leads to increased consumption of fuel: if large numbers of people start conserving fuel, this will lower the price of that fuel which, in turn, will encourage increased consumption. Thus, argues Jevons, increased energy efficiency results in raising demand for energy in the economy as a whole.

In the real economy a rebound effect is often observed: for instance, if householders switch from using 18W compact fluorescent bulbs instead of 75W incandescent bulbs, the energy saving should be 76 percent. But in reality this is seldom so. Because the lighting now costs less per hour to run, users are often less motivated to switch lights off. Thus, they 'take back' some of the energy savings by leaving more lights on for longer, particularly when past levels of energy services – lighting, heating or cooling – were regarded as inadequate.[23]

This observation reinforces the Jevons Paradox. Nevertheless, critics argue that this view is likely to break down when significant energy shortages and price rises occur, because these encourage conservation measures, whether people like it or not.

Efficiency or sufficiency: when enough is enough

Because vehicles last for years, and buildings and power plants last for decades, it is crucially important to initiate major changes through the introduction of significant national and international policies.

In Europe, America and Japan, significant efficiency gains have resulted from new technical developments, often driven by new regulations, policy standards and tax incentives. But is this enough to bring CO_2 emissions down to levels required for global climate security? The Austrian philosopher and social critic Ivan Illich (1926–2002) had some interesting things to say about energy matters. In an essay entitled

Energy and Equity, published in 1975, he questioned the wisdom of increases in energy use as a prerequisite of social betterment. He insisted that ever-greater energy use was also a step towards ever-greater alienation and social separation: "The energy policies adopted during the current decade will determine the range and character of social relationships a society will be able to enjoy by the year 2000. A low-energy policy allows for a wide choice of lifestyles and cultures. If, on the other hand, a society opts for high energy consumption, its social relations must be dictated by technocracy and will be equally degrading whether labelled capitalist or socialist. . . . While people have begun to accept ecological limits on maximum per capita energy use as a condition for physical survival, they do not yet think about the use of minimum feasible power as the foundation of any of various social orders that would be both modern and desirable. Yet only a ceiling on energy use can lead to social relations that are characterized by high levels of equity."[24]

This view is a fierce challenge to the widely held view that the rest of the world must play catch-up with the countries that have gone furthest in their use of energy. Illich's views, of course, are now highly topical because of the huge climate challenges facing humanity: we must all meet at a certain level of energy use that is compatible with climate stability as well as the limits to the use of fossil fuels, which are much better understood now to be a finite resource. It is interesting that Illich should argue for limited energy use from the point of view of social wellbeing and equality. This is certainly food for thought.

Illich again: "What is generally overlooked is that equity and energy can grow concurrently only to a point. Below a threshold of per capita wattage, motors improve the conditions for social progress. Above this threshold, energy grows at the expense of equity. Further energy affluence then means decreased distribution of control over that energy."

PACE: A New Policy for Energy Efficiency from Berkeley, California

Randy Hayes, World Future Council
Fundamental to achieving a renewable world is to maximize energy efficiency in the already built world. Property Assessment for Clean Energy or PACE is a method of financing the work of insulation, lighting, window replacement, appliance upgrade, etc.
Imagine that property owners can borrow from a special city fund to improve the energy efficiency of their property. They can even use the money to install renewable energy systems. Building owners pay the low-interest loan back over 20 years. Often, the annual savings on the energy bill will be greater than the annual payment!
Here is how it works: you apply for a loan from this special fund that your city can set up. An annual tax is added to your property tax bill. If your home or office building is sold, the changes to the building stay with the building. So the new owners pay the remaining tax obligation. Even the city's costs to administer the programme are covered in the programme.
The city of Berkeley, California came up with this model, which they call the 'Berkeley First'. The pilot programme is focused on financing solar power, but will expand to energy efficiency. For more information: **www.ci.berkeley.ca.us/ Content Display.aspx?id=26580**.
Where does the city get the money? They issue bonds. The way they issue the bonds is similar to how cities typically finance sewer upgrades and neighbourhood beautification projects. It is a well-known and trusted financing system therefore it should be easily replicated. Hundreds of cities across the US and in a few

other countries are looking into replicating this approach. Contact your city now and ask them to look into it. This is low-cost capital for building retrofits – an important part of the path to a renewable world.

The 2000-Watt Society

The idea that it is necessary to define a level of global energy use beyond which we should not go has a rapidly growing following. There is much evidence that it is necessary to define overall limits on energy use – both in terms of 'what is sufficient for us' and in terms of what is good for the planet. A really worthwhile proposal was made in 1998 by the Swiss Federal Institute of Technology in Zürich – the 2000-Watt Society. In this scenario each person in the developed world would cut their overall rate of energy use to no more than 2,000 watts – 17,520 kilowatt-hours per year for all energy use, by the year 2050 – by a range of energy efficiency measures. (The Swiss Solar Energy Society is pushing for a much more rapid move to 2,000 watts, namely by 2030.) The concept can be scaled up from personal or household energy use to the collective energy use of the whole society. Together with this energy limit, a 1 ton of CO_2 emissions limit per person per year was also stipulated.

Limiting the total energy use per person will be a critical goal in any future energy scenario. 2,000 watts corresponds to the average consumption of Swiss citizens in 1960 and is approximately the current world average rate of total energy use. It compares to current averages of around 6,000 watts in Western Europe, 12,000 watts in the United States, 1,500 watts in China, 1,000 watts in India, and only 300 watts in Bangladesh. The last time Switzerland was a 2,000-watt society was in the 1960s, but it currently uses a per capita average of around 5,000 watts.

In response to concerns about climate change and energy security, the scenario further envisages that the use of carbon-based fuels would be cut to no more than 500 watts per person, or a quarter of the 2,000 watt allocation, within 50 years.

The proposal is backed by major bodies such as the Swiss Federal Office of Energy and the Association of Swiss Architects and Engineers. It is envisaged that achieving a 2,000-watt society will require, among other measures,

- **a refocusing of research into new priority areas**
- **a major investment in the country's capital assets**
- **refurbishment of the nation's building stock to low-energy standards**
- **major improvements in the efficiency of road transport and aviation**
- **revisioning of energy-intensive materials use, and**
- **widespread introduction of renewable energy, district heating and microgeneration.**[25]

LIFESTYLE WITH 2,000 WATTS

Hans Zulliger

2,000 watts is today's continuous power requirement of an average world citizen. A central European inhabitant demands 3-4 times this amount and is responsible for about 8 times more CO_2 output than would be required to stop global warming. To put it in technical terms, we are challenged to use no more than 17,500 kWh equivalent per person and year and to discharge no more than 1 ton of CO_2. (1 litre of oil or gasoline contains about 10 kWh of energy and 2.5 kg of CO_2.) The energy balance presented here is the energy used by a private person, not including the consumption of the workplace.

What lifestyle would be possible if this were the consumption limit for a European of good social standing?

The first priority is to eliminate fossil fuels for heating the living space and hot water. Passive solar heat with thermal solar collectors can supply more than half of the energy required in a well-insulated house. The rest can be produced with a heat pump (the electricity must come from a renewable source like wind, hydro or waste biomass) or by burning biomass cleanly.

Credit: Hans Zulliger.

Our house (2 persons) requires 5,000 kWh for hot water and heating a year. Lighting, cooking, appliances (we have no dryer), computers etc. use about 3500 kW. This is primarily a matter of well-chosen investments and a conscious lifestyle. We have made the necessary upgrades and enjoy a very comfortable room temperature, typical for houses with low energy consumption.

A more serious challenge is the energy consumption and CO_2 output of transport. If all the energy allocation were to be used for transport only, each of us could consume 1,750 litres of gasoline for a small car or kerosene in an airplane. This would let us travel a distance of about 25,000 km a year. But 1 ton of CO_2 lets us drive or fly only 6,000 km, a goal we have not

yet achieved, since we have been flying too far.

We have opted to use mostly trains for our travels. In addition, we drive our hybrid car about 5,000 km a year, using 250 litres of gasoline. We could fly 8,000 km a year if we ignored the CO_2 limit. This is certainly a severe restriction, since air travel is cheap and there are many fascinating places in the world.

Overall, our lifestyle is very comfortable and satisfying and we find great joy through personal contacts with family and friends. We gladly forgo our desire to fly to exotic places, knowing that we are making a significant contribution to reducing the world's resource consumption.

Energy descent

The idea of a 2,000-Watt Society links closely with the concept of 'energy descent' that has been developed in Britain in recent years. This discussion has been raised primarily out of concern about the continued availability of fossil fuels and about global competition with developing countries that are demanding a fairer share of energy resources.

But even for developing and emerging countries, there are limits to increasing their use of fossil-fuel energy. An ever-growing number of energy analysts are coming around to the view that we are close to reaching peak oil, and that gas and even coal may also be approaching peak production rates in the coming decades.[26] With less and less fossil fuels available to us at an ever higher price, we need to move towards living within the annual energy supply available from the sun. Whilst there is no doubt that the harvest of renewable energy will grow as technologies develop, this means developing lifestyles that are better integrated with natural processes and cycles than we are presently used to.

In the global context, energy descent is used

as a term for a transitional phase during which humanity goes from the growing use of fossil fuels, which has occurred ever since the industrial revolution, to a diminishing use of fossil fuels. In the end we must ask ourselves 'What do we really need to be happy, healthy and vibrantly alive? 'There is much evidence to suggest that we could live very well on 80 to 90 percent less energy than we presently use. It is a matter of adjusting our lifestyles, values and priorities, and this may take some reorientation.

Whilst all energy efficiency improvements are helpful, we should start exploring what energy sufficiency could mean in practice. In the richer countries we will have to start climbing down the pyramid of energy slaves, which will require significant changes in our habits. But it will be apparent that gains in quality of life will emerge from this energy descent, that life will become less hectic, that there can be more personal contacts, more walking, less driving, better air quality and less noise. All of these changes, discussed in more detail in Chapter 8, are bound to be beneficial to both our mental and physical health.

We need to utilize a new kind of 'linking thinking', connecting concern about climate change and energy security with sustainable energy solutions. A fundamental change in the ways in which societies produce and consume energy is indispensable for global sustainable development.

This means that we must deal with the mismatch between what we know and what we are actually doing much of the time.

The effectiveness of energy capture is a central organizing principle in living organisms as well as in social systems. The performance quality of any energy system is determined by a complex combination of factors – physical, technical, economic, social and environmental. A much more sophisticated use of energy is called for at this time.

In order to guarantee every inhabitant of this planet a safe, reliable, efficient, accessible and affordable energy supply, future energy policies need to:

- **decouple energy consumption from utility company profits**
- **remove subsidies for fossil fuels and nuclear energy**
- **use energy performance contracting for retrofitting existing buildings**
- **define procurement specifications for transportation, office equipment and buildings**
- **shorten transmission distances between production and consumption**
- **reward competition between market participants to assure efficient solutions**
- **define necessary limits on per capita energy consumption**

Acknowledgements

Axel Bree *WFC staff*
Stefan Schurig *WFC staff*
Hans-Peter Dürr *WFC councillor*
Jeffery Kenworthy *Curtin University, Perth*
Iris Gust *Hafen City University, Hamburg*
Hans Zulliger *Foundation for the Third Millenium*
Dan Frybort *Solar Sailor*

Keeping warm

Keeping warm in winter, or keeping cool in summer under a tropical sun, need not require vast amounts of fossil fuel. When fuel resources seemed limitless, and when climate change was not an issue, living in an 'age of fire' seemed to make sense. But now we need the right incentives to insulate rather than to light a fire.

Being energy-efficient makes environmental sense. But it must also make economic sense. Governments have not shied away from subsidizing fossil-fuel burning with vast amounts of money. The challenge now is to assure that it becomes cost-effective for everybody to save energy rather than to use it.

Long-term thinking has been alien to governments driven by the desire to be reelected in a few years time. But it is up to all of us to assure that governments are inventive in the interests of both present and future voters. We the voters need to change the parameters under which governments make laws on behalf of all of us.

www.greenjobsnow.com

The Green-Collar Economy

" *We'll put people back to work rebuilding our crumbling roads and bridges, modernizing schools that are failing our children, and building wind farms and solar panels, fuel-efficient cars and the alternative energy technologies that can free us from our dependence on foreign oil and keep our economy competitive in the years ahead.* "

US President Barack Obama

" *Where your talents and the needs of the world cross, therein lies your vocation.* "

Aristotle

Introduction

'Green-collar jobs' allow all of society to engage in the two most critical objectives of the next decade: equitably protecting the environment and future-proofing the economy. Creating green jobs and a sustainable economy is a perfect example of two of the themes of this book, 'a logic too compelling to ignore' and 'opportunity in necessity'. In other words, we have to do these things anyway, and if we do, everybody wins.

> *"Gangs are never goin' to die out. You all goin' to get us jobs?" – Black youth in Los Angeles.*

The rapid transition to a low-carbon economy is not only vital for climate protection and human security, but will deliver many and varied employment opportunities for all levels of society. This brings environmental protection into the daily lives of many more people than is currently the case. If a society has a large percentage of the population connected to environmentally friendly products and services directly through jobs, they become more aware and more active stakeholders. This improves the conditions for making the popular mandate necessary for passing effective environmental legislation, and spurring positive behavioural change.

People can access the low-carbon sector via anything from driving, building and planting, to administration, financial and legal work, to journalism, design, research and engineering. The greening of existing jobs and the creation of many new green jobs is already a multi-billion dollar global reality. Ultimately, all jobs should be green.

Green-collar jobs have become a major issue in US politics, as the nation attempts to address the realities of environmental, economic and financial crises. While they had been held back

Credit: Clipper Wind.

by a regressive federal administration for many years, the focus on green jobs is now increasing rapidly, due to efforts at state and municipal level, as well as those of many non-profit initiatives, trade unions and partnerships. Under the leadership of President Barack Obama, the 'green economy' has been identified as a key strategy for restarting stalled industrial production, saving and re-visioning failing industries, securing energy supplies and protecting the environment. His economic stimulus package contains many billions of dollars for green industries and measures (as detailed below).

Over the past three decades, several European countries have been quietly moving ahead with a transition in their economies, mainly in renewables and energy efficiency. Studies come mostly from Germany, which has forged ahead in these areas, but countries such as Denmark, Sweden and the other Scandinavian nations have excelled in introducing renewable energy generation, insulation, heating and more efficient building design.

The green jobs agenda is one of the most important in the environmental and social justice movements. It unites people with responsibility and opportunity. It can attract votes, customers and employees. It can provide first steps on the employment ladder, and offers plenty of career advancement opportunities. It will become increasingly leveraged in efforts toward finally generating real momentum towards true sustainability.

This chapter will look at definitions, the spread of opportunities in the sector, projected growth, drivers and barriers. Although not a long-established area of investigation, there are now a number of very solid studies carried out at different levels to understand this field and advocate its advancement. This chapter draws from this excellent material.

What is a green-collar job?

'Green Collar' as a term arrived via a 1976 Congressional hearing in the US, when Professor Patrick Heffernan delivered a paper entitled 'Jobs for the Environment – The Coming Green Collar Revolution'. Since then the term had mostly lain dormant. However, in the last few years many individuals and groups in the US have been developing this approach. They have made the positive economic opportunities explicit, successfully describing the links between economy and environment and between poverty and pollution, and

comprehensively dispelled the myth that environmental protection can only come at a cost to the national budget. This was the logic voiced by the federal administration under President Bush when defending their decision not to sign up to the Kyoto protocol. The opposite is true, when decisions are made to prioritize green growth at the national level. The renewable energy industry alone has comprehensively demonstrated this.

Green-collar jobs can cover many sectors, from low to high skill levels. They are not necessarily brand new types of jobs, but can be 'greener' versions of existing job types, such as in research and development, or manufacturing and agriculture, with associated support staff and service sector positions. These jobs are all directly associated with addressing the vast panoply of environmental issues around the world, including food, water, ecosystems, energy, manufacturing, transport, buildings and waste.

> "... the burgeoning industry is claiming scores of experienced workers who can put to use the skills they've acquired in more established fields such as construction, finance, and marketing. In some cases, the high demand for green career-changers translates into a larger paycheck. But more often, the satisfaction of making a positive difference in the world is enough of a boost."[1]

The definition of a 'green-collar job' has been interpreted in slightly different ways. A major report by UNEP suggests that defining green jobs is a matter of defining a green economy. In other words, how green can a job be in a dirty economy? Could the greening of transport fuels make a driver's job greener, for example? The authors talk of 'shades of green':

Credit: Green Jobs Now.

A green economy is an economy that values nature and people and creates decent, well-paying jobs. Technological and systemic choices offer varying degrees of environmental benefit and different types of employment. Pollution prevention has different implications than pollution control, as does climate mitigation compared with adaptation, efficient buildings vis-à-vis retrofits; or public transit versus fuel-efficient automobiles. It is of course preferable that the most efficient, least polluting options receive priority. But these are not either-or choices, as all of these options are needed to bring about a more sustainable, low-carbon economy. But they do suggest 'shades of green' in employment. Greater efficiency in the use of energy, water, and materials is a core objective. The critical question is where to draw the line between efficient and inefficient practices. A low threshold will define a greater number of jobs as green, but may yield an illusion of progress. In the light of the need to dramatically reduce humanity's environmental footprint, the bar needs to be set high – best available technology and best practices internationally should be seen as the most appropriate thresholds. And, given technological progress and the urgent need for improvement, the dividing line between efficient and inefficient must rise over time. Hence, 'green jobs' is a relative and highly dynamic concept.[2]

In his highly recommended book on the subject, US green economy campaigner and author Van Jones defines a green-collar job as "a family-supporting career-track job that directly contributes to preserving or enhancing environmental quality".[3] He sets out three core principles which define a green economy: equal protection for all, equal opportunity for all and reverence for all creation. He has been instrumental in campaigning for green jobs, and extending the dimensions of what they can achieve.

In reports from the US, the language of description is often strong in terms of its equal opportunity arguments. Advocates draw attention to the fact that low-income workers can find attractive, meaningful employment in this sector, due to low barriers to entry and career prospects in an expanding sector.[4]

Credit: Bristol Wood Recycling Project.

BRISTOL WOOD RECYCLING PROJECT, UK

This award-winning social enterprise has three objectives: to save resources from waste; to provide affordable timber and resources to the local community; to enable social inclusion and offer learning opportunities through volunteer and work placement.

The idea started in 1998 in Brighton and Hove, and has since spread to 20 towns and cities, creating around 60 jobs in England and Wales. There is now a national umbrella organization, the National Community Wood Recycling Project. Since 2005, BWRP has collected over 1,000 tonnes of wood waste, transforming around a fifth from waste into reusable material. The wood is collected, cleaned up and transformed for re-use in the Wood Shop, or turned into wood chips. Retail sales amount to around £80,000 annually.

The wood or wood products are bought by customers in construction, house building and renovation, as well as by institutions and creative designers. These customers value the social and environmental benefits of the enterprise, as well as getting low-priced wood products to keep their costs down.

The project relies on time given by volunteers, who can come from many backgrounds, including 'marginalized groups' such as the long-term unemployed, those with substance abuse problems, those with learning difficulties or mental illness. The Project offers them an inclusive, sociable and practical environment in which they can gain work experience, skills and confidence to help better their personal situation.

The project is self-financing, and supports four full-time staff, some of whom started as volunteers themselves. They have created work and training opportunities for dozens of volunteers, entirely without grant funding. Bristol City Council supports the initiative by providing land at very low rental rates.

www.bwrp.org.uk

Others are more direct: "Put simply, if a job improves the environment, but doesn't provide a family-supporting wage or a career ladder to move low-income workers into higher-skilled occupations, it is not a green-collar job. Such would be the case with workers installing solar

GREEN AND DECENT JOBS? A SCHEMATIC OVERVIEW

GREEN BUT NOT DECENT
Examples:
- Electronics recycling without adequate occupational safety
- Low-wage installers of solar panels
- Exploited biofuels plantation day labourers

GREEN AND DECENT
Examples:
- Unionized wind and solar power jobs
- Green architects
- Well-paid public transit employees

NEITHER GREEN NOR DECENT
Examples:
- Coal mining with adequate safety
- Women workers in the cut flower industry in Africa and Latin America
- Hog slaughterhouse workers

DECENT BUT NOT GREEN
Examples:
- Unionized car manufacturing workers
- Chemical engineers
- Airline pilots

Environment

Decent Work

Source: Worldwatch Institute, 2008.[6]

panels without job security or proper training, or young people pushing brooms at a green building site without opportunity for training or advancement."[5]

So, while there is as yet no universally agreed definition in existing studies, there are several common features. Broadly, people exploring this area consider green-collar jobs to be those which:

- **are related to environmentally friendly products and services**
- **are relevant to all education and skill levels**
- **provide a living wage and health benefits**
- **offer career development**
- **are often locally based**

The range of green-collar jobs

Green jobs can fall into many categories. Technical, highly-skilled positions in research and development (R&D), engineering and manufacturing are only one part of the chain. In renewable energy, for example, investors do a great deal of work to develop a project; environmental impact assessments (EIAs) and consultations may be necessary before installations can be approved; the financial sector helps facilitate projects; legal and administrative support is essential; professionals are required to install the technologies, connect them to the grid and maintain them; policy work is vital to enable market development; civil servants develop legislation and other facilitating measures; independent standards agencies oversee industry and government behaviour; and media and advertising are used by all with related products and services.

As the green sector develops, many people will find jobs within it through various entry points. There are voluntary and entry level positions, some offering on-the-job training;

people can transfer skills from another profession, they can retrain specifically, or take courses of study. While it is highly competitive already, there are many openings.

MOVING IN TO THE GREEN-COLLAR SECTOR
Ben Cartland, Acre Resources Ltd

Your first step is to find out how your experience is relevant to the 'green space'. Which elements of the green sector would most benefit from your previous experience – whether the NGO, charity, public or corporate arenas? Many of the most senior green-collar executives are career switchers themselves – highlighting the most common route for people wanting to make the move. In the vast majority of cases, people will move into the sector within their organizations (rather than quitting to find a new job in this space). If you work in a large company, the chances are that green-related activities are going on somewhere within that structure. By seeking out the decision-makers, being clear about your ambitions and focused on adding value to their work, you should find that they're open to you helping their work as a small part of your role.

There is a large and growing workforce of highly experienced green professionals out there, and when you apply for the more 'senior' positions without an explanation of how your background is relevant, getting through to interview stage will be a challenge. So be sure to identify parts of your former or current experiences which can be relevant to positions, and underline the value in those transferable skills.

Whether you're a new graduate or a career switcher or community worker, your chances of getting that dream job will be hugely increased by two things – in-depth industry research and networking. Make sure you've done your homework – there are lots of resources where you can start to really understand the different elements to the green landscape and help identify where you'd best fit.

One of the great things about the green sector is that most people working in the space are genuinely passionate about what they do, and keen to share their experiences with new entrants into the market. There are lots of conferences, events, and online networking groups that can help you to meet people, make connections and open doors for yourself. For those approaching the sector from a standing start, internships and volunteering can be a good way to build experience and contacts. Most charities encourage volunteers and corporations positively encourage unpaid internships, but do make sure that it's both relevant to what you want to do, and is focused on an issue that you're genuinely passionate about.

If you're sure that a career in the green sector is right for you, then perseverance and dedication will get you where you want to be. There are lots of people who flirt with the idea of the green sector without putting their all into the job search. You need to be committed and focus your time, whilst being realistic about the timescales; you will find that your dedication will win out.

The table below and continued onto the following page gives an idea of the scope of green-collar jobs by sector with specific roles, and opportunities for advancement within them. It is an amalgam of related tables from research in the US. The entry level roles are general, while the advanced ones are more specific. In such fast-developing sectors, this is by no means universal or complete.

Green-Collar Jobs: Sectors, positions and opportunities for advancement

SECTORS	SUB-SECTORS	ENTRY LEVEL POSITIONS	ADVANCED POSITIONS
Renewable Energy	Solar, Wind, Wave, Tidal, Geothermal and Bioenergy deployment (for biofuels see transport & agriculture) Storage technologies (hydrogen fuel cells, molten salts, pumped storage, batteries etc) Smart grid development	Customer Service Sales Installation, Construction Maintenance Driving	R&D, Journeyman, Solar Electrician Service Technician, Project Manager Construction Managers Environmental Engineers Industrial Production Managers
Energy Efficiency	Energy efficiency retrofits HVAC (Heating, Ventilation, Air Conditioning)	Installation Evaluation Manufacture, Construction	Journeyman, Construction Managers, Building Inspectors Materials scientist, Engineer
Green Building	Efficient windows and lighting, Insulation, Building materials, Hauling and reuse of construction and demolition materials and debris	Construction, Carpentry Demolition Driving	Architect, General Project Manager Contractor
Water	Water conservation Rainwater harvesting Adaptive grey water reuse	Installation Construction, Maintenance Repair	Journeyman R&D Project Manager
Transportation	Public transportation, Bicycle supply and repair Energy-efficient cars, More fuel-efficient vehicles Hybrid-electric, electric, and fuel cell vehicles Car sharing, Non-motorized transport Reducing distance and dependence on motorized transport, Biofuels production	Dispatch, Assembly Finishing and repair Biofuel production Distribution driving Maintenance, Electrics Engineering, Purchasing	R&D, Shop manager, Production manager Biofuels research, Head mechanic, Civil engineers, Transportation supervisors Computer software engineers Chemists, Chemical engineers Chemical technicians
Agriculture & Horticulture	Biofuels production, Urban agriculture Farmers' markets, Specialty foods production Baking, Soil conservation, Water efficiency, Organic growing methods, Reducing farms-to-market distance Green (sustainable) landscaping Tree-cutting and pruning Peri-urban and urban agriculture Parks and open space landscaping	Biofuel growing and refining Growing, Packaging Delivery, Selling Set-up/tear-down Brewing, Roasting, Packaging Baking, Mixing, Cleaning Planting, Maintenance Tree surgery/pruning	R&D Production manager Market manager Floor manager Head baker Project manager Landscape architect Head gardener

Green-Collar Jobs: Sectors, positions and opportunities for advancement (continued).

SECTORS	SUB-SECTORS	ENTRY LEVEL POSITIONS	ADVANCED POSITIONS
Woodworking	Custom architecture, cabinetry, furniture, repairs	Assembly, Sanding, Finishing Carpentry, Installation	Journeyman Head Carpenter
Manufacturing	Pollution control (scrubbers and other tailpipe technologies) Cradle-to-cradle (closed-loop systems)	Manufacturing Distribution driving	Designer Technician Manager
Materials Management/ Waste Stream Diversion	Recycling and reuse Extended producer responsibility/ Product take-back De-materialization Durability and repairability of products Large-scale green waste composting	Waste facility operation Collection, Sorting, Driving Loading, Salvaging Warehouse Packaging and Composting	Yard manager, Designer Research scientist, Warehouse manager, Floor/Department manager
Retail	Promoting efficient products/eco-labels New service economy (selling services, not products) Locating stores closer to residential areas Minimize shipping distance from origin of products to store location	Research Policy work Retail sales	Research director, Urban planner Store manager Logistics manager
Non-Toxic Printing	Commercial printing services Clean production techniques (toxics avoidance)	Binding Post-press, Delivery	Press Op Pre-Press
Non-Toxic Cleaning	Residential & commercial cleaning	Cleaning Customer service	Team leader Manager

Adapted from: Green Collar Jobs Are Community Serving Work Force Opportunities, (Pinderhughes, p3); Jobs That Will Build the Green US Economy and Fight Global Warming (PERI, p3); Shades of Green: Pro-Environmental Measures in Major Segments of the Economy (UNEP, 2007, p5) and Twenty-two different sectors of the US economy currently provide workers with green-collar jobs (Pinderhughes, p2).

Renewables and efficiency job creation

Renewable energy and energy efficiency have so far been two of the greatest job-creating sectors. An impressive list of facts and figures from the US and Germany shows the kind of economic and employment opportunities that are already being seized in these areas, and how this could expand in the future. According to the American Solar Energy Society, in their 2008 report *Defining, Estimating, and Forecasting the Renewable Energy and Energy Efficiency Industries in the US and in Colorado*, the US has a huge industry in renewables and efficiency already, and this could grow enormously in the coming years with the right incentives:

We found that, in 2007, the US RE&EE industries generated $1,045 billion in sales and created over 9 million jobs – including $10.3 billion in sales and over 91,000 jobs in Colorado. The US RE&EE revenues represent substantially more than the combined 2007 sales of the three largest US corporations – Wal-Mart, ExxonMobil, and GM ($905 billion). RE&EE are growing faster than the US average and contain some of the most rapidly growing industries in the world, such as wind, photovoltaics, fuel cells, recycling / remanufacturing, and biofuels. With appropriate federal and state government policies, RE&EE could by 2030 generate over 37 million jobs per year in the US . . .[7]

ASES's oft-quoted report on renewables for 2007 – *Renewable Energy and Energy Efficiency: Economic Drivers for the 21st Century* – forecast that by 2030 as many as 1 out of 4 workers (40 million people) in the US will be working in renewable energy and energy efficiency industries which will be worth up to $4.5 trillion in revenue in the US, with the appropriate public policies in place. They claim that these industries already generate nearly $1 trillion in revenue, contributing more than $150 billion in tax revenues.[8]

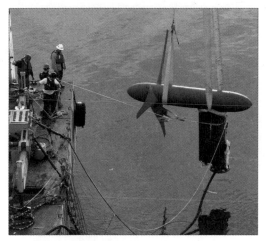

Credit: Marine Current Turbines Ltd.
Installing a marine current turbine.

Kammen et al, in a 2004 study on job creation from renewables, found that, per unit of delivered energy, the renewables industry provides more jobs than the fossil-fuel industry. Further, they suggest it is the comprehensiveness and coordination of energy policy that yields the biggest combined rewards for the various sectors.[9]

Germany has been an international beacon in terms of renewable energy job creation since the early 1990s, with a very active Federal Environment Ministry providing annual figures on these and other benefits of renewable energy.[10] Their spring 2009 press release summarizes the usual impressive data on the previous year's growth:

Renewable energies once again proved their importance for growth and employment last year. According to the latest figures, the number of employees in this sector rose from 250,000 in 2007 to almost 280,000 – an increase of more

than 10 percent. The reason: strongly increasing domestic turnover of around €30 billion in 2008 and a significant rise in the renewables' share in electricity and heat production. According to provisional estimates by the Working Group on Renewable Energies Statistics (AGEE-Stat), renewables enable savings of roughly 115 million tonnes of climate-damaging CO_2 per year in Germany – 57 million tonnes as a result of the Renewable Energy Sources Act (EEG) alone. With a share of around 10 percent in final energy consumption, renewables have further strengthened their role as a key pillar of sustainable energy supply. They have a share of 14.8 percent in gross electricity consumption and 7.7 percent in heat supply. In 2008 the renewables sector recorded a significant increase in turnover. Total investments and revenues from plant operations rose last year to around €30 billion – almost 4.5 billion more than in the previous year. With almost €13 billion, investments in plant construction were almost 20 percent above the previous year's figure.[11]

At the time of writing the economic downturn has not impacted the sector too significantly. Some job losses and bankruptcies have occurred, but oversupply has created a buyer's market, and whilst credit, finance and investment have taken a hit, the appetite for projects is still growing broadly in line with the industry trends of the last decade or so. Their guaranteed payments for renewable electricity generation through the feed-in tariff (see Chapter 3) have a major part to play in sustaining industry confidence.

Policy drivers

Some governments, national and local, have made great progress with environmentally-friendly laws and policies. Some companies are ahead of the curve in spotting opportunities presented by the need to address climate change and environmental damage, and to deal with fair trade issues, for example. Many members of the world's voting and shopping public are responding to the push and pull factors from government and business which are helping them to make greener lifestyle choices. All three groups influence one another, and are in turn influenced by energy costs. Getting away from fossil-fuel use is becoming easier as we learn from one another, and as new alternatives are developed. The rewards are immense, and first movers are securing valuable market share and supply chains. They are also future-proofing their country's economies and company's finances, and creating sustainable employment as a result.

These are some of the driving factors in producing changes in the world's economies. Green markets are growing as a result, and at present are estimated at €1,000 billion, with a projected ~€2,200 billion by 2020:

Green sectors, and present and future values

Energy efficiency technologies	€450 billion	€900 billion by 2020
Waste management/recycling	€30 billion	€46 billion by 2020
Water supply/sanitation/water efficiency	€185 billion	€480 billion by 2020
Sustainable transport	€180 billion	€360 billion by 2020

Policy drivers have been perhaps most apparent in renewables and recycling, but are becoming increasingly visible in many other key areas, including energy efficiency, manufacturing, waste, buildings and transport:

- **Renewable energy and energy efficiency targets, mandates and incentives (feed-in tariffs, solar roof programmes, solar thermal ordinances, tax credits, portfolio standards, fuel efficiency standards)**

- **Energy efficiency retrofits (government-funded schemes, mandates)**
- **Public and private sector green procurement (mandates for purchasing eco-friendly products and services)**
- **Ecolabelling (guiding purchasing choices by creating standards)**
- **Extended Producer Responsibility (product take-back, reuse and recycling laws)**
- **Recycling and anti-landfill mandates (e.g. obligations upon local authorities)**
- **Green Building standards (e.g. UK's Zero Carbon Homes by 2016 policy)**
- **Sustainable transport (walking and cycling promotion, alternative fuel mandates, tram or bus rapid transit systems)**

Feed-in tariffs, also known as Renewable Energy Payments (REPs) in the US, are by far the biggest job creation policy driver in renewable energy, and this growth will snowball as more and more interests see how proliferation of new energy systems can create new markets, such as electric vehicles, energy storage technologies and smart grids (see page 77), creating a self-reinforcing positive feedback (see pages 89-91). In Canada the province of Ontario is moving toward a FIT, with Deputy Premier George Smitherman announcing that it could generate over 50,000 new jobs within three years. In the US state of Michigan, also home to a dying automotive industry, they have been exploring how a FIT could revive their manufacturing economy. Many other North American states and provinces have been doing likewise.

As stated above, the German feed-in tariff for renewable energy (see Chapter 3) has helped to create well over a quarter of a million jobs and a world-beating industry with an annual turnover of nearly €25 billion per year, in less than twenty years.[12] The United States, Germany, Spain, India and China are among the most attractive countries to invest in for renewables,[13] due largely to their determination and the establishment of proactive support schemes. All of these countries have corresponding domestic manufacturing and supply capacity, producing many hundreds of thousands of direct and indirect jobs between them.

Green jobs have, somewhat controversially, also been created by incentives such as the Clean Development Mechanism (CDM), one of the Kyoto Protocol's market mechanisms (see Chapter 4). Despite much criticism of the system, over 1,000 renewable energy projects have been put in place in developing countries, and the system appears likely to continue into the new post-Kyoto climate agreement, mainly as it has helped create a new market in tradeable certificates.

Public sector procurement is another way of boosting the green products and services sector. The European Union produced the *Buying Green Handbook* to help guide the thinking of public authorities:

Public authorities are major consumers in Europe, spending some 16% of the EU's gross domestic product (which is a sum equivalent to half the GDP of Germany). By using their purchasing power to opt for goods and services that also respect the environment, they can make an important contribution towards sustainable development. Green public procurement covers areas such as the purchase of energy-efficient computers and buildings, office equipment made of environmentally sustainable timber, recyclable paper, electric cars, environment-friendly public transport, organic food in canteens, electricity stemming from renewable energy sources, and air conditioning systems complying with state-of-the-art environmental solutions.[14]

Energy-efficiency policies are required, just as with renewable energy, to boost the market development for efficiency products and services. The CERT (Carbon Emission Reduction Target) system in the UK puts an obligation on energy suppliers to achieve targets for promoting reductions in carbon emissions in the household sector. Suppliers must direct at least 40% of carbon savings to a priority group

Credit: ? Installing loft insulation.

of low-income and elderly consumers. During its existence, from April 2008 to 2011, the programme is expected to deliver overall lifetime carbon dioxide savings of 154 MtCO2 – equivalent to annual net savings of 4.2 MtCO2 by 2010, and equivalent to the emissions from 700,000 homes each year. It is further estimated to stimulate around £2.8 billion of investment by energy suppliers in carbon reduction measures.[15] Such policy-driven activity means jobs in various roles throughout the supply chain.

However, after the cheap measures are used, such as loft and cavity wall insulation and low-energy lightbulbs, how can more expensive measures be promoted, especially those dealing with single-skin brick buildings which have no cavities to insulate? The technologies themselves must be both available and affordable, and policy directives must be created to achieve this. Furthermore, energy companies and government are often mistrusted, which is why local authorities, community groups and other organizations are required to communicate with the public to encourage the take-up of additional efficiency measures. The Energy Sufficiency chapter contains further examples of new options.

A report by the UK Association for the Conservation of Energy concludes: "Though job creation was not the primary stated aim for any of the programmes studied here, the case studies and modelling exercises found that employment gains have been an indirect consequence in virtually every case. Macro-economic modelling suggests that where countries unilaterally initiate energy-efficiency programmes there can be some job losses at the EU level in the short term. However, at the national level negative outcomes are very rare in terms of employment, and in the longer term the outcome is always positive."[16]

> "Innovative policies can move the transition to sustainability forward at a much faster pace. Governments must establish an ambitious and clear policy framework to reward, support, and drive sustainable economic and social activity . . . this means a decisive and urgent shift in government policy at the global as well as national and local levels with regard to subsidy and tax policy, adequate financing flows and mechanisms, scaling up of promising projects and ventures, sharing of green technologies and relevant information, and replicating both successful regulations and incentives and best industry practices. With progress on these fronts, millions of new green jobs can indeed be generated in coming years."
>
> UNEP, 2007, p.xiii

A carbon tax, preferably a revenue-neutral one, could help to internalize the costs of fossil-fuel use – both in production and consumption. Hybrid systems with cap-and-trade systems are recommended as the cheapest way to introduce such measures. This sets a limit on the level or quantity of GHG emissions, issues permits equalling that quantity, and allows trading of the permits among entities who emit greenhouse gases. This creates a market for greenhouse gas reductions, and thus a direct monetary cost for GHG emissions.[17] Such a development could massively increase the economic attractiveness of renewables and efficiency measures, and hence boost those sectors dramatically.

Business drivers

Beyond these national and international policies, there are the innovators in business who are willing to go the extra mile first, helping to capture market share and set standards. Interface Carpets is a leading example, and their mission statement exemplifies this:

. . . We will strive to create an organization wherein all people are accorded unconditional respect and dignity . . . We will honor the places where we do business by endeavoring to become the first name in industrial ecology, a corporation that cherishes nature and restores the environment. Interface will lead by example and validate by results, including profits, leaving the world a better place than when we began, and we will be restorative through the power of our influence in the world.

It is clear that outdated, business-as-usual attitudes will not prevail in the changing market place. General Motors has seen a precipitous decline in its market share, while more forward-looking companies such as Toyota and Honda, who are making hybrid petrol-electric vehicles a common sight on US roads, have enjoyed rises in theirs. That said, UNEP research suggests that the profile for innovation is small to medium-term enterprises who favour employees with problem-solving skills and personal initiative.[18]

At the local level, Professor Raquel Pinderhughes' research on green jobs in the Bay Area of San Francisco showed that green businesses require support to flourish, especially in terms of adequate, appropriate, affordable space and a general stimulation of the sector to make them more viable and numerous. For the latter she recommends providing (a) procurement dollars and contracts to purchase goods and services that local green businesses provide; (b) assistance with marketing; (c) access to capital; and (d) technical assistance.[19]

The Apollo Alliance and Green For All in the US focus on green job creation in cities and local communities, and make the following recommendations:

1. *Identify your environmental and economic goals, and assess local and regional opportunities for achieving those goals.*

2. *Enact policies and programmes to drive investment into targeted green economic activity and increase demand for local green-collar workers.*

3. *Prepare your green-collar workforce by building green-collar job training partnerships to identify and meet workforce training needs, and by creating green pathways out of poverty that focus on recruitment, job readiness, job training, and job placement for low-income residents.*

4. *Leverage your programme's success to build political support for new and bolder policies and initiatives.*[20]

Green New Deals

As the global economic recession has tightened up private sector investment, a major cash injection has come to green markets by way of various 'Green New Deals'. The term has been used by many groups to promote the idea of boosting economic recovery through government spending, as US President Franklin D. Roosevelt did during the great depression of the 1930s. The New Deal was a sequence of central economic planning and economic stimulus programmes initiated between 1933 and 1938, with the goals of giving work relief to the unemployed, reforming business and financial practices, and initiating an economic recovery.

The New Economics Foundation (nef) in the UK, a think-and-do tank, came up with one of the first Green New Deal proposals in July 2008. It was "a response to the credit crunch and wider energy and food crises, and to the lack of comprehensive, joined-up action from politicians". It calls for massive investment in renewable energy and wider environmental transformation in the UK, leading to the creation of thousands of new green-collar jobs; reining in reckless aspects of the finance sector – but making low-cost capital available to fund the UK's green economic shift; and building a new alliance between environmentalists, industry, agriculture and unions to put the interests of the real economy ahead of those of footloose finance.[21]

UNEP released a joint statement advocating similar approaches in October 2008. They espouse the 'double-dividend' economic and environmental benefits of funding building retrofitting, sustainable infrastructure and green jobs policies. The intended outcomes are as follows:

- **Immediate economic stimulus and job creation, in particular through investments in retrofitting buildings;**
- **Longer-term steady generation of economic activity and job creation through infrastructure investments;**
- **Preparation for a low-emission future by reducing greenhouse gas emissions, improving energy efficiency and using our water resources more wisely;**
- **Promotion of export-competitive green industries and green-collar jobs; and**
- **Assistance to low-income and other vulnerable households to cope with economic uncertainty, housing affordability and fuel and electricity price volatility.[22]**

The UNEP final report of February 2009 on a Green New Deal advocates a mix of policies and incentives which should not only restart the global economy but improve its sustainability. Crucially, they highlight the need for an 'expanded vision' which takes in key global challenges such as water, ecosystems health, carbon dependency and poverty.[23]

The *Financial Times* published details of the economic stimulus packages introduced by various countries and regions, detailing the amounts pledged for green measures:

ECONOMIC STIMULUS PACKAGES
AND GREEN PROPORTIONS

COUNTRY / REGION	Stimulus ($ billion)	Green portion	Green percentage
Australia	26.7	2.5	9
Canada	31.8	2.6	8
China	586.1	221.3	38
EU	38.8	22.8	59
France	33.7	7.1	21
Germany	104.8	13.8	13
Italy	103.5	1.3	1
Japan	485.9	12.4	3
South Korea	38.1	30.7	81
UK	30.4	2.1	7
US	972.0	112.3	12

Source: adapted from Financial Times,
Which country has the greenest bail-out?[24]

The US Green Jobs Act of 2007 (H.R. 2847), introduced by Reps. Hilda Solis (D-CA) and John Tierney (D-MA), authorized up to $125 million in funding to establish national and state job training programmes to help address skills shortages that threaten to slow growth in green industries. The Green Jobs Act was signed into law in December 2007, but it was not until the new administration passed the American Recovery and Reinvestment Act in 2009 that the funds were actually made available to meet the goals. The Act provides funding for green sectors such as renewable energy, energy efficiency, electricity grid infrastructure and transport. This is as forceful a statement of intent as we have seen in getting to grips with greening a national economy.

CLEAN ENERGY DETAILS OF AMERICAN RECOVERY AND REINVESTMENT BILL [25]	
$4 billion	For job training with focus on green-collar job training
$32 billion	To transform the nation's energy transmission, distribution, and production systems by allowing for a smarter and better grid and focusing investment in renewable technology
$11 billion	Reliable, efficient electricity grid
$6 billion	To weatherize modest-income homes
$31 billion	To modernize federal and other public infrastructure with investments that lead to long-term energy cost savings
$20 billion	To local school districts through new School Modernization and Repair Program to increase energy efficiency
$16 billion	To repair public housing and make key energy-efficiency retrofits
$1 billion	Public Housing Capital Fund for projects that improve energy efficiency
$1.5 billion	HOME Investment Partnerships to help local communities build and rehabilitate low-income housing using green technologies
$6 billion	GSA Federal Buildings for renovations and repairs to federal buildings to increase energy efficiency and conservation
$6.9 billion	Local Government Energy Efficiency Block Grants to help state and local governments become energy-efficient and reduce carbon emissions
$2.5 billion	Energy Efficiency Housing Retrofits for a new programme to upgrade HUD sponsored low-income housing to increase energy efficiency
$2 billion	Energy Efficiency and Renewable Energy Research for development, demonstration, and deployment activities to foster energy independence, reduce carbon emissions, and cut utility bills
$500 million	For advanced energy-efficient manufacturing
$1.5 billion	Energy Efficiency Grants and Loans for Institutions for energy sustainability and efficiency grants to school districts, institutes of higher education, local governments, and municipal utilities
$500 million	Industrial Energy Efficiency for energy-efficient manufacturing demonstration projects
$10 billion	For transit and rail to reduce traffic congestion and gas consumption
$2 billion	Advanced Battery Loans and Grants to support US manufacturers of advanced vehicle batteries and battery systems
$1.1 billion	Amtrak and Intercity Passenger Rail Construction Grants
$200 million	Electric Transportation for a new grant programme to encourage electric vehicle technologies
$2 billion	To support advanced battery development
$2.4 billion	For carbon sequestration research and demonstration projects
$1.85 billion	For various clean energy projects to promote energy smart appliances, assist states and GSA to convert fleets to more efficient vehicles, electric vehicle technology research, developing renewable energy for military use
$400 million	Alternative Buses and Trucks to state and local governments to purchase efficient alternative fuel vehicles
$8 billion	Renewable Energy Loan Guarantees for alternative energy power generation and transmission projects
$350 million	Department of Defense Research into using renewable energy to power weapons systems and military bases
$2.4 billion	Cleaning Fossil Energy for carbon capture and sequestration technology demonstration projects
$400 million	For NASA climate change research

Barriers

The UNEP Green Jobs report makes an excellent assessment of the conditions militating against the growth of green jobs, which is worth reproducing in full:

. . . the encouraging growth of green jobs needs to be viewed against the sheer enormity of the tasks facing human society in terms of achieving a truly sustainable, low-carbon, and more equitable world. A number of inescapable realities need to be addressed:

1. *Green jobs are simply not growing rapidly enough. As the Stern Review points out, overall investment in green technologies remains inadequate, notwithstanding the very strong growth in renewable energy. Carbon markets (along with the necessary institutions and networks of climate cooperation) may eventually make an important contribution to financing green development, but for now are still on a distant horizon.*

2. *Green employment has gained an important foothold in the developed world, but with the major exception of China and Brazil, it is still quite exceptional in most developing countries. Yet these are the countries that account for some 80 percent of the world's workforce.*

3. *We see the emergence of green jobs inside a global labour market still largely driven by conventional job creation. The rising level of informality in the global economy constitutes a major challenge to green job growth. Moreover, the chronic and worsening levels of inequality both within and between countries are a major impediment. The effort to advance decent work and pro-poor sustainable development is critical to building green jobs across the developing world in particular.*

4. *Unsustainable business practices are still quite prevalent and often remain more profitable. Short–term pressures of shareholders and financial markets are not easily overcome. The early adopters of green business practices have to contend with companies that can command consumer loyalty through low prices (on the back of 'externalized' costs). And surprisingly often, market failures, coupled with lack of green knowledge, impede action.*

. . . *These do not have to be insurmountable obstacles. Innovative policies can move the transition to sustainability forward at a much faster pace. Governments must establish an ambitious and clear policy framework to reward, support and drive sustainable economic and social activity and be prepared to confront those whose business practices continue to pose a serious threat to a sustainable future. This means a decisive and urgent shift in government policy at the global as well as national and local levels with regard to subsidy and tax policy, adequate financing flows and mechanisms, scaling up of promising projects and ventures, sharing of green technologies and relevant information, and replicating both successful regulations and incentives and best industry practices. With progress on these fronts, millions of new green jobs can indeed be generated in coming years.*[26]

Pinderhughes makes the following points on impediments to more green growth: "Most firms are not adequately prepared to address the work force development issues that will accompany rapid growth. Seventy-three percent of the business owners / managers surveyed stated that there was a shortage of qualified green-collar workers for their sector, with the greatest needs in energy, green building, mechanics and bike repair."[27]

Credit: Miguel Mendonça. Recycling is already big business.

As above, parts of the new green economy plans in the US are aimed at addressing such skills shortages. The longer-term growth of green markets will depend to an extent on confidence in the relevant industries and services, which means that qualified and trained professionals are vital. Without such people, the technologies cannot be put to use in great numbers, and the development of economies of scale are held back. Furthermore, green technologies must come down in price quickly to be a viable alternative for consumers.

Conclusions

Given that a clean environment and a sustainable global economy are vital and non-negotiable for life on earth – yet have hitherto been politically unattainable – what can green job creation do to leverage public support for societal, economic, climate and environment-protecting measures? Despite it being an emerging area of practice and study, it is clear that green jobs and the green economy agenda are central to finally gaining momentum with the interlinked energy and environment issues – and can do so on the back of the precarious global economic situation. Longer-term, it is arguably the most likely route to the successful development of both bottom-up and top-down engagement with environmental protection in society. By attaching other concepts which directly involve citizens, such as participatory budgeting[28] and feed-in tariffs, it can help provide positive momentum in which government, business and society can move together. This synergy will be necessary in order to create a critical mass that reshapes global society in a sustainable way. Green job creation is about embedding this thinking in economic reality, creating a common goal, and ensuring buy-in from all relevant stakeholders. A new, transformative wave washing over the world's economies, building on successful developments in countries around the world such as Germany, Spain, China, Japan and the US, can bring many people into these sectors and unleash human creativity upon this transition.

Green jobs will need to be carefully monitored and studied, in order to build an accurate and useful picture of the development of this sector. Government, trade unions and business associations should monitor direct and indirect job creation, and its demographic spread.[29] Sooner rather than later, green job creation should be a standard aim of any employer, and policies should be in place to assure that this is so.

A carbon-constrained world will generate ongoing legislative, market and behavioural responses which will in turn lead to green job creation. Energy, transport, waste and building sectors are foremost in attracting investment, as outlined above, but many other sectors will also benefit. From manufacturing processes to food and energy production, these changes are all about minimizing inputs and losses – creating an efficient, less fossil-fuel-dependent economy. In nature, efficient design and behaviour is an iron law of survival, and one we must learn well in the coming decades. Creating efficient infrastructure and processes, for ourselves and future generations, is top of this century's 'things to do' list. The renewable energy transition, and climate change mitigation and adaptation more broadly, will provide many new roles, and in great numbers – both in the developed and the developing world. In the end, all jobs have to be green jobs. All activities must ultimately conserve, protect and enhance the environment and the world that future generations will inherit. In other words, green jobs are a central part of not only potential prosperity, but potential survival also.

For the growth of the green-collar economy, several factors are critical:

- Policy drivers such as carbon taxes, renewable energy and energy efficiency targets, ecolabelling, green procurement mandates, extended producer responsibility, recycling mandates, green building standards, sustainable transport, and economic stimulus packages
- Anyone must be able to access the green sector and gain a safe and decent job with longer-term career prospects
- Training programmes in the green sector are essential; a major barrier to a rapid greening of the economy is the lack of a trained workforce
- Unsustainable policies and practices, and perverse subsidies need to be removed if the economy is to move in a greener direction

Acknowledgements

Janet Sawin *Worldwatch Institute*
Michael Renner *Worldwatch Institute*
Raquel Pinderhughes
San Francisco State University
Steve Fischer *Clipper Wind*
Parin Shah *Green For All*
Ben Castle *Energy Savings Trust*

" *The point is this. When you think about the emerging green economy, don't think of George Jetson with a jet pack. Think of Joe Sixpack with a hard hat and lunch bucket, sleeves rolled up, going off to fix America. Think of Rosie the Riveter, manufacturing parts for hybrid buses or wind turbines. Those images will represent the true face of a green-collar America.*

If we are going to beat global warming, we are going to have to weatherize millions of buildings, install millions of solar panels, manufacture millions of wind-turbine parts, plant and care for millions of trees, build millions of plug-in hybrid vehicles, and construct thousands of solar farms, wind farms, and wave farms. That will require thousands of contracts and millions of jobs – producing billions of dollars of economic stimulus. "

Van Jones, from *The Green Collar Economy –*
How one solution can fix our two biggest problems

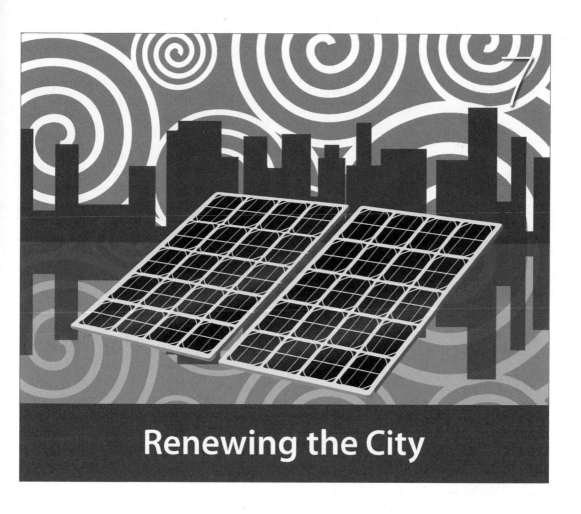

Chapter Seven

Renewing the City

" I'd put my money on the sun and solar energy. What a source of power! I hope we don't have to wait until oil and coal run out before we tackle that. "

Thomas Edison

What do the towns of Güssing, Dardesheim, Varese, Moura, Samsø, Thisted, Bourke, Fredrikshavn and Rockport have in common?[1] Few of us may ever have heard of most of them, but they stand out as 21st-century pioneers that have implemented 100 percent renewable energy strategies. These towns are examples of a new world in the making – a modern, comfortable world powered by regenerative energy. This would have been considered unthinkable just a few years ago, but is becoming a reality in an ever-increasing number and variety of places as supportive national policies make investments in renewable energy worthwhile. Some towns are striving to be entirely energy self-sufficient, others are integrating their efforts into regional sustainable energy strategies, while others again are building new regional economies based on exporting surplus energy.

The towns listed above can be found in different parts of Europe, Australia and the USA and they are each utilizing a different combination of wind power, solar energy, biomass, biogas, small-scale hydro or geothermal energy to make them largely self-reliant in electricity and heating. Various innovative storage systems are being utilized to assure a continuous energy supply. What is still an exception in 2009 is likely to become commonplace in the next decade.

In Chapter 1 we listed some of the breathtaking innovations that emerged from the industrial revolution and the 'carboniferous capitalism' (Lewis Mumford) it gave rise to. We described how new fossil-fuel-based technologies spread across the world, and how cities of unprecedented size started to emerge in many places in a process that one might call 'carboniferous urbanization'.

The last 300 years have seen the growth of ever-larger cities based on ever-increasing fossil-

Credit: Dardesheim Tourist Office. The East German town of Dardesheim combines electricity from PV roofs, wind turbines and biomass burners into a sustainable energy system. Dardesheim is not just self-sufficient but has become a net exporter of electricity to the national grid with considerable financial benefit to the local population.

fuel supplies from ever-larger refineries and power stations, often based on local or regional energy sources. In the second half of the 20th century cities of millions of people started to spring up across the world, increasingly dependent on fuel supplies from distant places. London, for instance, requires the equivalent of two supertankers of oil per week for its 7.5 million inhabitants.[2] Such vast urban structures depend on a continuous supply of energy – for powering high-rise city centres and low-density sprawling suburbs, as centres of production, consumption, services, transport and communication.

19th- and 20th-century technical innovations have made large-scale urbanization possible.

Some 80 percent of people in the richer countries now live in cities and about 50 percent worldwide. Built on just three to four percent of the world's land surface, cities use about 80 percent of its resources. The bulk of the world's fossil-fuel combustion is occurring in and on behalf of cities, and the resulting emissions are contributing very significantly to climate change.[3]

Whilst the per capita energy consumption in developed countries can be higher in rural areas than in cities, the fact that most people there live in cities makes the need to minimize their dependence on fossil fuel crucially important.[4] In developing countries the per capita use of energy is much higher in cities than in rural areas and here, too, the challenge is to assure the most efficient possible energy performance, and increase the use of renewables in urban settlements. According to Anna Tibaijuka, Under-Secretary-General of the UN and Executive Director of UN-HABITAT, "any serious attempt at climate change mitigation and adaptation must include our cities as front-line actors."

Whilst cities all over the world are the primary agents of climate change, they are also likely to become its primary victims – particularly those located near the sea, in river valleys prone to flooding or in areas vulnerable to droughts. A recent assessment suggests that a one-metre sea level rise, which is forecast for the 21st century, will have a direct impact on 150 million people. Indirectly it will affect hundreds of millions more as rising sea levels damage the productivity of farmland in coastal locations.[5]

Until recently, the use of fossil fuels to power cities was simply taken for granted. City planners did not see the need to consider alternative energy sources in their designs. But the start of the 21st century introduces the compelling logic of fundamental change in urban energy supply. Now planners are looking ever more closely at the potential of alternative sources for a secure and carbon-free urban energy supply. Can large 'carboniferous cities' exist by being powered by renewable energy instead?

Most cities that will exist at the end of the 21st century have already been built. London is already there, and so are New York, Tokyo, Shanghai and São Paulo, and they need to function differently in the future. It is crucially important to do every thing possible to help cities to become zero carbon rated.

The places listed at the start of this chapter are small towns. Unlike traditional towns and villages, which can still be found in many rural regions across the world, they don't rely on firewood, bullocks, horses or water wheels to supply their energy requirements. They are surrounded by open countryside and can take advantage of this for wind and solar installations and for biomass and hydro power. For a comfortable contemporary lifestyle they use electricity supplied by modern renewable energy technologies in combination with efficient energy-demand management – highly insulated buildings, low-energy lighting, etc. Transportation is often not included in the 100 percent renewable energy definition, though with the rapidly growing availability of new electric vehicles, this may also change before long.

A town called Moura

In one of the poorest but sunniest regions of Portugal, the municipality of Moura has made headlines recently. Moura and eight nearby villages, with a combined population of 16,500, have found a basis for new wealth in the form of solar energy which is now being used to drive the region's development.

In 2002 Moura's mayor, Jose Maria Pos-de-Mina, founded a municipal energy company, Ampercentral Solar SA, to meet the region's electricity needs in a sustainable manner. As a result the Girassol solar energy plant, one of the largest in the world, began its operation near the village of Ameraleja in March 2008, having cost some €250 million. It covers 112 hectares, equivalent to three-quarters of London's Hyde Park, with 2,520 large solar panels.

The station will have a peak capacity of 62 MW when it is completed in 2010. The solar panels tilt at a permanent 45 degrees using a newly developed tracking system to follow the sun's daily path. The plant will produce 93 gigawatt hours per year, equivalent to the electricity use of 30,000 households, nearly double the needs of the Moura municipality. The solar farm will supply twice Moura's own energy needs half of the time, producing a surplus for export to the grid during the day, and importing electricity during the evening and at night.

To implement the project, the local citizens agreed to take on much of its financial risk, and until 2006 they held 90 percent of the capital in company. However, it has since been sold to the Spanish renewable energy company Acciona SA for a substantial profit which has been shared by all stakeholders. [6]

Portugal, which does not have its own oil, coal or gas deposits, has some of Europe's most ambitious national targets for renewable energy. It is aiming to set up a pioneering low-carbon economy and intends to generate 31 percent of its energy from clean sources by 2020. It wants to develop a renewables industry to rival that of Germany, Denmark or Spain to generate much-needed new employment and expertise. It is Portuguese government policy to insist that foreign renewable energy companies team up with local engineering enterprises to establish new renewable industry clusters.

By the use of a feed-in tariff to assure that renewable energy investment is secure and profitable, Portugal has trebled its hydropower and quadrupled its wind power capacity in just three years, and is also making very substantial investments in wave power and photovoltaic arrays. Encouraged by long-term price guarantees by the state, firms are expected to invest £10 billion in renewables by 2012 and up to £100 billion by 2020.

Moura is an example of a smaller town that has secured its energy future by installing a solar farm in its hinterland. But what about larger cities? Interestingly, even cities of hundreds of thousands of people are now moving towards meeting an ever-growing proportion of their energy supplies from renewables. In Spain, very rapid development of renewable energy is now occurring, again facilitated by enlightened national legislation.

Solar Seville

In the vicinity of Seville, exciting things are going on. Rising out of the Andalusian countryside like a gigantic obelisk, a 90-metre concrete tower surrounded by concentric rings of mirrors is Spain's first major solar power station. The tower, known as PS10, is surrounded by 624 mirrors which produce some 60 MW, enough energy to power around 60,000 homes. The mirrors track the sun throughout the year, reflecting its light onto the solar receptor at the top of the tower. Water passes through and is heated up and turned into steam which powers a series of turbines to produce electricity. In addition there is also a nearby photovoltaic power plant consisting of 154 panels which will generate enough electricity for a further 1,800 homes.

Two more concentrating solar power (CSP) plants are already being built as part of a project whose final aim is to provide enough solar energy for 180,000 homes, or most of the electricity needs of the 600,000 people of Seville. The completed project will be able to

Credit: Abengoa. Seville is well on its way to become a city fully powered by solar energy. The solar towers above are about to be joined by several others using the latest solar energy technology which can store heat and supply electricity even after dark.

produce over 300 MW. In addition to the power towers, there will also be PV arrays and parabolic solar collectors. All these solar power plants will be operational by 2013. All in all, the solar energy schemes near Seville will prevent annual emissions of more than 600,000t of CO_2 into the atmosphere over their 25-year life. During manufacturing and construction the scheme will create more than 1,000 jobs, and an additional 300 service and maintenance jobs.[7]

Apart from the solar energy supplies from the vicinity of the city, Seville City Council is also taking advantage of the region's huge solar potential by installing PV panels on the roofs of municipal buildings all over the city – office buildings, schools, community centres and sports centres. By increasing the solar energy supply from within the city, the municipal electric bill, fossil-fuel dependency and CO_2 emissions are also being reduced, but an important additional aim is to increase awareness among Seville's citizens about the tremendous benefits of solar energy and to encourage them to install solar arrays on their houses as well.

Solar cities

The term solar city is increasingly widely used across the world. In Australia, Adelaide, Alice Springs, Blacktown, Central Victoria, Moreland, Perth and Townsville are all designated as solar cities. All of them have the ambition to rapidly increase their use of renewable electricity.[8] The same applies to India, where 60 cities have been listed as solar cities as part of a government programme. While none will be fully solar-powered for the foreseeable future, they will benefit from increased funding for solar energy development.[9]

In China, Rizhao City in Shandong Province calls itself a solar city. The city mandates all new buildings to incorporate solar panels in their design, 99 percent of households in the city's central districts have solar water heaters, and most public lighting is PV-powered. In the suburbs, over 30 percent of households use solar water heaters and many have solar cooking facilities as well. In nearby farming villages over 60,000 greenhouses are heated by solar panels. In total, Rizhao has some 500,000 square metres of solar water heating panels,

Credit: Himin Solar. Sun-Moon Mansion, Solar Valley, Dezhou, a building complex studded with solar heating panels and PV cells. The building is the headquarters of Himin Solar, the world's largest solar thermal technology company.

equivalent to about 0.5 megawatts of electricity. Across the city a combination of regulations and public education has spurred this remarkable development.[10]

Solar Valley, Dezhou

The city of Dezhou, also in Shandong Province, is building an ambitious complex of solar-powered buildings called Solar Valley. In 2010 it will host the 4th international Solar City Summit. China's solar industry is growing by some 30 percent a year. By 2010 rooftop solar water heaters will save China from burning 22.5 million tons of standard coal a year. This is part of China's very vigorous renewable energy strategy.[11] Zhang Xiaoqiang, vice-chairman of China's national development commission, stated in June 2009 that "China is aiming to have a massive one-fifth of all its energy from renewable sources by 2020."[12]

Whitelee and Glasgow

Back in the UK, surprising developments are occurring as well. Scottish Power Renewables completed Europe's largest on-shore wind farm at Whitelee near Glasgow, with a capacity of 322 MW at a cost of £300m in early 2009. (It is interesting to note that the investment cost per watt is about a fifth of that at Moura – wind power is still much more cost competitive than solar energy.) In the coming years Whitelee's capacity will nearly double to 614 MW, with the whole wind farm of 220 turbines taking up 7,500 hectares, producing about 2 watts per square metre. It will then generate enough electricity for all the homes in Glasgow, a city of around 600,000 people.

As with the other renewable energy schemes listed, Whitelee's power output will be fed into the national electricity grid and not just solely supply Glasgow. But the proximity of the wind farm to the city will effectively make it its local renewable energy source. About 40 percent of Glasgow's total electricity consumption will be supplied by the wind farm.[13]

Keith Anderson, the director of Scottish Power Renewables, describes Whitelee as a landmark for the country because of its size and scale. But much more is to follow. He says: "We're currently in conversations with the Scottish

Government about the development of an offshore wind farm off the west coast of Scotland which could be anything up to 1,800 MW, at least five or six times the size of Whitelee."[14]

The London Array

The UK's largest city, London, is also well on its way to getting a significant dose of renewable energy from an offshore wind farm called the London Array, to be built around 12 miles off the coasts of Kent and Essex. With a 1,000 MW capacity it is expected to become the world's largest offshore wind farm. It is being funded by a consortium consisting of E.ON UK Renewables, DONG Energy and the Abu Dhabi-based Masdar. The three companies will invest €2.2 billion in building the first 630 MW phase of the London Array. It will be constructed in two phases on a 23,400 hectare site in the Thames estuary and will ultimately supply the electricity needs of 750,000 homes, or a quarter of Greater London households.

The first 630 MW phase of the London Array with 175 turbines is expected to be completed in time for the London Olympics in 2012. The completed wind farm will consist of a total of 341 wind turbines of between 3 and 7 MW capacity. The decision by the three investment partners to go ahead with the project was taken after the UK government recently offered a higher unit price for offshore wind farm electricity. Because the three partners are now satisfied that the project is financially viable they are pushing ahead with construction.

The London Array will displace daily emissions of 1.9 m tonnes of carbon dioxide. It is an important part of the UK's plan to cut its CO_2 emissions by 80 percent by 2050 and to meet its future energy needs in a sustainable manner. It will be the start of a major expansion of UK offshore wind capacity and will also generate thousands of jobs. Together with other major offshore wind farm projects, such as the 500 MW Great Gabbard scheme off the Suffolk coast, the densely populated south-east of England will be getting a very substantial proportion of its electricity supply from renewable sources by 2015. [15]

Credit: London Array. Offshore wind power is a crucial energy source for large cities in coastal locations such as London. 25% of the UK's electricity is to come from offshore wind by 2020, or a total of 29 gigawatts. Higher wind speeds at sea and larger turbines of up to 6 MW offset part of the higher cost of producing electricity offshore.

Megacities and their resource use

For some time much thought has been given to the need for very large cities like London to become environmentally sustainable. The issue is not only how to increase renewable energy supplies but also to reduce overall resource consumption. For London to become an environmentally sustainable city, it would need to reduce its energy and resource throughput by some three-quarters, as suggested below. That is a huge challenge but also a huge new opportunity. [16]

Nicky Gavron, former Deputy Mayor of London, was one of the creators of the Clinton Foundation's C40 sustainability initiative which brings together some of the world's largest cities. At the launch of the initiative in 2005 she said this: "Leadership from national governments is crucial in tackling climate change, but when it comes to practical action on the ground, cities are centre stage. Cities have a special responsibility to cut emissions because they are huge consumers of energy and uniquely vulnerable to the impacts of climate change. And as the urgency for action increases, we cities need to build wider and stronger links across the world. . . . I want to see . . . long-term international city collaboration on climate change."

There is a growing understanding that such efforts do not just mean 'pain', but significant new business and job opportunities from renewable energy – from retrofitting buildings, from creating better transport systems, from waste recycling, and so on.

Excerpts from the C40 Large Cities Climate Summit Declaration, Seoul, May 2009
C40 cities hereby set a common goal of transforming themselves into low-carbon cities, by cutting greenhouse gas emissions to the largest extent possible, by adapting themselves to the various unavoidable climate change consequences, by making cities less vulnerable to climate change, and by enhancing cities' capacity for remediation.

C40 cities identify their current level of carbon emissions from all city operations and stages of community development including urban planning, design and infrastructure building. Cities reduce emissions wherever possible through policies, programmes and projects and taking steps to negate the impact of remaining emissions.

C40 cities actively work together to accelerate delivery of low-carbon technologies, programmes and financing, including through active coordination in the procurement of specific technologies through the C40 Secretariat.

In the run up to the COP15 United Nations Climate Change Conference in Copenhagen in December 2009, the leading role of cities in the global effort against climate change must be recognized. C40 cities and all cities with shared goals, must be engaged, empowered and resourced, so that cities can work together to deliver on greenhouse gas reduction targets and stop climate change.

The C40 Climate Leadership Group calls upon cities and their citizens to exert their efforts to address the threats caused by climate change for the benefit of all the people and future generations. [17]

Retrofitting existing cities

In an urbanizing world it is becoming apparent that global sustainable development must, above all else, mean sustainable urban development. All over the world the awareness is growing rapidly that modern cities have huge responsibilities – and great new economic opportunities – in reducing their environmental impacts.

The Stern Review, already cited elsewhere, reached the very simple conclusion that the benefits of strong and early action on climate change far outweigh the economic costs of not acting. Decision-makers all over the world have realized that a large proportion of the actions required to deal with climate change need to be taken in cities. Major international efforts, such as the C40 initiative, recognize this fact. It has attracted very substantial funding to retrofit major urban buildings in order to make them much more energy-efficient.

Internationally, UN Habitat complements the work of the C40 initiative. It now focuses much of its work on sustainable urbanization. Its World Urban Campaign "is a platform for member States and Habitat partners to elevate policies and share practical tools for sustainable urbanization. . . . The campaign in this way seeks to position sustainable urbanization as a priority issue of the international community and as a national policy priority for individual member States."[18]

The International Council on Local Environment Initiatives (ICLEI), has a programme called 'Cities For Climate Protection' that works with some 800 cities and local governments worldwide to support their efforts to reduce their greenhouse gas emissions. The campaign helps them understand how their decisions affect energy use and how appropriate decision-making can mitigate global climate change whilst also improving community life.[19]

In Europe, Energie-Cités, the association of local authorities promoting local sustainable energy policy, has more than 150 members, mainly municipalities. There are other regional groupings such as the European Climate Alliance [20] under which hundreds of local authorities are organized. Members have resolved to cut their CO_2 emissions by ten percent every five years in the future.

All these initiatives are starting to make an important contribution to the implementation of policies on sustainable energy development. They are now being complemented by the World Future Council's Cities and Climate Change Commission that is seeking to accelerate renewable energy supply to cities all over the world. Our starting point is to track really significant reductions in urban greenhouse gas emissions and comprehensive efforts to utilize renewable energy to power cities, as this chapter demonstrates.

In a world facing climate chaos it is crucially important to do every thing possible to retrofit existing cities with sustainable energy systems. Much work has already been done across Europe. Cities such as Heidelberg, Freiburg, Vienna, Barcelona, London, Helsinki and Stockholm, to name but a few, have already initiated substantial investment in the energy efficiency of buildings and new infrastructure, as well as renewable energy.

Nevertheless, the global challenges are simply enormous. A recent report by Booz Allen Hamilton, the global strategy and technology consulting firm, suggests that the world's urban infrastructure systems need an astonishing $40 trillion investment to bring them up to date. According to the report, the vast and complex systems used to deliver water, electricity and transport services in urban areas are inadequate in both older cities that are suffering from decaying infrastructures, as well as in newer cities that are still developing their infrastructures. The report says that water, sewage and electricity schemes should be developed jointly rather than separately to assure maximum synergies.[21]

The report does not even take into account the vast challenge of retrofitting cities to enhance their environmental sustainability rather than simply to improve their service provision. For cities to meet the environmental challenges of the 21st century requires a global investment programme to make them truly compatible with the integrity of the earth's fragile ecosystems on which their wellbeing depends and without which they are ultimately doomed.

CARBON-NEUTRAL COPENHAGEN

"In Copenhagen, we are looking for solutions that will save the world. Our target is to be an inspirational city and our main goal is to be the world's first carbon-neutral city by 2025." So says Claus Bondam, the environment mayor of a city that is already renowned for its enlightened planning policies, with a pedestrian centre, 7 kms of dedicated cycle routes and most electricity supplied by combined heat and power and offshore wind parks.

The new zero-carbon plan for Copenhagen involves 50 initial projects to reduce CO2 emissions by a further 20 percent by 2015. The business community and the local inhabitants have been invited to work closely with the city's administration towards achieving this ambitious goal. The city government is making a substantial investment in new wind turbine projects, which will allow citizens to invest in green energy. Other initiatives include the use of hydrogen-powered and electric cars that could be parked for free and recharged on street corners.

Another step towards achieving a carbon-neutral Copenhagen by 2025 is to increase the production of geothermal heat by 600 percent to generate up to 50 percent of the city's district heating requirements at a cost of about $180 million. A recent survey reports that the ground a few kilometres beneath Copenhagen contains about 70 times more energy than required by Denmark to fulfil its heating, electricity and transportation needs. Jesper

Magtengaard, an engineer of DONG Energy, Copenhagen, has said that new calculations show that it is economically feasible to allow building heating systems to absorb heat from water, send the used water back underground, allowing it to be reheated, and then reuse it for district heating.

www.rudi.net

Cities and transport

COMPARISON OF THE SUSTAINABLE TRANSPORT CLUSTERS OF 84 CITIES				
Least sustainable transport	Less sustainable transport	Sustainable transport	More sustainable transport	Most sustainable transport
Houston	Bologna	Manchester	Paris	Zurich
Phoenix	Montreal	Glasgow	Madrid	Berne
Denver	Wellington	Newcastle	Helsinki	Shanghai
Atlanta	Toronto	Copenhagen	Jakarta	Cairo
San Diego	Nantes	Johannesburg	Amsterdam	Vienna
Riyadh	New York	Rome	São Paulo	Munich
Los Angeles	Kuala Lumpur	Graz	Manilla	Prague
San Francisco	Sydney	Tehran	Bogota	Berlin
Calgary	Tel Aviv	Taipei	Dusseldorf	Cracow
Chicago	Ho Chi Minh City	Milan	Tunis	Mumbai
Washington	Lyon	Guangzhou	Budapest	Beijing
Ottawa	Marseille	Harare	Stuttgart	London
Perth	Athens	Oslo	Seoul	Osaka
Melbourne	Ruhr	Stockholm	Brussels	Dakar
Vancouver	Geneva	Cape Town	Singapore	Chennai
Brisbane	Bangkok	Frankfurt	Sapporo	Tokyo
	Curitiba	Hamburg	Barcelona	Hong Kong

List of cities researched and compiled by Prof. Jeffrey Kenworthy.

From this list of 84 cities it is apparent that low-density cities in the US, Canada, Australia and the Middle East have a much higher per-capita use of transport fuels than European,

Asian and North African cities. Invariably the cities on the left are very low density, and the ones on the right are high density. This is primarily a function of 1) availability of cheap fuel, and 2) deliberate policy decision to invest in public transport. Thus some cities have much more sustainable transport systems than others, but all have to improve in different ways.

News from the US

In 1932, John Nolen, a prominent, Harvard-educated urban planner and landscape architect, said, "The future city will be spread out, it will be regional, it will be the natural product of the automobile, the good road, electricity, the telephone, and the radio combined with the growing desire to live a more natural, biological life under pleasanter and more natural conditions." This was the idea behind suburbs, and it's still seductive. But it's also a prescription for sprawl and expressways and wasteful use of energy. [22]

'Smart growth' is a 21st century response to the problems associated with suburban sprawl. In 1996 the Environmental Protection Agency helped establish the Smart Growth Network in conjunction with environmental groups, historic preservation organizations, professional organizations, developers, real estate interests and city and state governments. The purpose of smart growth planning is the reduction of sprawl and car-dependency, and the promotion of liveable and more sustainable communities. Its specific propositions are:

1. New developments that are connected to public transport;
2. Park and ride at public transport stations;
3. Bicycle parking at public transport stations;
4. Car-free walkable city centres;
5. Increased density, and mixed used developments.

Across the USA smart growth principles are being employed by an ever-growing number of cities. Under the Obama presidency, it is likely that national smart growth legislation will help local authorities to speed up smart growth initiatives.

Ironically, New York City, seen by many as an urban jungle, is increasingly cited as a model of smart growth. It was recently called the "greenest city in the US" because so many of its residents live in compact multi-storey buildings, and use public transit, bicycles or their own feet to commute to work. City residents also consume about half as much electricity as those who live in more spread-out suburban areas elsewhere in the United States. [23]

Smart growth is also part of the agenda of hundreds of US mayors. In 2005, lack of commitment by the Bush administration forced the US Conference of Mayors – representing towns of over 30,000 people – to initiate the US Mayors Climate Protection Agreement. Its stated goal is to help all towns and cities to counter climate change. By November 2007, 710 mayors from all 50 US States had signed the Agreement. The participating cities are committed to take the following three actions:

- **Strive to meet or beat the Kyoto Protocol targets in their own communities, through actions ranging from anti-sprawl land-use policies to urban forest restoration projects to public information campaigns;**
- **Urge their state governments, and the federal government, to enact policies and programs to meet or beat the greenhouse gas emission reduction target suggested for the United States in the Kyoto Protocol – 7 percent reduction from 1990 levels by 2012; and**

■ **Urge the US Congress to pass the bipartisan greenhouse gas reduction legislation, which would establish a national emission trading system.**

The mayors recognized that by implementing energy efficiency and renewable energy schemes, and by better transport planning, cities can become a key part of the solution to climate change – as well as becoming better places to live. It can be expected that under a new US government much more effort will be taken to assure that national policy brings about such changes at the local level.[24]

Regarding solar development, major projects are underway across California. In February 2009 Southern California Edison announced a deal with solar company BrightSource to provide 1,300 megawatts of solar power, which is enough to power almost 845,000 homes. Upon approval by the California Public Utilities Commission, construction will begin on seven projects to install the solar arrays which drive steam turbines. The first project is scheduled to be completed by 2013. The system is used in desert locations, such as the Mojave desert which has had solar-powered steam turbines since the 1970s.

Meanwhile wind power development is becoming big business in the US and particularly in Texas, partly due to the efforts of one T. Boone Pickens, a well known oil man. The town of Sweetwater, until recently a high unemployment trouble spot, has become the Wind Turbine Capital of the US and it is claimed that newcomers have a job in the green industry before they can even unpack their bags. Texas is the top wind energy producer in the US, with over 4,000 megawatts installed. In July 2007, the Texas Public Utility Commission approved additional transmission lines that can deliver as much as 25,000 megawatts of wind

energy to urban centres by 2012. By then all Texans will be able to access the state's vast wind resources.[25]

Towards the solar suburb

For decades, Americans have fled to the suburbs in search of clean air and open space. But is this trend under threat? In 2004 a documentary was made in the USA called *The End of Suburbia* which was a stark warning to urban planners as well as citizens: the suburb cannot survive in an era of expensive gasoline.[26]

It is certainly true that the growth of suburbia since the Second World War is largely a function of cheap private transport. Millions of people invested their newfound wealth in suburbia. As suburban populations exploded, so did the use of the motor car. What started out as the American Dream soon also became the dream of Australians, Canadians and Europeans. But at the start of the 21st century, serious questions about the viability of this way of life are being asked. As global demand for fossil fuels begins to outstrip supply, what is the future of suburbia?

Credit: Tessera Solar. Solar dishes with sterling engines are a technology of major potential for low-density locations, suitable for public spaces within suburbia.

The End of Suburbia paints a nightmare scenario of suburbia which has run out of gasoline. And an ever-growing number of planners and developers are seeing the logic of creating compact settlements that emphasize the opportunities inherent in local community living. Meanwhile wherever possible existing low-density suburbia should be augmented with new retail and office clusters and activity centres which offer new opportunities for both community living and public transportation nodes.

Meanwhile it is possible also to think of the solar suburb: retrofitting the fossil-fuel suburb into renewable energy systems, with solar systems and wind power within the suburb to power not only houses themselves but also to power electric vehicles.

In Australia a quiet solar revolution is starting so sweep suburbia. The concept is simple – buy solar panels in bulk and rally fifty or so households in a geographic area to get together to share the cost of installing a 1KW photovoltaic panel system for each house. Solar communities have started popping up around Australia. In addition to householders, local councils and community groups have also got on board, as have commercial programmes. The panels are ordered in bulk to reduce shipping and labour costs. The homeowners have been taking advantage of the Federal Government's rebate scheme that makes the PV panels affordable. Over 100 solar neighbourhoods are already established in Victoria, and NSW, South Australia and Queensland are following suit.

Whilst at present solar panels are mainly being installed for a limited electricity supply, future solar suburbs could supply a much larger proportion of its people's energy needs, even electricity for limited travel with electric cars. The very spaciousness of the suburb holds the potential for electricity supply from solar arrays and wind turbines that would be much harder to achieve in densely built-up areas. And in the suburbs the potential for local fruit and vegetable supply can be much more easily realized once it becomes part of suburban culture as originally envisaged by Frank Lloyd-Wright who, like John Nolan, developed his concept of the 'Broadacre City' in 1932 at the height of the Great Depression.[27]

MASDAR CITY

What about creating new solar cities from scratch? Abu Dhabi has started to build what it says is the world's first purpose-built new zero-carbon, zero-waste, car-free city which will be powered by the sun. Masdar City, which will extend to 6 million square metres, will cost $22 billion, take eight years to build and be home to 50,000 people and 1,500 businesses. It uses traditional planning principals of a compact, walled city, together with new technologies, to achieve a carbon-neutral community. The shaded walkways and narrow streets will create a pedestrian-friendly environment suitable for

Source: Foster and Partners.

Abu Dhabi's extreme climate. Residents will move around on foot or in travel pods running on magnetic tracks. The city forms part of an ambitious plan the government of Abu Dhabi has to develop clean energy technologies, including Masdar PV, which is to become one of the largest solar technology companies in the world. Masdar City will consist mainly of low-rise low-energy buildings. They will be constructed to allow air flow in but to keep the sun's heat out. Wind towers will ventilate homes and offices using natural convection. Water will be provided through a solar-powered desalination plant. The city will need only a quarter of the power required for a similar-sized community, while its water needs will be 60 percent lower. The land surrounding the city will contain photovoltaic arrays, wind farms and food-growing areas. Master planned by Foster + Partners, the initiative has been driven by Dr. Sultan Ahmed Al Jaber, CEO of the Abu Dhabi Future Energy Company.

The metabolism of cities: from linear to circular

Given that for the time being urbanization is a global trend, this means first and foremost that ways have to be found for cities to minimize their systemic dependence on fossil fuels and the unsustainable use of resources. Their need to develop sustainable relationships to the ecosystems from which they draw their resources – be they farmland, forests or marine ecosystems – has already been raised in Chapter 2.

Whilst the sustainable energy supply to cities is a crucially important issue, efforts to make them into fully sustainable systems need to go beyond that. The metaphor of relevance here is that of the *metabolism of cities*.

Like other organisms, cities have a definable metabolism. The metabolism of many modern cities is essentially linear, with resources flowing through the urban system without much concern about their origin, or about the destination of wastes. Inputs and outputs are considered as largely unrelated. Fossil fuels are extracted from rock strata, refined and burned, and the waste gases are discharged into the atmosphere. Raw materials are extracted, combined and processed into consumer goods that ultimately end up as rubbish which cannot be beneficially reabsorbed into living nature.

In distant forests, trees are felled for their timber or pulp, but all too often forests are not replenished. Similar processes apply to food: nutrients and carbon are taken from farmland as food is harvested, processed and eaten. The resulting sewage, with or without treatment, is then discharged into rivers and coastal waters downstream from population centres, and usually not returned to farmland. Rivers and coastal waters all over the world are polluted by both sewage and toxic effluents, as well as the run-off of mineral fertilizer applied to farmland feeding cities. This linear, open-loop approach is utterly unsustainable.

The linear metabolic system of most cities is profoundly different from nature's circular metabolism, where waste does not exist: every output by an organism is also an input which replenishes the whole living environment. Planners seeking to design sustainable urban systems should start by studying the ecology of natural systems. On a predominantly urban planet, cities will need to adopt circular metabolic systems to assure their own long-term viability as well as that of the rural environments on which they depend. Outputs will need to become inputs into the urban production system. It is certainly true that in recent years a very substantial increase in recycling of paper, metals, plastic and glass has

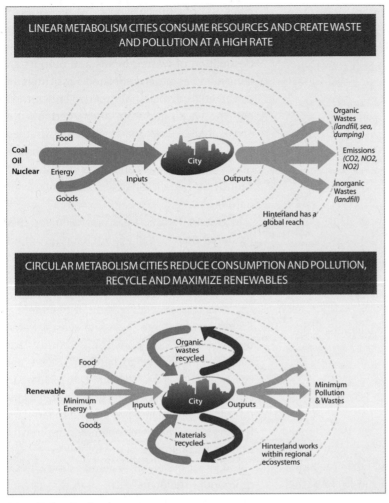

LINEAR METABOLISM CITIES CONSUME RESOURCES AND CREATE WASTE AND POLLUTION AT A HIGH RATE

Coal
Oil
Nuclear   Energy

Food

Goods

Inputs   City   Outputs

Organic Wastes (landfill, sea, dumping)

Emissions (CO2, NO2, NO2)

Inorganic Wastes (landfill)

Hinterland has a global reach

CIRCULAR METABOLISM CITIES REDUCE CONSUMPTION AND POLLUTION, RECYCLE AND MAXIMIZE RENEWABLES

Organic wastes recycled

Food

Renewable
Minimum Energy

Goods

Inputs   City   Outputs

Minimum Pollution & Wastes

Materials recycled

Hinterland works within regional ecosystems

Source: Herbert Girardet.

Other materials, such as heavy metals, have discernible environmental effects as they gradually leach from the roofs of buildings and from water pipes and accumulate in the local environment. Nitrates, phosphates or chlorinated hydrocarbons build up in soils and water courses, with potentially negative impacts for the health of future inhabitants.

The critical question today, as humanity continues to urbanize, is whether living standards in our cities can be maintained whilst their local and global environmental impacts are brought down to a minimum. To answer this question it helps to draw up balance sheets comparing the resource flows of cities across the world. It is becoming apparent that similar-sized cities supply their needs with a greatly varying throughput of resources. Most large cities have been studied in considerable detail and in many cases it won't be very difficult to compare their use of resources. It is certainly clear that large cities in developing countries have a much lower per capita resource throughput, and much higher recycling rates than cities in the richer countries.

Overleaf is a transition scenario for London which also has relevance for other wealthy cities across the world:

occurred. But as suggested in Chapter 3, much more needs to be done and to convert organic materials into compost, and to return plant nutrients and carbon to farmland to assure its long-term fertility.

The local effects of urban resource use also need to be better understood. Cities accumulate large amounts of materials within them. Vienna, with 1.6 million inhabitants, every day increases its actual weight by some 25,000 tonnes.[28] Much of this is relatively inert materials, such as steel, concrete and tarmac.

LONDON SUSTAINABILITY SCENARIOS

	UNSUSTAINABLE	TOWARDS SUSTAINABILITY	SUSTAINABLE
RESOURCE, ENERGY & LAND USE	'FACTOR 1' – 2000 Per capita footprint: 6.6 ha = Total ecological footprint – 300 x London's surface area	'FACTOR 2' – 2015 Per capita footprint: 3.3 ha = Total ecological footprint - 150 x London's surface area	'FACTOR 3' ~ 2030 Per capita footprint: 1.6 ha = Total ecological footprint - 75 x London's surface area
Food	Long-distance supply of highly packaged food as norm Intensive processing High meat consumption 30% food waste Very energy-intensive Only 2% organic, most of this imported Limited allotment growing and peri-urban fruit and vegetable cultivation	Reduced long-distance supply Less processing & packaging Reduced meat consumption Some food waste recycling More energy-efficient 30% organic, mostly locally grown 40% UK grains 50% increase in allotment growing 40% peri-urban fruit & vegetable supplies	Regional supplies emphasized Minimal processing and packaging Low meat consumption Routine food waste recycling Highly energy-efficient 50% organic, incl. use of sewage 60% UK grains A further 30% increase in allotment growing 60% peri-urban fruit & vegetable supplies
Water/ sewage	Water from Thames & Lea High-flush toilets as norm No run-off storage Single household water system Little sewage recycling	More use of London water table Variable-flush toilets as norm Some run-off storage Efficient household water system Some sewage recycling	Much use of London water table Low-flush toilets as norm Substantial run-off storage Dual household water systems Processing of solids into bio-char
Energy	Dependence on fossil fuels 18% nuclear Low building insulation standards Much use of inefficient appliances Minimal end use efficiency Minimal renewable energy	Reduced fossil-fuel use/more CHP/ 40% renewable Improved building insulation standards More efficient appliances and increased end-use efficiency	CHP/solar/wind/biomass & fuel cells as main energy technologies High building insulation standards Common use of high-efficiency appliances and smart metering. From energy efficiency to sufficiency
Transport	Emphasis on private transport Minimal car-sharing Little cycling and walking Fossil-fuel-powered transport Low transport interconnection	Better transport mix More shared vehicles Much cycling and walking Petrol, electric & fuel cell transport Good interconnections	Optimal transport mix Widespread vehicle sharing 'Urban village', cycling and walking Fuel cell & solar-electric transport Optimal interconnections
Materials	Wasteful use of materials Only imported materials Little product durability Everything is packaged Few regional supplies No regional timber Unsustainable sources as norm No consumption limitation	More local and reused materials Minimal use of virgin materials Increasing product durability Reduction in use of packaging Emphasis on regional supplies Some regional timber Sustainable sources common Some consumption reduction	Minimal waste of materials Maximize sustainable sources High product durability Minimal packaging Emphasis on local supplies Regional timber in common use Shared use of products Large consumption reduction
Waste	Linear system 8% recycling Little waste separation Minimal recycling Most waste disposed in landfills Some incineration No remanufacturing	Towards a circular system 50% recycling Enhanced waste separation: Reduce, reuse, recycle Restricted landfill disposal Minimal incineration New remanufacturing industries	Circular system 80% recycling Waste separation as norm: Refuse, reduce, reuse, recycle Remanufacture of metals, glass, paper and consumer waste into new products has become routine

Herbert Girardet, 2002 and 2009

The ecological footprints of cities

Human impact on the planet today is primarily from urban consumption patterns. Cities have an enormous ecological footprint on the global environment. They take up huge areas outside their own territories in order to supply the food and materials we take for granted in our daily urban life.

Concentration of intense economic processes and high levels of personal consumption increase the resource demands of an urbanizing humanity. Apart from a monopoly on the use of fossil fuels and metals, humans now consume nearly half the world's total photosynthetic capacity as well. Cities are the home of the 'amplified man', an unprecedented amalgam of biology and technology, transcending our biological ancestors. Beyond their limits, cities profoundly affect distant ecosystems as a result of their demand for exotic timber, rare plants for domestic display, caged birds and unusual pets. The annual turnover of illegal wildlife trade, emanating from cities, is second only to the drugs trade.

As city people we need to know what levels of production and consumption are sustainable, i.e. within the earth's environmental limits. In order to assess our impacts, the Canadian ecologist William Rees and his colleague Mathis Wackernagel developed the concept of the ecological footprints of nations and cities.[29] They define these as the areas required to supply them with food and forest products, and to absorb their output of wastes, and particularly their output of CO_2.

They estimate that a North American city with 650,000 people requires some 30,000 square kilometres of land to meet domestic needs, without even including the environmental demands of industry. In comparison, an Indian city of this seize would require just 2,800 square kilometres, or less than ten percent of that required by an American city.[30]

Using this methodology, in 1995 I (H.G.) made a study to attempt to quantify London's footprint. I found that this extended to around 125 times its surface area of 159,000 hectares, or to nearly 20 million hectares. I calculated that London, with 7 million people, or 12 percent of the population of the UK, required the equivalent of its entire productive land.[31] Of course, in reality this area stretches to far-flung places such as the wheat prairies of Kansas, the tea gardens of Assam, the forests of Scandinavia and Amazonia, the soy fields of Mato Grosso and the greenhouses and orange groves of Spain. According to my figures, each individual Londoner had a footprint of some three hectares of land.

London is one of the world's most thoroughly researched cities, and a second study called 'City Limits' conducted in 2000 went into much more detail than my own. It also calculated the energy used in agricultural production, transportation and processing, the land surface required for producing pet food, and the ocean regions required to supply London with fish. If these additional areas are included, London's footprint actually extends to more than double that of my original estimate, to twice the UK's surface area, or 6.63 hectares per Londoner.[32]

If all 6.8 billion people now living on this planet were to have the same footprints, this would add up to three times the productive land on earth: we would need three planets rather than the single one we have. Canadian, Australian and American cities have even larger footprints, extending to between eight and ten hectares of productive land per person. If everybody lives like Los Angelinos, we would need five planets.

Says WWF's Living Planet Report 2002: "The ecological footprint of the world average consumer in 1999 was 2.3 hectares per person, or 120 percent of the earth's biological capacity of 1.9 hectares per person. In other words, humanity now exceeds the planet's capacity to sustain its consumption of renewable resources. We are able to maintain this global overdraft on a temporary basis by eating into the earth's capital stocks of forests, fish and fertile soils. We also dump our excess carbon dioxide emissions into the atmosphere. Neither of these two activities are sustainable in the long term – the only sustainable option is to live within the biological productive capacity of the earth."[33]

The 2008 WWF Living Planet Report states that "over three-quarters of the world's population live in nations that are ecological debtors – their national consumption has outstripped their country's biocapacity. Thus, most of us are propping up our current lifestyles, and our economic growth, by drawing (and increasingly overdrawing) upon the ecological capital of other parts of the world."[34]

These processes are largely driven by urban consumption patterns. A growing number of studies have been conducted in recent years focussing on the ecological footprints of cities. The Swedish academic Carl Folke and his colleagues make this important point: "The capacity of ecosystems to sustain city development is becoming increasingly scarce as a consequence of rapid human population growth, intensified globalization of human activities, and human overexploitation and simplification of the natural resource base. The web of connections linking one ecosystem and one country with the next is escalating across all scales in both space and time. Everyone is now in everyone else's backyard."[35]

Folke and his colleagues have done particularly interesting work on fishing. They have established that the bulk of fish that is eaten is consumed in cities remote from the sea. In 1996 the largest 744 northern European cities consumed 25 percent of the world's annual sea fish catch. For their resource consumption and waste assimilation, the cities of Baltic Europe appropriate an area of forest, agricultural, marine and wetland ecosystems that

is 565-1,130 times larger than the area of the cities themselves.[36]

Clearly people across the developed world have a major job on their hands to significantly reduce their ecological footprints. The concept of One Planet Living developed by the BioRegional Development Group and WWF aims to get to grips with the need to reduce our ecological footprints is described in Chapter 8.

New opportunities for cities

It is often said by urban analysts that cities should be seen as the places where solutions to the world's environmental and climate problems can most easily be implemented because as places where most people live

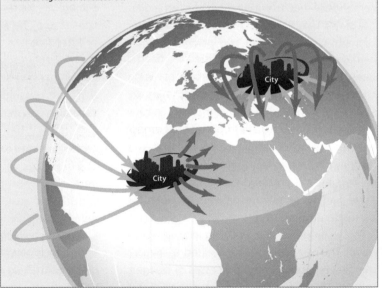

A GIANT FOOTPRINT

The city on the left wastes resources:

It gorges itself on meat, with animals fed mainly on imported feeds

It uses timber and paper products without concern about their forest origins

It emits vast amounts of CO2, requiring vast areas of vegetation to reabsorb it

A NIMBLE FOOTPRINT

The city on the right takes another chance:

Its citizens limit their meat consumption, preferring vegetable foods

Timber and paper are used frugally and efficiently

Tree-planting schemes assure assure reabsorption of its limited CO2 output

Credit: Rick Lawrence. The ecological footprints of modern cities stretch across the world. The challenge now is for cities to become much more nimble footed, with resource efficiency becoming the basis for sustainable local economies.

closely together they have the potential to make efficient use of resources. Recycling materials, conserving rather than burning fossil fuels and tapping into renewable energy can create many new local jobs. As described in Chapter 7, low-carbon urban development can be good for local business, the environment and citizens.

In many cities, and particularly in very large conurbations, large numbers of people cannot find jobs because economic globalization has caused the relocation of manufacturing jobs to other parts of the world. In addition, vast amounts of money are spent on importing fuels from distant places. Creating resource-efficient cities, with a substantial component of renewable energy as part of their energy supply, invariably means relocating jobs back to cities.

A US initiative called 'Climate Prosperity' sees three major new opportunities:

1) Green Savings – reducing waste and cutting costs;
2) Green Economy – expanding businesses and jobs by increasing market share;
3) Green Talent – investing in technical, entrepreneurial and workforce skills. [37]

To deal with these opportunities, we need a new form of comprehensive urban planning concerned with making cities environmentally sustainable, but also to enhance cultural sustainability. It is crucially important to harness the great variety of human experiences into city planning. In a world faced with a huge variety of challenges, it is critically important to use the huge variety of talents present in cities for better decision-making.

For instance, in the Brazilian city of Porto Alegre the city government decided to involve the general public in the processes of budget-setting. All citizens can now have a say about what their tax money should be spent on – better schools, better transport, playgrounds,

renewable energy installations, and so on. This creative process challenges citizens to actively contribute their views. Through this novel participatory process Porto Alegre has become a truly dynamic city, and the ideas pioneered there are being copied in other cities.

We need creativity and initiative at the local level, but we also need appropriate national policies to enable useful things to happen locally. Without enlightened national policy, the necessary changes won't happen fast enough. The more promising developments that are occurring in cities around the world are often the result of enlightened national policy driven by lively discussions within a country. For example, feed-in tariffs for renewable energy in Denmark and Germany came out of public discussion and from vigorous public demand.

Credit: Herbert Girardet. Half the people in developing countries live in squatter settlements such as the vast Kibera slum in Nairobi. Poverty and unemployment results in much more resource-efficient lifestyles than in richer cities and city districts. To improve living conditions and to provide renewable energy is one of the great challenges for places like Kibera in the coming years and decades. (See also Chapter 4.)

Towards the renewable city

The great challenge for city planners, architects and developers today, is to internalize the message that we cannot take the resource and energy supply to our cities for granted.

The characteristic of a truly sustainable city is, first and foremost, that it switches to renewable energy systems. What has been happening in and around Moura, Seville, Glasgow and even London is now starting to happen in many parts of the world. More and more towns and cities, and their regions, are working towards increasing their energy supply from the sun, the wind and other renewables. It is easier for smaller settlements to achieve energy self-reliance than very large cities, but it is becoming apparent that even cities of millions of people are aiming to become 'solar cities'.

The evidence from an ever-growing number of cities, as presented here, shows that cities of varying sizes can supply their energy needs from within their own territory and, beyond that, from their hinterland. Very ambitious renewable energy and energy efficiency schemes, such as the one now being undertaken in Copenhagen, are being envisaged by more and more cities. The evidence suggests that national enabling policies, such as feed-in tariffs, are best implemented at the local level where the energy is actually used.

In many cases such efforts cannot strictly be described as energy self-sufficiency because towns and cities are linked to electricity grids which can supply power from elsewhere. In the case of Moura, it is commercial companies rather than the cities and citizens themselves that can end up as the ultimate owners of renewable energy installations. Like it or not, this trend seems unavoidable in an era of privatization and economic globalization.

Of course, environmental sustainability is not everything – a pleasant urban environment with clean air, public meeting places, many parks and gardens and safe streets is also essential for a good urban quality of life.

Nevertheless, without substantial supplies of energy cities cannot exist. One of the great challenges of our time is to build a modern civilization based on renewable energy. Pioneering countries like Germany and Spain are striving to become 100 percent renewable by 2050.[38] A very ambitious agenda is also being pursued by Al Gore for the United States as well: he has proposed that the USA can supply the bulk of its energy supplies from renewables within ten years or so. It still remains to be seen whether the Obama administration can see the sense of working towards this goal.

These are the main challenges:

- **Raising public awareness of the role of cities in climate change**
- **Assuring effective knowledge exchange within and between cities**
- **Enabling renewable energy and energy efficiency development through new approaches in urban governance and planning**
- **Assuring widespread public understanding of opportunities for more efficient use of resources**
- **Creating public awareness of the economic benefits of sustainable urban development**

Acknowledgements

Peter Head *Arup*
Stefan Schurig *WFC staff*
Iris Gust *Hafen City University, Hamburg*
Peter Droege *University of Liechtenstein*
Marc Weiss *Climate Prosperity*
Stefan Behling *Foster and Partners*
Jeff Kenworthy
Curtin University of Technology, Perth
C.S. Kiang *WFC councillor*
Nicholas You *UN Habitat*

All eyes on China

Pudong, Shanghai's new business district, is China's Manhattan, symbolizing its ever-increasing economic prowess. In this business heart of a country of 1.2 billion people, many investment decisions about the world's future energy use, about cement production and iron ore mining, about logging and/or reforestation, are being made. Will China face up to the systemic environmental problems and impacts linked to its rapid economic growth?

Pudong is also a symbol of China's urban growth. Each year the country is currently building about 7.5 billion square feet of commercial and residential space, more than the combined floor space of all the malls in the United States, according to the US Energy Information Administration. Many buildings do not meet China's own codes for energy efficiency, requiring twice as much energy to heat and cool as those in similar climates in Europe or America. What will it take for China to become a leader in eco-technology? Will Pudong put Manhattan to shame by mainstreaming investment in industrial ecology projects?

Chapter Eight

From Global to Local?

*" As physical resources are everywhere limited, people
satisfying their needs by means of a modest use of resources
are obviously less likely to be at each other's throats than people
depending upon a high rate of use. Equally, people who live
in highly self-sufficient local communities are less likely
to get involved in large-scale violence than people
whose existence depends on world-wide systems of trade. "*

E. F. Schumacher, *Buddhist Economics*

The last few decades have been characterized by economic globalization resulting in an ever-greater expansion of worldwide trade, and violent conflicts linked to this have never been far away. Since this book seeks to address a multiplicity of interconnected issues around sustainability and resilience, localization – as a challenge to globalization – is a theme of great relevance, particularly in the context of energy use and climate change. Today, as we are heading ever closer to peak oil, the primary fuel of globalization, are we also heading ever closer to peak globalization?

For some forty years, alternative economists such as E. F. Schumacher, Manfred Max-Neef and Hermann Daly have been challenging neo-liberal economic orthodoxies of competitive advantage and a global division of labour striving for continuous economic growth. They commit the heresy of emphasizing the importance of local production for local consumption, and the impossibility of infinite growth in a finite world. They also emphasize the need to limit the use of fossil fuels in the long-distance transport of people and goods. But, by and large, these views have been falling on deaf ears, and economic decision-making by governments and companies has changed little in recent decades.

As World Future Council member Kaarin Taipale says in her book *Cities for Sale*: "Privatization of public assets and outsourcing of services has been deemed a rational, non-ideological measure to increase efficiency. The same is true of globalization, which is seen as both the cause and effect of international outsourcing, enabled by the technological possibilities of information and communication technology."[1]

Harvard economist Professor Stephen Marglin, in his recent book *The Dismal Science*, argues that "thinking like an economist undermines community".[2] There is no doubt that, under the pressure of ever-expanding economic globalization, the yearning for local community-based lifestyles has never been far away. Whilst many of us now belong to social networks stretching across the planet, we are also tied into neighbourhoods and communities, particularly in the context of family living. The argument for strengthening local social bonds, and beyond that, local economies, is becoming ever stronger as the uncertainties associated with ever-increasing global dependencies become clearer. These are particularly apparent in the globalization of our fossil-fuel-based energy system. Whilst the industrial revolution was initially based on exploiting local coal deposits, the supply of coal, oil and gas from all over the world is now being taken for granted in underpinning modern economies and lifestyles.

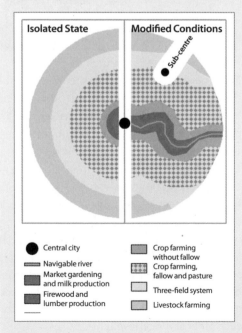

THE ISOLATED STATE: from local to global

Isolated State | Modified Conditions

Sub-centre

- ● Central city
- ▬ Navigable river
- Market gardening and milk production
- Firewood and lumber production
- Crop farming without fallow
- Crop farming, fallow and pasture
- Three-field system
- Livestock farming

Johann-Heinrich von Thünen's famous diagram from his 1863 book The Isolated State[3] *contrasts a town that is not connected to transport routes (on the left) with one that is (on the right). The 'isolated town' is surrounded by four concentric rings of land use. Dairying and intensive farming lie closest to the town as vegetables, fruit and milk must get to market quickly. Timber and firewood would be produced in the second ring since wood is very heavy and difficult to transport. The third zone consists of extensive field crops such as grain that last longer and are much lighter, reducing transport costs. Ranching is located in the final ring since animals are 'self-transporting'. Von Thünen's rings are busted wide open once new transportation systems blur local land use patterns. A river or canal is replaced by rail and road, and then air transport, food, fuel and manufactured products can be cheaply brought to local markets from virtually any distance. But will rising fuel costs and concerns about climate change challenge this 'march of progress'?*

Can localization get a grip?

Industrialization and globalization have created many useful and important things, but increasing dependency on forces beyond the control of most of us is certainly one of them. The argument that local economic resilience is a desirable goal has been further strengthened by the recent upheavals in the international financial system. A profound sense of insecurity came to affect the people who had been persuaded to overstretch themselves by the false promise of cheap loans and 'fail-safe' prosperity. This new kind of 'insecuritization' has triggered a search for alternatives, with many people seeking mutual support from each other at a local level.

The 'localization' movement originated in the mid-1970s, partly in response to the oil crisis and the subsequent increases in fuel prices, but in later years it was of fairly marginal significance as a glut in oil and a sense of prosperity in the wealthier countries encouraged people to consume more and more, regardless of the consequences. Now the combined effects of rising fuel prices, growing financial insecurity and concern about climate change have brought localization back as an option to be considered seriously.

The globalization vs. localization debate has been of particular relevance for many developing countries where rail and road infrastructure was created primarily for transporting raw materials and products to ports and airports, with markets in developed countries as their final destination. Due to poor internal transport connections and high prices for (often) imported fuel, local production for local consumption is still common. Even rapidly emerging economies such as China, where very substantial investments in transport infrastructure are being made, government policies are still supporting urban-fringe or peri-urban agriculture to assure easily accessible supplies of fruit and vegetables.[4]

Source: Herbert Girardet. In China local food production for local consumption is still being strongly encouraged. Shanghai is surrounded by a farm belt of 300,000 ha, the same as the surface area of the city, to assure a steady supply of fresh vegetables to the city's markets.

Vulnerability to the effects of high fuel prices is not restricted to developing countries. Picture a comfortable middle-class suburb in America, Australia or Europe and think through its most basic inputs, or 'dependencies': food, water and energy. If the area was suddenly cut off, most likely by serious problems in the oil supply chain, how would people survive? How would they feed themselves, source their water or heat their homes? And beyond an immediate crisis, how could such areas become as self-reliant as those of medieval times?

More choice from abroad – of food, wine and manufactured products – has kept prices low, but at what cost? Critics of globalization say that the fundamentals of life are now, within a couple of generations, far from certain. As conditions have been created to allow capital to become ever more footloose, the outsourcing of jobs has become common practice and has come to be feared and loathed in many countries. Insecurity, bitterness and frustration grow as employees find that their jobs have been transferred to cheap labour regions such as Eastern Europe, China, Taiwan, India or Malaysia. Governments are largely unable to prevent this, as globalized capital has no sense of loyalty to any particular nation.

Just-in-time supply of just about any component or product has now assumed global dimensions as a multiplicity of interconnecting transport systems now covers our planet. A critique of fossil-fuelled globalization, a potentially fragile set of interdependencies is central to many of the issues addressed in this book. In this chapter we wish to provide some examples of innovative thought and action dealing with localization from around the world. We portray some examples of existing and proposed policies and approaches for making local areas more resilient which are worthy of exploration.

LOCAL VERSUS GLOBAL

Colin Hines

Globalization is occurring increasingly at the expense of social, environmental and labour improvements, and is causing rising inequality for most of the world. Localization, by contrast, is a process that reverses the trend of globalization by discriminating in favour of the local. The policies bringing about localization are those which increase control of the economy by communities and nation states. The result should be an increase in community cohesion, a reduction in poverty and inequality, and an improvement in livelihoods, social infrastructure and environmental protection, and hence an increase in the all-important sense of security.

ideas.repec.org/a/tpr/glenvp/
v3y2003i3p1-7.html

Many people involved in the burgeoning localization movement start by pointing out the social benefits. They speak of a better sense of community spirit, of empowerment, of meaningful relationships, of neighbourhoods that have become safer and more interesting places in which to live. A major priority is the urge to reduce the daily, routine dependence on fossil fuels. This is to be achieved without a sense of having to 'give things up'. Options for 'energy descent', local resilience and richer community living are all on offer here, but certainly not by creating a hermetically-sealed neighbourhood cut off from the rest of the world.

In due course Localization, or 'Relocalization', may be replaced by a term not defined by what it is reacting to but by what it can offer. The active and deliberate creation of a more localized world will need more than civil society buy-in: it will require significant policy initiatives from government and active support from business to develop an historic momentum. It is not about the 'what' so much as the 'how', and 'how much'. Deliberately reducing reliance on external trade for the benefit of local resilience is a difficult undertaking: expansion (rather than reduction) of trade, after all, is a powerful engine that drives most developed economies, and that gives developing countries much needed foreign income.

Food from afar

A move towards local food is at the heart of the localization movement – and yet food was also the start of historic moves towards globalization. The modern world of global food trade started in Britain in 1846. That was the year in which parliament abolished the Corn Laws which had protected British farmers, and particularly grain growers, from foreign competition. For centuries the Corn Laws had formed an integral part of Britain's mercantile system, regulating export and import of cereals in order to maintain adequate supplies for consumers as well as secure prices for producers. In 1846 the Anti-Corn Law League, a free trade lobby, succeeded in having the corn laws repealed because they were seen as an unwarranted tax on food. The new 'open' free-trade economy was designed to decrease the price of basic foods, particularly for the inhabitants of Britain's rapidly growing industrial cities, and to weave stronger commercial bonds with other nations and with Britain's colonies, where vast areas of land were put under the plough.

Ever since 1846 urban markets in countries such as Britain and Holland have been the drivers of the globalization of food production. In the mid-20th century this process was further accelerated as ever more mechanized food production on ever-larger farms became possible, as well as long-distance transport via steamship became possible. This is not the place to go into more detail; suffice it to say that there is an increasingly strong reaction to the globalization of the food system, which is changing the way customers are looking at food.

In the United States, food typically travels between 1,500 and 2,500 miles from farm to plate – 25 percent further now than it did in 1980.[5] Even food grown locally can rack up a lot of 'food miles'. This is a commonly used term which refers to the distance food is transported from the sources of its production to where it is consumed. It is a useful measure for assessing the environmental impact of food. The potatoes you buy at the local shop could have been transported from a local farm to be washed and packaged hundreds of miles away and then sent back to be sold near where they were produced in the first place. This applies even more to processed food. Ingredients and packaging materials travel around from farm to factory to supermarket at enormous energy cost.

A classic case study from the Wuppertal Institute is represented by the diagram reproduced overleaf. It is of a plastic pot of strawberry yoghurt sold in Germany. 8,000 kilometres of roads are used for producing and distributing the yogurt in question. A single 150g strawberry yogurt purchased in a supermarket in southern Germany will be responsible for moving one 44-tonne lorry nearly ten metres. With growing concern about long-term fossil-fuel availability and about climate change, such long-distance food trade is coming under increasing scrutiny.

The energy dependence built into our current global food system is of astonishing proportions. Agriculture contributes in the region of 20 percent of global greenhouse gas emissions as:

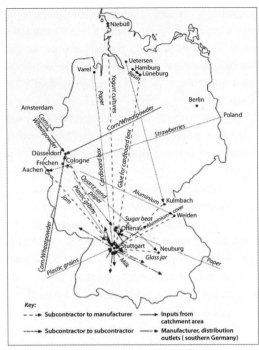

Source: Stefanie Böge, Wuppertal Institut 1993. The diagram shows the transportation involved in assembling the materials and contents of a yoghurt pot.

- **larger farms are worked with bigger machines**
- **food supplies originate from fewer, larger enterprises**
- **more and more inputs such as fertilizers and pesticides are used**
- **delivery patterns become progressively more centralized**
- **processing and packaging increase**
- **food travels greater distances[6]**

FOOD DILEMMAS

Ken Hayes, Soil Association

The UK government believes that a resilient and secure food system can be achieved through high yields and global trade. Unfortunately, you don't have to look far to find flaws in this strategy: the industrialization of agriculture over the past 50 years has not alleviated poverty and hunger in developing countries; in 2008, the volatility in global markets caused escalating food prices which compromised the food security of millions.

These events demonstrate that global markets are not resilient to shocks and are prone to instability. Climate change and dwindling fossil-fuel reserves are predicted to further undermine global markets as they currently function.

It can be difficult for us to relate these global issues to our individual food choices. The solution to our precarious position is not as simple as abandoning global trade and buying all our food locally. International food supply is just as important for us culturally as it is economically for developing country farmers. We do, however, need to radically rethink how global trade is conducted in a way which improves access to markets for disadvantaged, small-scale farmers and rewards good environmental practice.

The experiences of farmers in East Africa show that a diverse farm system using organic techniques has the potential to alleviate poverty and improve food security. There is little or no reliance on costly inputs, and by producing a range of crops, total on-farm productivity is increased. This greatly reduces farmers' vulnerability to crop failure and fluctuations in the export market.

What remains unresolved is how to ensure farmers get a fair share of the price we pay for the food they grow. Parallels can be drawn between fair trade and local food. Both attempt to create a more direct social and financial link between farmers and consumers. However neither fair trade nor local trade exist in isolation from mainstream markets, and do not necessarily deliver environmental sustainability. As consumers, we have a degree of choice in what we buy and where we shop. There is also a clear need for governments to put more *importance on social and environmental issues when agreeing trade rules.*

Trying to address trade, production, and consumption as distinct and separate issues is a key cause of our damaging and risky food system. An integrated, diverse farm system based on organic principles provides a platform on which we can restructure trade, if we want to try to avoid such fault lines in the future.

From globavores to locavores?

'Locavores' is the term for those who subsist on produce from their local area. Amusingly, the term was voted 2007 Word of the Year in the *New Oxford American Dictionary*. The 'locavore' movement encourages consumers to buy from farmers' markets or even to grow or pick their own food, arguing that fresh, local products are more nutritious and taste better.

The issue of local food is one of the most commonly and enthusiastically embraced of all the issues around localization. From British allotment gardening, to community supported agriculture, to Cuban urban agriculture, to Japanese rooftop gardens – there are more and more examples of intra-urban and peri-urban areas being transformed into productive food-growing land. Direct marketing of farm products through farmers markets has become important for many agricultural producers.

Community Supported Agriculture (CSA) is a producer-consumer partnership that allows members to own 'shares' in the harvest on a farm. CSA enterprises involve their members actively in the growing and harvesting of crops. Participants make an agreement in advance to purchase a particular crop from a producer, and they often also help out in the fields. Some groups even set out to the purchase or rent land and to employ a farmer or farm worker.

Today there is a vigorous movement of consumers in many countries who want to base their diet on local production. Slow food, community supported agriculture, vegetable box schemes and shared garden schemes are all part of the picture. Supermarkets are increasingly paying lip service to this development by showing the picture of farmers on joints of meat or lumps of cheese, giving consumers a sense of connectedness with the source of the food on the dinner table.

But, not surprisingly, the idea that 'only local is good' has come under scrutiny. Is food that is grown locally but with high inputs of fertilizers and by the use of large tractors a climate-friendly alternative? Is it better just because it has travelled a shorter distance?

In Europe, critics of the dominant food system often take green beans that are being air freighted from places like Kenya to European supermarkets as an example of unacceptable supplies. But others point out that beans in Kenya are produced in an environmentally - friendly manner. "Beans there are grown using manual labour – nothing is mechanized," says Professor Gareth Edwards-Jones of Bangor University, an expert on African agriculture. "They don't use tractors, they use cow muck as fertilizer, and they have low-tech irrigation systems in Kenya. They also provide employment to many. So you have to weigh that against the air miles used to get them to the supermarket. Long term, the only fair option is to ensure the prices of the goods we consume, including organic produce, cover the environmental costs wherever the goods are from. We also need a labelling system that tells consumers about how the product is reducing poverty."

In short, the issue of trying to reduce the emissions produced by food is bedevilled by complexity. A dietary point is stressed by Tara Garnett of the UK's Food Climate Research Network: "There is only one way of being sure that you cut down on your carbon emissions when buying food: stop eating meat, milk, butter and cheese. These come from ruminants – sheep and cattle – that produce a great deal of harmful methane. In other words, it is not the source of the food that matters but the kind of food you eat."[7]

Cuba's great experiment

In recent years Cuba has become a world-beating laboratory for the development of organic urban agriculture: local food produced for local consumption. It demonstrates how a major crisis can be turned into an opportunity through deliberate policy. Following the collapse of the Soviet Union in 1989, food security in Havana and other cities became a major concern. Cuba had lost its main sugar market and 85 percent of its export earnings, and the US trade embargo caused further economic hardship. When food shortages due to the lack of fuel for tractors and lorries caused serious food supply problems, the government decided to encourage people to practise agriculture within Cuba's cities. Soon gardens sprouted up everywhere – at housing estates, schools, community centres, hospitals and factories.

Cuba's urban agriculture programme aims to provide each person with at least 300 grams of fresh vegetables per day, a figure considered by the FAO as appropriate for maintaining good health. Among the most popular crops are tomatoes, sweet corn, lettuce, onions, cabbage and carrots. Urban food growing is a source of employment for many people, and provides fresh produce with zero transportation costs. By 2002, more than 35,000 hectares of urban land were used for the intensive production of fruit, vegetables and spices. Some 117,000 people work in the urban gardens, which produce over half the vegetables grown in Cuba.

It was Cubans of Chinese origins who were a major inspiration behind the urban agriculture revolution, persuading Cubans whose diet did not include copious amounts of vegetables, that they should change their diet. With cookery classes conducted at the urban farms, Chinese-style cooking seems to be catching on. In Havana vegetarian restaurants are doing good business, and people from all walks of life have come to expound the health benefits of fresh organic, locally grown food.

Urban agriculture is particularly evident in Havana. It has become a world leader in the subject, as food production was decentralized from large mechanized state farms to urban cultivation systems. With some 3 million people, Havana is the largest city in the Caribbean, with nearly 20 percent of Cuba's population. Today more than 50 percent of Havana's fresh produce is grown organically within the city limits, using organic compost and simple but effective irrigation systems. The workers in many state enterprises grow their own food. The government has also helped hundreds of thousands of people to set up vegetable gardens, to plant fruit trees and to raise chickens and rabbits.

Urban farming has evolved into three main forms – state-owned research gardens (*organoponicos*), private gardens (*huertos privados*), and popular gardens (*huertos populares*). Organic crops are mainly grown on raised vegetable beds, which make very efficient use of whatever plot of land is available. The main source of compost is bagasse trucked in from Cuba's sugar cane fields. Ironically, the sugar cane is grown with artificial fertilizers, but the bagasse is composted and effectively becomes an organic growing medium. Cuba's urban agriculture programme provides good quality seeds, advice on composting and crop rotations, and on dealing with bacterial and fungal diseases without relying on chemical pesticides.[8]

In recent years Cuba's 200 biotechnology centres have opened a significant new export market by offering advice on successful organic cultivation methods to other countries such as Jamaica and Venezuela. In Caracas, Cuban-style vegetable gardens can now be found amid the chaos of busy inner-city streets. Inspired by what he saw in Cuba, President Hugo Chavez ordered intensive urban farming schemes across Venezuela's cities in a bid to enhance food self-sufficiency.

Source: Herbert Girardet. Jac Smit, the founder of the international Urban Agriculture Network, at an 'organoponico' garden in Havana.

Navdanya – seed sovereignty in India

Localization of food is not only a matter of producing local food for local markets but also keeping control of the seeds used in growing agricultural crops. This is a particularly important issue for farmers in developing countries who, since time immemorial, have based their food production on saving their own seeds. They are now targeted by multi-national seed companies determined to make them dependent on newly introduced crop varieties, which require extensive use of artificial fertilizers and pesticides.

In India, Vandana Shiva, a World Future Council member, decided to counter this trend by setting up an organization called Navdanya. It has pioneered the movement of seed saving, in the realization that the conservation of agricultural biodiversity requires the active participation of the communities who have evolved and protected the plants and animals that form the basis of their systems of agriculture.

Navdanya works for economic and food security by promoting ecological agriculture based on biodiversity. For 25 years Navdanya has worked with local communities and farmers' organizations, now serving more than 200,000 men and women farming across 14 Indian States. Navdanya's efforts have resulted in the conservation of more than 2,000 rice varieties from all over the country, many of which have been adapted over centuries to meet different local ecological conditions. Members have also conserved 31 varieties of wheat and hundreds of millets, pulses, oilseeds and vegetables, as well as a great variety of multi-purpose plant species, including medicinal plants.

To reflect its philosophy of seed sovereignty, Navdanya has initiated 34 Community Seed Banks with many partners across India, encouraging them to become self-sufficient and self-supporting. The seed banks operate in different eco-zones, facilitating the rejuvenation of India's agricultural biodiversity, farmers' self-reliance in seed and farmers' rights.

Navdanya has also established a conservation and training centre at its farm near Dehradun in Uttarakhand, in a region where more than 70,000 farmers are members of Navdanya. These farmers in turn are spreading the movement to their neighbouring villages.

Today, biodiversity conservation programmes which are directly run or supported by Navdanya are underway in Uttaranchal, Uttar Pradesh, Madhya Pradesh, Rajasthan, Orissa, West Bengal, Karnataka and Haryana.[9]

Local energy – national and regional policy

As we discussed in Chapter 3, the concept of energy subsidiarity advocates the greatest production of energy as near to the point of use as possible. Renewable energy development has been discussed to an extent, but we want to provide some historical background on why local energy supplies can expect much growth in the coming years.

The story starts in Denmark. The 1970s oil shocks gave a boost to the steady grassroots development of the Danish wind energy sector, and it was this work, done by backyard enthusiasts and cooperative groups, that directly laid the foundations for today's huge and rapidly growing global RE industry. With financial support measures from a supportive government at the time, there was a positive top-down response to the bottom-up enthusiasm of these amateur pioneers. This case can be considered a good example when addressing the present situation. Once again, we have fluctuating fossil-fuel prices and global instability, allied in this case with enormous uncertainty in the financial sector. Local renewable energy makes increasing sense against this backdrop, as well as pushing in the right direction with regard to climate change mitigation.

When we talk of 'local', for the purposes of this book we need to define a scale. The chapters on cities, renewable energy and energy equality overlap here, so we are mainly thinking of districts and suburbs in developed countries: areas of low to moderate density. High density areas are dealt with in the Cities chapter, and developing countries in the Energy Equality chapter.

In terms of promotion policies for getting small-scale renewables into the built environment especially, there are several approaches. Aside from grant programmes, low interest loans and tax incentives, there are a few common promotion policies. One is net metering, which allows home generators to feed their energy into the grid and run their meter backwards, but this effectively values renewables-derived electricity at the same level as electricity from fossil fuels. This unfortunately discounts the environmentally-friendly nature of the energy.

SOLARSIEDLUNG, FREIBURG

Credit: Rolf Disch.

Freiburg, in south-western Germany, has only half the solar potential of southern Spain, but for many years it has been at the forefront of Europe's renewable energy revolution. With a population of 200,000, it has more solar roofs than the whole of the United Kingdom which has 60 million people. This development was driven partly by the national feed-in tariff policy and partly by local initiative.

Freiburg's new Solarsiedlung, or solar village, designed by 'solar architect' Rolf Disch, is probably Europe's most influential housing project of this kind, indicating that cities have the potential to produce a surplus of energy from within their own territory. The rooftop PV panels produce 6,300 kWh per home per year, or nearly three times more than each home consumes. By a combination of passive solar heating and high levels of insulation with novel Vacuum Insulation Panels, the 58 residential *units consume only 2,200 kWh per year, just one-third of the average consumption of a typical California home.*

In addition to its solar arrays, the Solarsiedlung also excels because of its use of sustainable materials and construction methods, choice of energy-efficient appliances, and urban design that optimizes opportunities for pedestrian living, cycling and public transport. The Solarsiedlung, with its mix of owner-occupied and rented homes, offers a compact, pleasant living environment for all its residents. It is widely regarded as a model for sustainable urban living for the 21st century.

The deployment of renewable energy has been spurred more by the feed-in tariff model (FIT) than any other, which is detailed in the renewable energy chapter. Microgeneration is best served by a feed-in tariff set at an appropriate level. Solar PV in particular does well from FITs as they are simpler for householders to negotiate than certificate schemes, but can also benefit from grant programmes which supply some of the up-front costs of the technology.

The UK's 'Merton Rule' is a mandate to use renewable energy on-site to reduce CO_2 emissions from the built environment. This planning policy, which was developed by the London Borough of Merton in 2003, has now become part of national planning guidance. The wording of the policy reads: "All new non-residential developments above a threshold of 1,000 sq.m. will be expected to incorporate renewable energy production equipment to provide at least 10 percent of predicted energy requirements." This mandate is not only leading to big CO_2 reductions, but is helping to create an industry that can respond to the need for affordable renewable energy. How the 10 percent criterion is met is up to the developer.[10]

The Barcelona Solar Thermal Ordinance of 2000 is a mandate for buildings to use solar hot water heating systems to supply 60 percent of their running hot water requirements. This has also spread across the country to 35 cities, including eight provincial capitals. It is estimated to have saved the equivalent of 19,626 MWh/year (based upon a city of 35,000 people), €1,087,301 per year in energy costs and the equivalent of 3,451 tonnes of CO_2.[11]

Since the early 1990s Woking Borough Council in the UK has used a combination of measures to reduce its own carbon dioxide emissions by around 77 percent, and those of the borough as a whole by 17 percent. Importantly, this has been achieved without financial support from central Government. Woking has incrementally expanded its local energy capacity, funding growth of that capacity by reinvesting money saved through its energy efficiency projects. Since 1999, local energy development in the town has been taken forward by a public/private joint venture energy service company (ESCO), Thameswey Energy Ltd (TEL). It is wholly owned by the council and is allowed to operate outside the capital controls of local government. TEL provides local energy, including cooling, heat and electricity to all Woking's institutional, commercial and residential customers.

In 2002, Woking was the first local authority to adopt a comprehensive Climate Change Strategy, aimed at meeting the Royal Commission on Environmental Pollution's target of a 60 percent reduction in carbon dioxide emissions by 2050. The town has now built up a network of over 60 local generators, including cogeneration and trigeneration units, photovoltaic arrays and the UK's first hydrogen fuel cell station. A key feature of the Woking example is that its energy system runs on a local private wire network, which allows unlicensed generation and supply to take place outside the main electricity market.

In Woking this private network is able to provide electricity connections for the whole town. Because the operator is unlicensed, it can avoid costs such as the UK Renewables Obligation, Climate Change Levy and the Energy Efficiency Commitment. This helps promote the financial viability of the more expensive low-carbon energy sources used in Woking. However, there are also some disadvantages to the use of private wire networks. Customers are not protected in the same way as those supplied by licensed energy companies and cannot easily switch energy supplier. When necessary, these networks are also still dependent on the external public networks for back-up power.[12]

The potential of local RE will be seen increasingly in projects such as the 'bioenergy village' of Jühnde in northern Germany. This award-winning project shows that 100 percent of energy needs can be supplied by renewables. A bioenergy plant composed of a 700 kW biogas installation and a 550 kW wood chip heating plant provide electricity and heat for over 140 households. The heat is distributed via a short-distance pipeline. The plant is fuelled from local organic waste resources, which in turn is beneficial to the region. The biogas is produced from the manure of 800 cows, 1,400 pigs, and from grass and other plants. It fuels a power station that generates 4,000,000 kWh of electricity annually. In summer the heat generated by the bio energy plant is sufficient for the village's hot water requirements, and for drying the woodchips ready for the winter, when the wood chip heating plant is switched on. Jühnde demonstrates that rural areas can become self-sufficient in energy, saving money and making excellent use of organic by-products.

Credit: Jühnde Village Council. Jühnde bio-energy village using biomass and biogas as its primary energy source.

Making local economies work: Mondragón Corporacion Cooperativa

The revival of local economies in the face of globalization is a difficult thing to achieve. However, there is one example that stands out because of the sheer magnitude of its success: The Mondragón Corporacion Cooperativa (MCC) in the Basque country in Spain. It is a regional group of manufacturing, financial and retail companies which has subsequently extended across the rest of Spain and abroad. It is considered the world's largest worker cooperative and an important example of workers' self-management.

The company was founded in Arrasate, or Mondragón in Spanish. The town had suffered badly during the Spanish Civil War and there was mass unemployment. In 1941 a young priest, Father José María Arizmendiarrieta, arrived and decided to set up cooperatives to facilitate economic development of the town. Co-operatives had a long tradition in the Basque Country but had died away after the Civil War.

In 1943, Arizmendiarrieta set up a Polytechnic School which came to play a key role in the development of the co-operative movement. In 1956, five young graduates of the school set up the first cooperative enterprise named ULGOR after their surnames, which focused on the manufacture of gas heaters and cookers. In 1959, they set up the Caja Laboral Popular ("People's Worker Bank"), a credit union that allows its members access to financial services and provides start-up funds for new co-operative ventures. New companies started up in the 1960s, including Fagor Electrónica, Fagor Ederlan and Danobat.

The cooperatives have a variety of functions: they also provide insurance and pension funds and discounts at Eroski stores which, in turn, are supplied by cooperative trucks. When a cooperative gets into financial trouble, workers usually prefer pay cuts over layoffs or redundancies. If the situation deteriorates, redundant workers are usually offered positions in other group cooperatives.

In the 1980s, the various companies responded to pressures of globalization by joining together as the Mondragón Cooperative Corporation. The MCC is now the Basque Country's largest corporation and the seventh largest in Spain. In 2006 the MCC contributed 3.8 percent towards the GDP of the Basque Country.

Education has always been key to MCC and its development. Members may have studied at a group-owned school and can attend the Mondragón University which was set up in the 1990s and which aims to promote further cooperative development in the Basque country. Some 4,000 students attend the university campuses in Oñati, Eskoriatza and Mondragón.

MCC now constitutes over 150 companies, with important manufacturing and engineering interests as well as retail, financial and educational arms. Eroski is the largest Spanish-owned supermarket chain and the third largest retail group in the Basque government. The tax authorities of the Basque provinces have initiated special measures to help cooperatives. All of these measures have contributed to local economic resilience and they have helped to ensure high employment rates even during times of economic crisis.

New currencies support regional development

by WFC adviser Prof. Dr. Margrit Kennedy

The introduction of regional currencies offers an opportunity for decentralized development that is that is sensitive to social, cultural aspects of our global societies. As the world experiences financial and economic crisis, peak oil and the dangers of climate change at the same time, we need to direct our focus toward smaller, pragmatic solutions. The development of regions as an economic unit may present one of the most successful ways of moving toward another form of globalization, and the introduction of its own currency is the fastest way of strengthening this development.

Regional currencies complement the national currency within a defined geographic area that people relate to personally and emotionally. They prove useful in different respects: from the protection of cultural identity to marketing regionally grown foods, from the ecologically sensible choice of the shortest transportation routes to exercising ethical concern when utilizing non-renewable resources. As an integral component of regional economic cycles, a regional currency can sustainably curb the dangers of inflation and deflation, and connect unused resources with unmet needs.

There are many historic precedents and examples of dual currency systems in the world demonstrating their unique contribution in building social capital. There are at least 1,300 complementary currency groups operating in

Europe, on which regional currencies would build their constituencies. They are forming or have already established networks of information and mutual support with an increasing number of websites demonstrating a growing need for information and exchange of experiences. In the context of a worldwide monetary crisis the public interest in complementary and regional currencies increases rapidly.

One example of the most successful regional currencies in Germany is the 'Chiemgauer'. In use since 2003, it aims at creating customer, producer and trade loyalty for a region instead of aiming at customer loyalty for a commercial enterprise. The term 'Regio' is being used by most of the 60 existing currency initiatives, of which 30 have already issued their own currency. The vast majority of them belong to the Regiogeld Federation (Regiogeldverband), and exhibit many common features:

- **It allows a partial de-coupling of a region from the global economy and assures that a significant proportion of economic exchanges are carried out in the region's own currency**
- **It keeps the added value of regionally exchanged goods within the regional economy and thus helps to reduce unemployment in that region**
- **Its creation is transparent and therefore can be democratically controlled**
- **It encourages ecological projects and promotes the shortest efficient transportation route**
- **It enhances regional identity, cooperation and responsibility among participants and creates new relationships between consumers and producers**

Belonging to the 'Regiogeldverband' guarantees certain rules and standards:

- **The Regio is not an 'official' means of payment – nobody is obliged to accept it**
- **Because it is voluntary, it will only function as long as people consider it to be useful, i.e. as long as it can be spent on regional products**
- **Its use is limited by geography; the currency in each region bears a different name**
- **Converting Regios into national currency usually incurs an exchange fee**
- **Regios do not normally earn interest but carry a circulation incentive – i.e. a fee – if not passed on.**

After the first years – when growth in turnover and number of participants begins to accelerate – the economic advantages for the different actors will become more evident: businesses, administration, non-profit organizations, and employment offices all profit from a complementary currency, which makes use of local resources and replaces social welfare programmes without becoming a welfare system itself, making people independent and building on the creativity of individuals and groups to resolve their specific problems in specific ways.

Regional currencies complement national and international currencies and may one day be introduced in cooperation with national banks and the European Central Bank. The current crises and the long-term outlook seem to indicate a thorough revision of existing monetary policies and professional attitudes toward the smaller siblings of the Euro, Dollar and Yen.

The solution presented here will be a surprise for conventional economic thinking, which invariably assumes monopolies for national monies as an unquestionable given. The regional currency examples, and other complementary currency models which exist for different purposes, show that monetary sustainability will be enhanced by a diversity of currency systems, allowing multiple and more diverse monetary systems to emerge. While they are proving their capacity to play a stabilizing role on a small scale today, they may well help to sustain the global economic system tomorrow, if they can be implemented on the scale necessary to make a difference.

The Lewes Pound

The Lewes Pound is an initiative of Transition Town Lewes as the first step towards increasing the localization of the Lewes economy. It is a tool to help reconnect and rebuild the once-vibrant web of local businesses and traders, by bringing people together. It can only be accepted by locally owned traders, ensuring that most of the money spent with Lewes Pounds stays within the community. It aims to become a complementary currency to Sterling, but not a replacement.

Well over 50 percent of all local traders accept the Lewes Pounds. They are issued in exchange for Sterling at four issuing points across town, including Lewes Town Hall, at a 1-to-1 exchange rate. Traders who take Lewes Pounds are encouraged to give them to customers as change or pay their suppliers and employees with them. They can also trade them back into Sterling at any time.

This initiative is part of a longer-term plan that may include LETS, local banks and the decoupling of the Lewes Pound and Sterling, but the objective of this initial phase to raise awareness about the importance of local trade, to give people a reason to shop locally and to start a conversation on these issues. Its success

has far exceeded the expectations of the founders, helped in no small part by the fact that the currency was launched in the middle of an economic crisis. The Lewes Pound is seen to buck the trend of economic doom and gloom, and has as a result has become a mainstream news story, hopefully giving birth to many similar initiatives.

www.thelewespound.org

at the earlier stage of 'mulling' whether or not to become Transition groups.

Rather than simply offering a menu of responses or actions, the Transition approach is one that acts as a catalyst, using awareness raising and networking to focus people's minds and their creative thinking on the practicalities of relocalization. They are based on four key assumptions:

1. That life with dramatically lower energy consumption is inevitable, and that it is better to plan for it than to be taken by surprise

2. That our settlements and communities presently lack the resilience to enable them to weather the severe energy shocks that will accompany peak oil

3. That we have to act collectively and we have to act now

4. That by unleashing the collective genius of those around us to creatively and proactively design our energy descent, we can build ways of living that are more connected, more enriching and that recognize the biological limits of our planet.

Central to the Transition concept is the idea of resilience. Resilience is a different concept from sustainability. The term sustainability implies that our current ways of doing things can continue indefinitely, i.e. global trade, economic growth and so on, we just need to lessen its impact on the environment, run the cars on hydrogen and put solar panels on the roof. Resilience on the other hand, is about the ability of our settlements, businesses and economies, to withstand shock from the outside. It focuses on increasing diversity (of livelihoods, food systems, businesses, etc.) and increasing modularity (increased local self-reliance and localized supply chains). As we enter a time when the likelihood of such shocks is increasing, whether it be from climate change,

high energy prices or interruptions in supply, we need resilience perhaps more than ever, yet we have dismantled and discarded much of it over the past 40 or so years. Urban market gardens lie beneath car parks, farmers have been driven from the land, and our high streets, which once boasted a wide diversity of local, family-run businesses, now all look largely the same.

The Transition approach is about looking at the practicalities of relocalization, seeing the move towards more localized approaches as being an inevitable change in direction for mankind. It is not so much 'Small is Beautiful' as, when one removes cheap fossil fuels from the picture, 'Small is Inevitable.' It is a transition from a time when our degree of economic success and personal prowess depended entirely on our degree of oil consumption, to one where our degree of dependency is our degree of vulnerability. It is a transition that will not be successfully managed without an extraordinarily high level of co-ordination, creativity and determination.

Any talk about the Transition movement always includes a mention of 'The Cheerful Disclaimer', which is at the heart of the concept. This states that Transition is an iterative process, one that is evolving as it goes along, based on the experience of those applying it. No-one claims that the Transition model as it exists definitely works – what matters is the process, the collaborative experimentation. Although it is a very young movement, some notable practical initiatives are starting to emerge. These include:

• The towns of Lewes and Totnes have begun experimenting with their own printed currencies. The Lewes Pound is now accepted in over 100 Lewes businesses

• The 'Garden Share' concept, begun in Totnes, is now being developed in a number of other towns, and inspired River Cottage's 'Landshare' initiative

• *Transition BS3 in Bristol has created a Community Small Holding and a Community Garden with land donated by the Council*

• *Transition Waiheke in New Zealand has begun an initiative to plant 20,000 fruit and nut trees across the island*

• *Somerset and Leicestershire County Councils have both passed resolutions to support their local Transition initiatives and to work towards becoming 'Transition Authorities'*

• *There are now pools of Transition Trainers in many countries*

• *A number of Transition initiatives are setting up their own energy companies, usually based on the ESCO model*

One of the key objectives of a Transition initiative is the creation of an 'Energy Descent Action Plan,' that is, a Plan B for the settlement in question. This aims to set out a practical pathway for how the town can move away from oil dependency and thrive in the process. Totnes in Devon is currently creating the UK's first such pathway, as well as developing many of the tools and approaches needed for its creation.

In terms of the limitations of the Transition concept, there are several:

• *The degree of community engagement they manage to achieve*

• *Their ability to manage conflict, and to transform ideas and discussions into practical action*

• *Their ability to sustain engagement over a period of time*

Although financial support is vital, it is rarely an adequate substitute for enthusiasm, and most initiatives achieve a great deal on little or no funding. It is also important to observe that Transition initiatives see themselves as one of many responses required on a broad range of scales, from international legislation through to national government action as well as local initiatives. The Transition Network was set up in 2007 in order to support, encourage, inspire, network and train Transition initiatives.
For more information, visit www.transitionnetwork.org

The Low Carbon Communities Network (LCCN) was set up in response the growing number of grassroots communities who recognize that reducing CO_2 emissions in the shortest possible timescale is imperative. They are autonomous and do not subscribe to a set model or set of guiding principles. There are several hundred across the UK and abroad, some of whom grew out of Local Agenda 21 initiatives and are well established in their locality. LCCN recognizes the need to work with government, business and communities to ensure that policy encourages personal behaviour change and empowers business to take up the challenge to a low carbon economy.

Their 'Smart Living' theme, running through 2009, has three key messages:

1. We need to reduce our demand for energy from the world's finite resources

2. The energy we use to heat and power our homes should to be used as efficiently as possible

3. Householders and communities should be able to make informed choices about renewables technologies which are the most appropriate and cost-effective for their situation.

The work of LCCN is clearly complementary to that of the Transition movement. Energy self-reliance and decarbonization for climate change purposes are two key elements which are shared globally. These local initiatives are especially useful in building grassroots activity and awareness, but they will always require top-down government policy to facilitate further development and activity, and avoid hitting a political ceiling.

Living on one planet

The challenges and opportunities of localization are, perhaps, best summarized in the ten principles defined under One Planet Living, a concept initiated by the London-based BioRegional Development Group and adopted by WWF. It sets out ten principles for global sustainable living at the local level, combining energy, transport, materials use, food and biodiversity conservation into one comprehensive package. This is all about staying within nature's bounds.

1	Zero carbon
2	Zero waste
3	Sustainable transport
4	Sustainable materials
5	Local and sustainable food
6	Sustainable water
7	Natural habitats and wildlife
8	Culture and heritage
9	Equity, fair trade and local economy
10	Health and happiness

One Planet Living is, above all else, concerned with reducing our ecological footprints by deliberate measures of living better on less. The concept has been successfully applied in innovative housing estates, such as the Beddington Zero Energy Development (BedZed), designed by architect Bill Dunster, and by BioRegional's numerous entrepreneurial activities.

The challenge now is to add together and scale up the numerous examples in this chapter to a comprehensive framework of action on renewing local economies as an important basis for resilient living and working in the 21st century. Localization has an important role to play in the climate and energy-constrained world in which we now live. It is about both constraints and new opportunities for making better use of resources in a globally connected world. There has been much lip-service paid to the concept of the Global Village. Today, it has come to mean global cooperation for achieving sustainable, resilient local economies that assure that a substantial proportion of local consumption is met by local production. Trade could be increasingly dematerialized, with ideas rather than products being exchanged worldwide. Let us trust that the global human community is getting ready to meet this historic challenge.

These are the main challenges:

- **Making the transition towards resilient communities a socially and economically attractive proposition**
- **Implementing national enabling policies for local sustainable development, including renewable energy**
- **Making local food supplies an essential part of the local diet**
- **Empowering local communities to build resilient local economies**

Acknowledgements

Margrit Kennedy *MonNetA*
Rob Hopkins *Transition Network*
Tracey Todhunter
Low Carbon Communities Network
Oliver Dudok van Heel *Transition Lewes*
Ken Hayes *Soil Association*
International Society for Ecology and Culture
www.isec.org.uk

Credit: Herbert Girardet. Pedestrian area, Lisbon City Centre.

" *To sum up the reason for the success of old and the failure of modern city planners in one paragraph: ancient city planners, recognizing the unchanging purpose of why people live in communities, put all their talent into the construction of the communal nucleus – inns, churches, city halls.*
The rest of the city – residences, schools, factories, trade – followed by itself. Modern city planners are forever building the rest of the city. But without nucleus nothing can hold together. And the nucleus they cannot build because of their conviction that every age has a different purpose which, by the time they have discovered it, has melted away from underneath their feet. "

Leopold Kohr, The Inner City, From Mud to Marble, 1989

9

Problem Technologies

*"And Lord, we are especially thankful for nuclear power,
the cleanest, safest energy source there is.
Except for solar, which is just a pipe dream."*

Homer Simpson

As we explore the potential for getting us off fossil fuels as quickly as possible, there are certain subjects which tend to dominate the mainstream debate. The issues of nuclear power and biofuels technologies are so forcefully pushed from one side and resisted from another that it is a huge challenge to attempt to explore them without incurring the wrath of many – and we would be equally damned if we avoided the subjects altogether. So we will attempt to wrestle with these issues as best we can, set aside the propaganda from both sides, and see if there is anything here we should in fact be supportive of, despite having 'deep green' backgrounds. The urgency is such that we must determine if any of these much-maligned technologies may be necessary as perhaps bridging technologies, or solutions in their own right.

Importantly, the question must be raised as to whether or not there will ever be a realistic and constructive process of engagement and cooperation between all those who are in essence seeking the same goal: generating clean energy. In the end, this issue is a matter of life or death, and must be resolved. However, writing this introduction after speaking to both sides, it is hard to imagine any calm and rational engagement ensuing. It may be trench warfare for some time yet. Nuclear and renewables do not seem destined to be good bedfellows, no matter how politicians may call for 'all options' to be included in the energy mix. Biofuels have set the cat among the pigeons, and caused no end of debate within the renewables community and in the wider environmental and policymaking communities. Equally contested subjects such as Coal-to-liquids (CtL) could also have been explored here, if space permitted, and Carbon Capture and Storage (CCS) is addressed in Chapter 1. These debates are likely to run and run.

Nuclear

For many of us who lived through the 1980s, the attempted nuclear renaissance which lurched into action in the early years of the 21st century is somewhat surprising to say the least. After Chernobyl and the 'end of the cold war', one could be forgiven for thinking that the oft-quoted laundry list of reasons why nuclear is not a good bet in any of its applications would have been sufficient to kill it off once and for all. However, like a horror-movie villain, it is back from the dead once more with profit in mind, and we have to deal with it. This time however, it is doing its best to fly the green flag, claiming to be a win-win solution to energy security and climate change. As British environmentalist George Monbiot observed, "For 50 years, nuclear power has been a solution in search of a problem."

"Don't forget to tell your grandchildren to make sure they let their grandchildren know how to instruct their grandchildren to show their grandchildren how to clarify to their grandchildren in what way their grandchildren could enable their grandchildren to look after our nuclear waste." – One Million Europeans Against Nuclear Power[1]

The promotion of nuclear power seems often to be more about personal interests and values than about solving the climate and energy problem. For example, no recent energy conference has been complete without someone on a panel espousing the green credentials and *necessity* of nuclear power – whether it was on the agenda or not. And more and more people are hearing this message. Unexpected luminaries within the green movement have come forward to urge this technology upon us for some time now, and more are still joining these ranks.[2]

Nuclear supporters argue that it:

- **is low-carbon**
- **can provide steady baseload power**
- **can be built quickly and safely**
- **can find a solution to nuclear waste**
- **is not going to lead to nuclear proliferation**
- **can be made terrorist-proof**
- **can be economical**

For many reasons, there are few who sit on the nuclear fence. We shall look here at what the opponents are suggesting is actually the case.

For starters, here is the opening of a prize-winning article on nuclear versus renewables:

Nuclear power plants are a poor choice for addressing energy challenges in a carbon constrained, post-Kyoto world. Nuclear generators are prone to insolvable infrastructural, economic, social, and environmental problems. They face immense capital costs, rising uranium fuel prices, significant life-cycle greenhouse gas emissions, and irresolvable problems with reactor safety, waste storage, weapons proliferation, and vulnerability to attack. Renewable power generators, in contrast, reduce dependence on foreign sources of uranium and decentralize electricity supply so that an accidental or intentional outage would have a more limited impact than the outage of larger nuclear facilities. Most significantly, renewable power technologies have environmental benefits because they create power without relying on the extraction of uranium and its associated digging, drilling, mining, transporting, enrichment, and storage.[3]

From another nuclear versus renewables paper:

Nuclear power has been promoted as a solution to climate change and an answer to energy security. It is neither. On the one hand, as a response to global warming it is too slow, too expensive and too limited. On the other hand, it is more of a security risk in an age of terror-related threats, than a security solution.[4]

From an economic analysis of the current UK government plans:

The economics of new nuclear power stations for the UK do not add up. It is not possible to achieve what the Government says it will do – build a new generation of nuclear stations in England without public subsidy. New build will not be possible without large sums of taxpayer's money being pledged, and extending the unlimited guarantee to underwrite all the debts of the existing and future nuclear industry.[5]

From a paper on the arguments against nuclear power:

Nuclear power is not an inevitable feature of energy supply systems. It has many attractive characteristics, but also a unique combination of problems, including military connections, problem of civil liberties, of safely and environment, of regard for future generations and, above all, of deteriorating economy.[6]

From the International Atomic Energy Agency's executive director:

The spent-fuel issue is the most critical one for nuclear. It will not develop if there is not a credible and satisfactory answer to the management of spent fuel and one which is convincing for the public.[7]

And from an article on carbon mitigation:

Nuclear plants are mutual hostages: the world's least well-run plant can imperil the future of all the others.[8]

So, in contradiction of the pro-nuclear view, we have here the basic arguments against nuclear, and especially new nuclear build:

- Cost
- Time
- Waste
- Proliferation
- Fuel supplies
- Security and safety

One could add, from the pro-renewables side, that a new nuclear programme could be a long-term distraction from investment in and development of the renewables industry. It would not be the first time. As renewable energy suffers from none of the problems outlined above (unless one argues the current cost of PV perhaps), one might conclude that we are dealing with a fundamentally political issue – more to do with the desires of the nuclear industry and government than truly with climate and environment-friendly energy generation.

Although nuclear is being touted as a friend to climate change, the relationship is not reciprocal. Sea level rises, now predicted to occur at double the rate suggested by the IPCC fourth assessment report of 2007,[9] could also threaten nuclear stations which are often sited on coasts. Reactors require large volumes of water for cooling. Droughts in 2006 caused the shutdown of reactors in France, Germany and Spain, and have threatened installations in North America. As nuclear plants are not designed to be shut down and restarted under normal conditions, this puts extra pressure on their systems. They run best when providing steady baseload power, meaning that they would ideally need to take precedence over renewables in the case of a full grid. If so, this would mean that the best low-carbon generation would have to be taken out of the grid in favour of nuclear.

However, the fact that these reactors cannot be built fast enough to make a difference to climate change is perhaps the most important. The lull in new build after Chernobyl has meant that many reactors will be decommissioned in the next decade, and that skilled workers are lacking. Even with new build therefore, new capacity would not create much in the way of extra low-carbon electricity generation. However, as renewable energy installations are generally modular, they can begin operation immediately. A wind farm with one hundred turbines can begin producing energy from the very first turbine commissioned, whereas a nuclear plant requires every single nut, bolt, valve and switch to be perfectly safe, secure and operational before the installation can begin operation: "A typical nuclear plant, for example, usually contains approximately fifty miles of piping that has been welded at 25,000 different points, and 900 miles of electrical cables. The electrical system has thousands of necessary components. The cooling system is equally complex."[10]

On operational safety, a cataloguing of accidents, costs and fatalities of major nuclear accidents from 1952 to 2008, recorded 4,100 fatalities and costs of $19,076 millions of (2006) US dollars.[11] The quantity and diversity of accidents is staggering, and given the reported tendency towards covering up nuclear accidents and safety alerts, is likely to be an incomplete picture. Health issues are not to be discounted either. Many claims have been made that communities living downstream or downwind of a reactor tend to exhibit notably higher rates of cancers.

Uranium mining is another major issue. It is dangerous and extremely damaging to the environment. Mines are either open pits up to 250 metres deep, or underground caverns similar to conventional coal shafts. Another extraction technique "involves subjecting natural uranium to in situ leaching where hundreds of tons of sulphuric acid, nitric acid, and ammonia are injected into the [uranium-rich rock deep in the earth's] strata and then pumped up again after three to twenty-five years, yielding uranium that has been leached over time from treated rocks. . . . Mined uranium must undergo a series of metallurgical processes to crush, screen, and wash the ore" before a series of chemical processes removes the remaining impurities. "After enrichment, about 85% . . . [is discarded] as waste in the form of depleted hex, known as 'enrichment tails'."

Source: istockphoto. Derelict uranium quarry.

These toxic wastes must be stored under strict safety conditions to prevent leaks into the natural environment. "Each year . . . France [alone] creates 16,000 tons of enrichment tails that are then exported to Russia or added to the existing 200,000 ton [sic] of depleted uranium stored within the country."[12]

A major argument over nuclear concerns its level of carbon emissions, with findings in qualified studies ranging from 1.4g to 288g of carbon dioxide equivalent per kWh: [13]

When the energy required for construction of a nuclear facility is added to the energy consumed in decommissioning as well as the energy required to mine, mill and enrich the uranium fuel, the nuclear fuel cycle consumes nearly half of all the electricity that a typical reactor is expected to produce during its lifetime, and this number does not include the energy needed to store spent fuel for thousands of years. . . . A majority of a nuclear reactor's generation is consumed by the nuclear life-cycle before a single kWh is available for use by electricity consumers.[14]

The mean value of emissions over the course of the lifetime of a nuclear reactor (reported from qualified studies) is 66g CO_2e/kWh, due to reliance on existing fossil-fuel infrastructure for plant construction, decommissioning, and fuel processing along with the energy intensity of uranium mining and enrichment. Thus, nuclear energy is in no way 'carbon-free' or 'emissions-free', even though it is much better (from purely a carbon-equivalent emissions standpoint) than coal, oil, and natural gas electricity generators, but worse than renewable and small-scale distributed generators.[15]

It cannot have gone unnoticed by even the most fervent nuclear advocate that various nations have been at great pains to prevent North Korea and Iran from developing a civilian

Life-cycle CO₂ estimates for electricity generators

Technology	Capacity/configuration/fuel	Estimate (gCO2e/kWh)
Wind	2.5 MW, offshore	9
Hydroelectric	3.1MW, reservoir	10
Wind	1.5MW, onshore	10
Biogas	Anaerobic digestion	11
Hydroelectric	300kW, run-of-river	13
Solar Thermal	80 MW, parabolic trough	13
Biomass	Forest wood Co-combustion with hard coal	14
Biomass	Forest wood steam turbine	22
Biomass	Short rotation forestry Co-combustion with hard coal	23
Biomass	FOREST WOOD reciprocating engine	27
Biomass	Waste wood steam turbine	31
Solar PV	Polycrystalline silicone	32
Biomass	Short rotation forestry steam turbine	35
Geothermal	80MW, hot dry rock	38
Biomass	Short rotation forestry reciprocating engine	41
Nuclear	Various reactor types	66
Natural Gas	Various	443
Fuel Cell	Hydrogen from gas reforming	664
Diesel	Various generator and turbine types	778
Heavy Oil	Various generator and turbine types	778
Coal	Various generator types with scrubbing	960
Coal	Various generator and without scrubbing	1050

Source: Sovacool, Valuing the greenhouse gas emissions from nuclear power: A critical survey, p2950.

nuclear power programme. Given that the industry has apparently vigorously denied that a 'dirty bomb' could be produced using material from a nuclear power station, what could their reasons be? Either civilian nuclear power is benign or it is not, and the attitude of the Bush administration in the US suggested that they felt it is not.

Something like an either/or argument has been suggested with regard to transmission also. The argument goes that nuclear plants are larger than any other generating installation (aside from large hydro), with third generation plants producing up to 1,600 MW. As many national electricity grids are rather ailing and in need of replacement, nuclear plants would require that they are significantly sturdier, to cope with the voltages required and prevent major line losses. Smaller, distributed generation installations do not require this kind of infrastructure, and tend to distribute the power more locally. So if a new nuclear programme were to be pursued, a major investment in updating grid capacity would be necessary, and this could create more transmission and distribution issues for renewables.

Supporters of nuclear point to the potential of so-called fast-breeder reactors, which are supposed to solve nuclear waste problems. But the fact is that they have so far not been scaled up successfully, and they have also been linked problematically with nuclear proliferation and national security issues, due to the creation of fissile plutonium in the process.[16,17]

Another objective is the development of a fusion reactor, which would effectively create a star on earth. One of the fusion fuels, deuterium, exists in huge quantities in the world's oceans. If it could be extracted economically, this approach could theoretically supply energy for 60 billion people for 1 million years.[18] Experts suggest that it might be possible to show that continuous fusion will be demonstrated in about 30 years and power generation in 50 years if all goes well. This programme will therefore do little to solve the current climate and energy crises.

The problem is that reactors usually take between five and ten years to build. Yet is its becoming apparent that within that time frame we must cut our carbon emissions massively.[19, 20] By comparison, renewable energy technologies can be installed far more quickly.

The nuclear industry also has a major issue with insurance, in that it is often described as being underinsured, leaving taxpayers to foot the bill.[21] These governmental subsidies are both substantial and often hidden.[22] In 2003 Swiss Re, a global reinsurer, called for contractual and legal measures to insulate the reinsurance sector from the nuclear industry.

The legacy issue should be considered for two reasons. Firstly, as the earlier quote suggests, there will be an obligation imposed on many future generations to look after the waste, and protect the next generation from it, long after the reactors themselves and the users of that energy have gone. Secondly, the limited nature of uranium supplies means that the more reactors get built, the less fuel available per reactor. According to the basic law of commodities, demand will raise the prices and the electricity will become more expensive. The most accessible and cheapest uranium will be exhausted, and the fact that the plants exist will require that they be fed, so as not to strand the investment. More expensive fuel will be required, and it will be potentially more destructive to the landscape to access it. Lower concentration mines will have to supply the rising demand, and the processing cost and energy requirements will rise until the energy necessary exceeds the energy supplied by the reactor.

So, the more reactors built, the faster the run-down of supplies, and the sooner we are left with gaps in generation once again – with present and future generations having to find a solution. This is of course predicated upon the performance of current reactor designs and the lack of successful, commercial-scale fast breeders.

The industry has been almost at a standstill in recent years. World nuclear capacity reached 372 GW in 2007, up from about 341 GW in 2000. Investment in nuclear power has not been attractive compared to other power generation options despite the vocal support of politicians. So, what do supporters present as evidence for a bright future? James Lovelock, the well-known developer of the 'Gaia' hypothesis, has been largely unqualified in his support for nuclear energy. His pro-nuclear arguments inspired Shirley Siluk Gregory, a 'progressive' green blogger to put together 10 'devil's advocate' pro-nuclear arguments. They suggest that nuclear's problems are not as bad as often stated, and that it is an important part of low-carbon energy generation.[23] To bring Lovelock's views up to date, when asked in a January 2009 interview if he still considered nuclear power to be a solution to climate change he responded, "It is a way for the UK to solve its energy problems, but it is not a global cure for climate change. It is too late for emissions reduction measures."[24]

Other environmentalists such as Britain's Mark Lynas, author of *Six Degrees*, have begun to give qualified support to nuclear energy, believing Generation IV reactors to be a climate change solution. He cites the work of Tom Blees, the American author of *Prescriptions for the Planet*, stating that such designs promise to meet criteria on sustainability, economics, safety and reliability.

Paul Brown, the former Guardian newspaper environment correspondent and author of *Voodoo Economics and the Doomed Nuclear Renaissance*, has the following response to

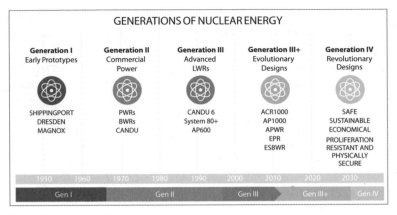

GENERATIONS OF NUCLEAR ENERGY

Generation I	Generation II	Generation III	Generation III+	Generation IV
Early Prototypes	Commercial Power	Advanced LWRs	Evolutionary Designs	Revolutionary Designs
SHIPPINGPORT DRESDEN MAGNOX	PWRs BWRs CANDU	CANDU 6 System 80+ AP600	ACR1000 AP1000 APWR EPR ESBWR	SAFE SUSTAINABLE ECONOMICAL PROLIFERATION RESISTANT AND PHYSICALLY SECURE

1950	1960	1970	1980	1990	2000	2010	2020	2030
Gen I			Gen II			Gen III	Gen III+	Gen IV

Source: US Department of Energy.
Note: the titles below each generation denote reactor models, with Generation IV being desired qualities. The progression of designs shows that the most environment(alist)-friendly blueprints are still just that – none are yet in existence.

Lynas's views:

There are no grounds for saying that a fourth generation of nuclear power would prevent proliferation. There are three generations at present; the third generation is the one being constructed in Finland and another in France. It is the type the government wants to build in England. Many 'new' designs for new nuclear power stations exist, all of them called fourth generation reactors. What this means is they could be the new form of reactors adopted after this present third generation. For all of them it is claimed they will be cheaper, safer, and better in every way than the present generation. All this is unproved hype. . . . The reason they have not been built is essentially because the first one (of every design) would be very expensive to build and might not work. No government is prepared to fund them so far.

The fourth generation that Lynas is talking about is a design that will burn existing stocks of plutonium and uranium thereby reducing stocks of these bomb-making materials, therefore reducing proliferation dangers. The UK government was asked by British Nuclear Fuels to sanction research and development into

building one of these at Sellafield but was refused on the grounds of cost.

No one knows whether an 'integral fast reactor breeder plant' would really work. Fast breeders only worked on small-scale dustbin-size projects and broke every time France, Japan, and Russia tried to scale them up.

Note the 'close to' fail-safe [argument]. [He] could have said in theory the design is fail-safe. In other words it has not been tried, so how can you know? Nuclear fission is a controlled nuclear explosion. It is virtually impossible to make it fail-safe.[25]

In summary, Brown is stating that the case for fourth generation nuclear reactors is purely theoretical. Third generation reactors are the models currently being built around the world. To get a reactor design to market inevitably costs millions of dollars just for the design work, and reactors are likely to be modified slightly from plant to plant as improvements are required or developed, adding to the expense. The overall impression from the research undertaken for this chapter is that next generation nuclear technologies can theoretically be safer, but the drawbacks, when compared to renewable energy, make nuclear appear a somewhat ridiculous option for mass deployment.

Renewable energy, compared with nuclear technology, can be empowering and engaging, and can aid community cohesion and self-reliance. However, a vast multitude of small generators invites complexity, which governments have often been apparently loath to deal with. Government and big business are similarly large, centralized and bureaucratic and they can meld their interests very well. By comparison, the general public, individually and collectively, can be chaotic, wilful, contrary and unpredictable. Yet in these times, when humanity is so numerous and has so much impact on the earth's environment, ordinary people must be engaged as an extraordinary resource. Renewables provide options for this which nuclear can never offer.

Conclusions

When one spends any amount of time whatsoever around the nuclear question, it rapidly becomes apparent that no matter what statistics, diagrams, arguments or evidence are put forth from one side, they will be immediately and absolutely countered by the other side. The decisions around replacement and/or expansion of existing nuclear facilities will in all likelihood follow the traditional pattern of dominant interests seeking all avenues to advance their agenda, while an infinitely poorer, decentralized opposition will seek to stop it in its tracks.

In the UK, the links between government and the nuclear industry are very close. At the time of writing, the Prime Minister's brother Craig Brown is Communications Director at EDF, the French 85%-state-owned nuclear giant. EDF have taken over British Energy, the sole UK nuclear company, paving the way for several reactors to be built in Britain. The first 'public consultations' held on the UK's nuclear future in recent years ended up in the Royal Courts of Justice in London in 2007, where Mr Justice Sullivan called the consultation process "seriously flawed", "misleading" and "manifestly inadequate and unfair".[26] In the US, the 2008 Washington International Renewable Energy Conference (WIREC) was addressed by President Bush, but he spoke largely about nuclear energy. One delegate described it as an "almost hallucinogenic" advert for nuclear power and biofuels, with very little of substance on actual renewables.

This 'friends in high places' strategy by the nuclear industry is one of the most troubling aspects of the issue, could be considered undemocratic, and does nothing to develop trust in the industry. It also serves to underline that it is not necessarily a matter of what makes sense in terms of energy investment and planning for the future, but of who has the power to decisively influence government policy in their favour.

Interestingly however, as this chapter was in the final drafting stage a press release arrived saying that a major nuclear company, Areva, is facing bankruptcy after hoped-for deals have not emerged, including South Africa pulling out of a new nuclear programme, citing cost. The future for nuclear energy has rarely looked rosy, but fast-changing circumstances and the financial and economic crises could see it stranded by a lack of taxpayer's money to guarantee its expensive development. The pro-renewables side would surely see this as the time to finally get serious about truly 'clean' energy.

Biofuels

Just a few years ago, as oil prices stared to rise, biofuels produced from agricultural crops entered the arena of future energy options. Yet what seemed to be a carbon-neutral solution to fuel production soon became a new object of fear and loathing by green groups as they pointed out that using food crops to feed cars instead of people was an unethical and impractical solution.

However, the debate has moved on apace, and so has the technology. As with every other issue in this book, biofuels are hotly contested, complex and rapidly evolving, and it requires great perseverance to get to grips with and keep up with the topic. Researching the matter becomes an effort to hit a moving target, but this chapter will offer a summary of the main issues. To begin with, it is useful to summarize definitions and basic production processes.

> "Worldwide, efforts to replace oil with biofuels are at a critical juncture. Double-digit growth in ethanol and biodiesel use during the past three years has contributed to a rapid increase in food, feed grain and soybean prices, as well as a sharp environmental backlash. Evidence is building that the biofuels industry is creating a host of ecological problems while failing to deliver real reductions in greenhouse gas emissions. Demand for biofuels is also creating global pressure for carbon-emitting deforestation and land conversion, as food and fuel compete for scarce resources."
>
> **Worldwatch Institute and Sierra Club,**
> **Smart Choices for Biofuels, p3**

Biofuels are a type of bioenergy, which is created from biomass – generally plant matter, but animal 'matter' also. Bioenergy is a common term for thermal or electrical energy derived from biomass sources, which are by nature renewable. Fuelwood and animal dung are used as traditional heating and cooking fuels (as discussed in Chapter 4. The term 'biofuel' is most commonly used when referring to liquid transport fuels. This relies on recently dead biological matter, whereas fossil fuels derive from long-dead biological matter.

Crops with high levels of sugars (sugar cane, sugar beet and sweet sorghum) and starches (corn/maize) are favourite for producing ethanol, and oil crops (oil palm, soybean, algae, jatropha, or pongamia pinnata) for biodiesel. Fruit, seed or sap can be used. Wood and wood by-products can also be converted into woodgas, methanol or ethanol.

Being a type of alcohol, ethanol is produced in a similar way to beer, by fermenting carbohydrates such as starches, sugars or celluloses. It is commonly used as a fuel additive to cut down vehicle emissions. 'Flex-fuel' vehicles can use mixtures of gasoline and up to 85 percent ethanol. Brazil's vehicle fleet has run on ethanol from sugarcane for many years.

Biodiesel is a combination of alcohol and vegetable oil, animal fat or recycled cooking greases. It can also be used as an emissions-reducing additive, or in its pure form as a renewable alternative fuel for diesel engines.

> "The world is on the threshold of an epochal transition from the petroeconomy, fuelled by carbon from the past, to the bioeconomy, fuelled by biomass created through photosyn-thesis."
> **John Mathews**

Criticism of biofuels produced from farm crops led to research into producing fuel from crop and forest wastes. 'Second-generation' biofuels use enzymes and other processes to convert cellulose from grasses and waste wood into ethanol and other fuels, and to process animal waste and fat, algae and urban wastes into biodiesel. Other technologies produce not only ethanol and biodiesel, but also bio-butanol, methanol, liquid hydrogen, bio-gasoline and synthetic diesel.[27]

First generation

In response to America's self-confessed 'addiction to oil', the Bush administration saw corn ethanol as the way to get off their habit. If oil = heroin, then ethanol = methadone. However, such 'first generation' (1G) biofuels have not worked out as a solution. A report by the Worldwatch Institute and the Sierra Club entitled *Smart Choices for Biofuels* summarizes the critique of first generation biofuels, with a focus on US ethanol production. They break it down into sections on: climate; land, soil and conservation; water; air pollution; economics, markets and prices; and job creation. Evidently the approach has been an epic failure, but has provided a comprehensive lesson in how not to do it.

The climate issue relates to net emissions balance; in other words, what quantity of emissions is absorbed compared to what is emitted throughout the life-cycle of the material? 1G production can involve land use change, in this case land clearance for growing, as well as oil-based fertilizer and pesticide manufacture and use, and energy use in farm machinery, biofuel refining, transportation and final use. "The total global warming footprint depends on what feedstock is used, how and where this feedstock is grown, any land-use changes, and how the fuel is processed. Scientists disagree about the potential benefits of corn ethanol; some estimates suggest that it provides a 12 to 18 percent net reduction in emissions compared to gasoline, but these figures assume that the refineries are fuelled by natural gas. If more-polluting coal power is used, the life-cycle emissions are higher than those associated with gasoline."[28]

The net energy balance is related to net emissions. Given the fossil-fuel inputs and energy losses for producing the biofuel, will it take more energy than it gives?

Marginal 'set aside' land can be brought back into production if corn demand is high enough, putting extra pressure on land which was being rested, and slowing recovery of fertility and structure. The land could also be used for watershed improvement or wildlife habitat. Overuse of land reduces the carbon-absorbing capacity of soils, a subject explored in Chapter 2.

Not only does agriculture draw an enormous amount of water – around 70 percent of the

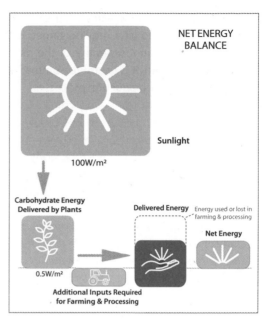

Source: MacKay, p45.

world's fresh water use – but it can lead to nitrogen and phosphorous pollution. This will only increase if large targets for corn ethanol production are set. Aquifer depletion is a serious problem for water supplies as water tables are lowered.[29] If aquifers are slow to recharge, the drawing of water can overwhelm the recharge rate and lead to plummeting yields for crops.

In addition to greenhouse gas production, smog-forming compounds and particulates result from the various stages of biofuel production. These include particle pollution, ozone, carbon monoxide, sulphur oxides, nitrogen oxides and lead. "Additionally, some research indicates that compared to gasoline, high-level ethanol blends may increase the formation of ground level ozone, which contributes to smog and is linked to some human illnesses."[30]

As far as the market and job creation potential are concerned, the news has not been good either. The trend towards industry consolidation emerges here, and has meant that smaller businesses and communities have not seen the economic and employment benefits they expected. Initial estimates of 700 jobs per ethanol plant have now been revised down in practice to more like 140.[31]

An influential and somewhat controversial study by Searchinger et al from 2008 analysed the impact of land use change arising from biofuels cultivation. The thesis of the study was that forest and grassland would be converted into new cropland to replace cropland converted to biofuel production. Their modelling found that "corn-based ethanol, instead of producing a 20% saving, nearly doubles greenhouse emissions over 30 years and increases greenhouse gases for 167 years. Biofuels from switchgrass, if grown on US corn lands, increase emissions by 50%."[32]

Corn-based ethanol also received a stern review from the International Forum on Globalization and the Institute for Policy Studies in their 2007 report *The False Promise of Biofuels*. They suggest three principles for guiding development of a comprehensive global framework for choosing energy systems to deal with the global crises:

First and foremost, our energy systems must be ecologically sustainable. The present climate crisis should make evident the need for maintaining critical global ecosystem services upon which we are dependent. Sustainability across generations is also a justice issue, making this criterion the most basic and vital condition for planning our energy future. Secondly, social justice demands that we choose energy systems, that if scaled up globally to their sustainable limits, are accessible to everyone. Fair distribution of scarce energy resources should be regarded as a basic human right. Finally, we must choose energy systems that meet the first two criteria while providing the highest level of net energy available.[33]

Their conclusion was that agrofuels fail to satisfy any of these principles.

The deforestation, food price and greenhouse gas emissions arguments were refuted by Goldemberg and Guardabassi in an article on the feasibility of biofuels:

The area used for soybean has not increased since 2004. The reality is that deforestation in the Amazonia has been going on for a long time at a rate of approximately 10,000 km^2 per year. Therefore, very recent increases are not due to soybean expansion, which has been very small since 2004, but instead due to cattle grazing.[34]

The point has been made that higher crops prices will not necessarily harm the poorest people; many of the world's 800 million undernourished people are farmers or farm labourers, who would ultimately stand to benefit from increased prices.[35]

The reduction in greenhouse gases can be assessed by a life-cycle analysis of the energy balance involved in the preparation of the ethanol. The results are sensitive to assumptions about growing conditions and the use of fertilizers, pesticides and other inputs in the agricultural phase as well as the use of fossil fuels in the industrial phase of production, which involves distillation of ethanol from a dilute solution. In the case of ethanol from maize, the ethanol plants are net importers of processing energy. In contrast, sugarcane distilleries are exporters of energy since most of their energy needs come from the sugarcane bagasse. As a result, the energy balance for maize and for sugarcane are approximately 1.4 and 10.2 respectively. Therefore, compared with gasoline, ethanol from maize emits 18% less CO$_2$, while ethanol from sugarcane emits 91% less CO$_2$.[36]

Credit: Greenpeace/Anderson. Palm oil plantation = deforestation.

As with nuclear, it is often found that both sides are able to provide facts and figures to counter any argument. Nonetheless, with these issues in view, what has been the response? With so much momentum in the field, driven by much the same raft of issues as renewable energy in general – security of supply, oil prices, new market opportunities, climate and environment – there has been a rush to 1G biofuels. But the US ethanol market has hit the skids in a major way, with numerous bankruptcies occurring.[37] This is partly thought to have resulted from over-zealous support from the Bush administration, without adequately assessing the available feedstocks to meet national targets. One could legitimately ask how many in the industry were truly serious about the emission reduction angle, given all of the above. However, anti-biofuels groups, academics and others have been working hard at keeping the industry honest, and second generation biofuels appear more promising than first generation.

Second generation

Non-food crops and inedible waste products are the starting point for second generation (2G) biofuels, which can help exclude animal and human food chains from the process, and are said to be superior in terms of net energy yields (see table below) and net greenhouse gas production, as well as having "potentially positive effects on soil and water quality and wildlife habitat".[38] These feedstocks include crop residues such as wheat stalks and 'waste' biomass, corn, wood, and grass crops such as Miscanthus and switchgrass. Other 2G feedstocks include non-plant sources such as fats, manure and the organic material found in urban waste.[39] Many 2G biofuels are under development such as biohydrogen, biomethanol, DMF, Bio-DME, Fischer-Tropsch diesel, biohydrogen diesel and wood diesel. Some experimental work is also being done on increasing biofuel potential through genetic engineering of organisms.[40, 41]

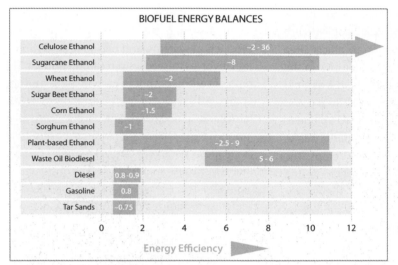

BIOFUEL ENERGY BALANCES

Celulose Ethanol	-2 - 36
Sugarcane Ethanol	-8
Wheat Ethanol	-2
Sugar Beet Ethanol	-2
Corn Ethanol	-1.5
Sorghum Ethanol	-1
Plant-based Ethanol	-2.5 - 9
Waste Oil Biodiesel	5 - 6
Diesel	0.8-0.9
Gasoline	0.8
Tar Sands	-0.75

Energy Efficiency

Source: Worldwatch Institute, Smart Choices for Biofuels, p8.
Note: Energy balance is a comparison of how much fossil energy goes into making a fuel against how much energy is provided by the fuel. The higher the energy balance, the more efficient the fuel. Figures provided above represent best estimates, not averages.

be grown on marginal lands, rather than on prime plots. However, these so-called 'marginal lands' may in fact be of use to many of the groups already, particularly in developing countries. These groups include communities, herders, pastoralists and hunter-gatherers, and it may be the only type of land available to women, who often have no property or

A key issue of contention with 2G is the use of crop residues. They are often termed 'wastes', but are important for soil quality and ecosystem functions including nutrient and carbon cycling, erosion control, hydrologic and energy balance and biodiversity. In addition, returning crop residue to the farmland is generally essential to maintaining and enhancing the soil organic carbon (SOC) pool, sustaining crop yields and achieving global food security.[43] An exception to this may be in high crop yield conditions and specific soil management regimes in temperate climates. Soil and environmental degradation have become widespread in Asian and African farmlands due to indiscriminate and long term removal of crop residues. It is argued that further soil degradation cannot be reversed without returning crop residues and adding additional biosolids to the soil.[44] See Chapter 2 for further discussion on this.

To maintain the food chain benefits of grass crops used in 2G, it is argued that they should

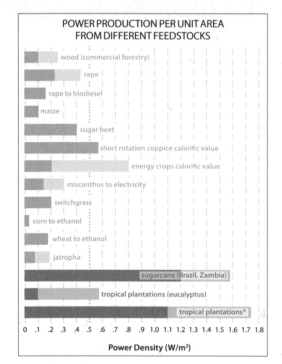

POWER PRODUCTION PER UNIT AREA FROM DIFFERENT FEEDSTOCKS

wood (commercial forestry)	
rape	
rape to biodiesel	
maize	
sugar beet	
short rotation coppice calorific value	
energy crops calorific value	
miscanthus to electricity	
switchgrass	
corn to ethanol	
wheat to ethanol	
jatropha	
sugarcane (Brazil, Zambia)	
tropical plantations (eucalyptus)	
tropical plantations*	

Power Density (W/m²)

Source: MacKay, p43.
Note: These power densities vary depending on irrigation and fertilization; ranges are indicated for some crops, for example wood has a range from 0.095–0.254W/m². The bottom three power densities are for crops grown in tropical locations. The last power density (tropical plantations) assumes genetic modification, fertilizer application, and irrigation. In the text, I use 0.5W/m² as a summary figure for the best energy crops in NW Europe.[42]*

inheritance rights. Lack of formal title to a parcel of land does not mean that local people do not value and use it, but according to official area maps, it can often be marked as empty. In the US and EU, marginal or set-aside land is of great benefit in protecting water, soils and biodiversity, but is becoming planted up due to the growth in commodity prices – partly due to biofuel production absorbing food crops. The marginal lands 'benefit' is therefore contested also, and it is argued that they exist in far smaller amounts than assumed by proponents of 2G approaches.[45]

In a land-use study on biofuels, Professor Lal found that some biofuel plantations can produce a variety of co-benefits, including protection from erosion, carbon sequestration and extra income from carbon credits:

> Risks of soil erosion by water and wind and of pollution from dispersed sources are generally less under perennial crop land use (e.g. Jatropha). Biofuel plantations are also beneficial to increasing biodiversity. Moreover, there is a distinct benefit of enhancing the terrestrial (e.g. soil and vegetation) carbon pool. When woody biomass (e.g. mesquite Jatropha) is established on cropland or very low productivity degraded soils, then there is an increase in the biotic carbon sequestered above ground, as well as an increase in the SOC (soil organic carbon). The carbon thus sequestered (and verified) can be traded in international markets such as the Clean Development Mechanism (CDM) of the Kyoto Treaty and the BioCarbon and Prototype Carbon Fund of the World Bank. There is an emerging market in carbon trading, which can provide an additional source of income to resource-poor farmers and land managers.[46]

Lal recommends using a holistic approach when assessing the sustainability of biofuel production systems, and basing it on an "index that involves the ecosystem carbon budget. The ratio of carbon output to carbon input must be computed considering all components at the farm and industrial plant levels. Farm-level inputs (e.g. tillage operations, fertilizers, pesticides, irrigation) are extremely carbon-intensive. These inputs must be considered in assessing the ecosystem carbon budget and their use optimized through reducing losses. Another useful index is the one that reflects the net life-cycle carbon intensity of a unit of biofuel. It is defined as the fossil carbon consumed on the farm plus fossil carbon consumed in the plant minus net positive change in SOC pool per energy unit of biofuel."[47]

Mathews suggests biofuels can be rendered carbon negative by "returning a portion of the biomass to the soil in more or less permanent form. The most straightforward means of doing so is through production of biochar – setting aside a portion of the biomass and, instead of converting it into fuel, reducing it to biochar through pyrolysis. It is a strategic choice how much of the biomass to convert into biofuel and how much into biochar – a choice that can be made by farmers and fuel producers."[48]

Evidently, 2G is challenged to get its facts right also. High-level independent research towards clearing up the various areas of contention is urgently needed to prevent a repeat of the 'too much too soon' rush towards 1G.

Third generation

Algae biofuel is often referred to as a third generation (3G) biofuel. It also goes by the name 'oilgae'. The first mention of algae biofuels was in an MIT report in the early 1950s, when microalgae were mass cultured for the first time.[49] Yet half a century later biofuel from algae is still comparatively nascent, and seems to be at the stage that 1G and 2G biofuels were in their infancy – a fossil-fuel substitute welcomed by many in industry, yet eyed with a degree of suspicion by green groups. However, algae biofuel has seemingly done quite well in convincing people of its merits and lack of drawbacks. This is partly due to the fact that biofuel can be produced from algae by feeding these fast-growing organisms (up to 30 times faster than other terrestrial plants[50]) on CO_2 exhaust gases direct from a coal power plant. Although the CO_2 gets released when the biofuel is burnt, the fact that a vehicle has also been run on pollution from the plant means that you have a net reduction in emissions from the combination of plant and vehicle, relative to running the vehicle on ordinary petrol or diesel.

> "Algae production has great promise because algae generate higher energy yields and require much less space to grow than conventional feedstocks. Algae also would not compete with food uses and could be grown with minimal inputs using a variety of methods."
>
> **Worldwatch Institute and Sierra Club**

According to developers GreenFuel Technologies Corporation, "Algae are the fastest-growing plants in the world. Like other plants, they use photosynthesis to harness sunlight and carbon dioxide, creating high-value compounds in the process. Energy is stored inside the cell as lipids and carbohydrates, and can be converted into fuels such as biodiesel and ethanol. Proteins produced by algae make them valuable ingredients for animal feed. GreenFuel uses a portfolio of technologies to profitably recycle CO_2 from smokestack, fermentation and geothermal gases via naturally occurring species of algae. Algae can be converted to

transportation fuels and feed ingredients or recycled back to a combustion source as biomass for power generation. Industrial facilities need no internal modifications to host a GreenFuel algae farm. In addition, the system does not require fertile land or potable water."[51] What helps make this approach work so well is that plants photosynthesize more easily if the carbon dioxide has already been concentrated for them.[52]

According to Paul Dickerson, chief operating officer of the US Department of Energy's Office of Energy Efficiency and Renewable Energy, "Its basic requirements are few: carbon dioxide, sun and water. Algae can flourish in non-arable land or in dirty water, and when it does flourish, its potential oil yield per acre is unmatched by any other terrestrial feedstock."[53] In ponds fed with concentrated CO_2 (concentrated to 10%), Ron Putt of Auburn University in the US says that algae can grow at 30g per square metre per day, producing 0.01 litres of biodiesel per square metre per day.[54]

However, algae is arguably best handled in closed systems, as open systems require topping up with fresh water due to evaporation. Closed systems, usually using long tubes, can be lit with LED lights, thereby improving access to light and overcoming the problem of 'self-shading' – dense algal growth at the surface blocking out light below. The company Bionavitas has produced Light Immersion Technology (LIT) for this purpose. They recommend it as a scalable and cost-effective way of producing an order of magnitude more growth.[55]

But algae is still unlikely to be a silver bullet for replacing transport fuels for the full US vehicle fleet, given that the US Department of Energy has estimated that the land area required to replace the nation's petroleum would be 15,000 square miles (38,849 square kilometres), or

Credit: GreenFuel Technologies. Algae biofuel plant.

roughly the size of the state of Maryland.[56] The land area required can be reduced by growing the algae in upright tubes instead of open pools, but still requires a concentrated source of CO_2.

At MIT's test facility designed by Isaac Berzin, a 20-megawatt cogeneration plant is linked to an algae system, which bubbles the flue gases through algae tubes. They found an 82 percent reduction in CO_2 emissions on sunny days and 50 percent on cloudy days, with an 85 percent cut in nitrogen oxides. Berzin and his co-workers 'tailor' algae to perform well at a specific power plant using a type of miniature bioreactor first developed for the space programme. The environment is gradually converted to conditions the algae will encounter at the plant, and within three months the algae are living on flue gases instead of air. Genetic engineering is therefore unnecessary, as they instead exploit the natural tendency of

algae to adapt to any environment.[57]

Many other companies and institutes are working on improving various aspects of the process, from production and harvesting to oil extraction, genetic modification and experimenting with the many different species of algae. Momentum and positive results will lead to more breakthroughs, improvements and cost reductions. The process is still costly, as are all early-stage energy technologies, but costs are dropping and interest is rising.

Could algae even be used to produce hydrogen? According to Professor David MacKay, it is a good idea because "it cuts out a load of chemical steps normally performed by carbohydrate-producing plants. Every chemical step reduces efficiency a little. Hydrogen can be produced directly by the photosynthetic system, right at step one. A research study from the National Renewable Energy Laboratory in Colorado predicted that a reactor filled with genetically-modified green algae, covering an area of 11 hectares in the Arizona desert, could produce 300 kg of hydrogen per day. Hydrogen contains 39 kWh per kg, so this algae-to-hydrogen facility would deliver a power per unit area of 4.4W/m². Taking into account the estimated electricity required to run the facility, the net power delivered would be reduced to 3.6W/m². That strikes me as still quite a promising number."[58]

So does this mean that 'deep greens' should welcome the net reduction in emissions, the improved land and water aspects relative to 1G and 2G biofuels, and the biodegradable nature of the feedstock, or condemn the arguable 'propping-up' of the coal industry? Historically, national self-interest has trumped any attempts to push coal out of the picture, whether by taxes, international agreements, carbon pricing or other means. If realistic and cost-effective alternatives, plus binding international agreements, are not set out, it is likely to be around for a long time, no matter what the environmental cost. There is not yet a big enough constituency active in attempting to displace it. High level calls for a moratorium are falling on conspicuously deaf ears. Nor can the conventional energy industry be expected to pack it in voluntarily. Their work to promote 'clean coal' is evidence enough of a will to remain the dominant providers of energy. Therefore, if algae can indeed reduce net emissions, and not compromise land and fresh water, then that may be a better bet than the other biofuel options discussed above.

Conclusions

Biofuels look set to continue development around the world, and so, for those with environmental, practical, ethical and social justice concerns, their job is to continue to police these developments. In the EU, this has resulted in some improvements to the sustainability criteria for biofuels.

The conclusion of Will Thurmond, an expert on biofuels, is that the US cannot meet their national biofuels targets from corn and soy, or Europe from oilseed rape. Because sustainability criteria are being introduced into the pursuit of increased biofuels targets, he advises investors and governments to go for non-food, non-rainforest crops. In the relatively near future carbon negativity may be made a condition of being accepted and defined as a biofuel.

Algae certainly appears to combine CO_2 reduction and fuel production more successfully than other feedstocks, along with its ability to operate in relatively closed systems, and produce high yields with a good net energy balance. However, every expert consulted and opinion read has ventured that biofuels are at best part of a post-oil portfolio – not a silver bullet. The precautionary approach is

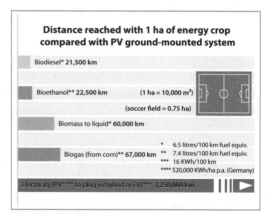

Distance reached with 1 ha of energy crop compared with PV ground-mounted system

Biodiesel* 21,500 km

Bioethanol** 22,500 km   (1 ha = 10,000 m²)

(soccer field = 0.75 ha)

Biomass to liquid* 60,000 km

*   6.5 litres/100 km fuel equiv.
**   7.4 litres/100 km fuel equiv.
*** 16 KWh/100 km
**** 520,000 KWh/ha p.a. (Germany)

Biogas (from corn)** 67,000 km

Electricity (PV**** to plug-in hybrid or EV)*** 3,250,000 km

Presentation: New materials for energy management at BASF. Dr. Joachim Rösch, BASF Future Business GmbH.

fundamental to related technologies, policies and practices – few solutions do not create problems of their own.

It may be interesting to end this chapter with a single slide showing the distances covered by running a vehicle on a variety of energy crops – and on photovoltaics produced on a surface area of one hectare. According to work from mid-2007, PV wins hands down, delivering a distance 147 times greater than biodiesel. And yet, Christoph Podewils' article on the subject draws on panels with lower efficiencies than today – 15 percent as against 18 percent.[59]

The upward trend in PV efficiency is worth bearing in mind, given that biofuel crops can be subject to crop pests and diseases, drought, fertilizer and pesticide shortages and so on. This is not to play cheerleader for the PV industry at the expense of what may be a useful part of the transport fuel solution. Many opponents of biofuels take the position that biofuel crops, produced on a small scale and under local control, should be supported. They argue that no large-scale approaches have yet proven themselves both sustainable and ethical. Whether or not algae biofuels will prove to be beyond reproach, or offer the yields required, they certainly appear to be the least problematic technology to date.

Although touted as solutions to climate and energy issues, nuclear and biofuels technologies have thus far failed to prove themselves to be either:

- Removing perverse subsidies from 'problem energy technologies'
- Assuring full cost accounting for all energy sources, including nuclear energy
- Facilitating active democratic decision-making in the implementation of new energy technologies
- Assuring a full understanding of the local and global land use implications of biofuels

Acknowledgements

Jim Duffy
Paul Brown
Helena Paul
Polly Higgins
Benjamin Sovacool
Hans Zulliger *Foundation for the Third Millenium*
Anders Wijkman *MEP*
Nathan Argent *Greenpeace*
Almuth Ernsting *Biofuel Watch*
Mark Anslow *The Ecologist magazine*
Christoph Podewils *Photon magazine*
Ward Crawford *The Converging World*
Will Thurmond *Emerging Markets Online*
Jeremy Gordon *World Nuclear Association*
Stephen Lacey *RenewableEnergyWorld.com*

Chapter Ten

Going Deeper, Looking Further

*" The choice is ours: form a global partnership to care for Earth
and one another or risk the destruction of ourselves
and the diversity of life. Fundamental changes are needed
in our values, institutions, and ways of living. "*

Earth Charter

*" Hope remains only in the most difficult task of all:
to reconsider everything from the ground up, so as to shape
a living society inside a dying one. "*

Albert Camus

In writing this book, we have placed a strong emphasis on climate change mitigation strategies and the social and economic benefits that come from them. This is not to deny the necessity of adaptation measures, but these would be more specific in terms of local and national strategies to take account of conditions on the ground. We take the view that even if climate change were not happening, we would still need to change our energy systems, restore the health of ecosystems, create more livable cities, vibrant communities and resilient localities, use less resources, spread wealth, increase international peace and leave behind a world fit for our children and grandchildren. So climate change could be seen as the final wake-up call to create an ethical, sustainable world. It is simply a choice, but determined joint action on the above issues is the only sane, viable choice, if we truly mean what we say about our love and care for our children.

The previous chapters should have conveyed to the reader, above all else, a sense of possibility – that many positive things are already happening around the world. We can see from this survey of proven and emerging solutions to climate, energy and ecosystem-related issues that the tools exist to remodel our ways of doing things. But we can go deeper, and look further. The challenges this book addresses may be seen as the most vivid narrative of human endeavour today. They encompass the full gamut of lived human experience and philosophical concerns, raising questions on everything from equality and justice, to governance and power, to psychology and geopolitics, to identity and meaning.

But there is no doubt that this entire field is riddled with arguments, power struggles, ego, hypocrisy, hope, fear, mistrust, confusion and desperation, as with so many other human undertakings. Many will look at the international negotiations on climate and sustainable development and want to give up. Others will celebrate the increase in recycling rates and feel the job is almost done. Others again will proclaim that challenging the current way of doing things is nothing but a left-wing conspiracy to create some kind of unrealistic utopia. And yet others will say that we need to start all over again with a complete change of paradigm in all areas of human activity.

Refusal for the protection of a better future for us children by governments, parents and civil society leaders is a violation of our fundamental human right as children! Stop Global Warming!
Musa Sesay, Freetown, Senegal, West Africa

Our view is that we must exercise the precautionary principle, assume that the predictions of climate scientists are a good guide to what may come our way, and take vigorous action soon. The public at large needs to know that we face severe challenges, yet we can create a better world in the process of saving it, and that they can play a critical role. All the talk we continually hear of a lack of 'political will' is surely a red herring: the political will for almost anything can exist in moments if sufficient numbers of voters impose their will publicly. Government and business must be subject to the will of the people, not the other way around. When it is suggested that 'they' will find a solution to climate change, it must be understood that 'they' includes everyone. Two members of the World Future Council, Frances Moore-Lappé and Jared Duval, provide the backbone of this chapter with an essay on how we can participate in our democracy, and apply our technology, to make the positive changes we so urgently require.

A wildfire of common sense

Frances Moore Lappé and Jared Duval

From the examples and lessons in this book, it is clear that we have many of the tools to make the turn. So what will it take from us, all of us?

In building confidence and positive energy, we believe it's helpful to keep in mind that the calamity we've created for ourselves and millions of other species is not 'business as usual.' It is not the norm of human existence, but a gigantic failed experiment, based on cheap, abundant fossil fuels, from which we can recover. Having grown up and lived in such a world, many of us understandably find it hard to imagine complex societies organized in different ways. It is difficult not to assume that the end of the fossil-fuelled period of human existence means loss.

But we believe it is quite possible that centuries hence humanity will look back on the 21st century and see liberation as much as loss. Consider that fossil fuels are by their very nature concentrated spatially and require concentrated capital to extract and distribute. Their development as the driver of our economies was accompanied therefore by enormous concentrations of wealth and power. Today the world's largest oil companies control more wealth than many of the poorer countries. Providers of fossil fuels are positioned to make the rest of us dependent on their power, literally – not because they are 'bad people' but because of the power structures on which our societies are based, and their ability to influence them. The 'curse of oil' has become a tragic reality – think of the devastation of the peoples of Nigeria's Niger delta, for example, even as the energy flowing from their piece of earth generates tens of billions of dollars every year.

People looking back on this time may see release from fossil-fuel dependency as one essential step towards humanity realizing its full potential. This release may allow us to create social systems more positively aligned with our intrinsic human nature, which does poorly when power is in a few hands. Like water, money is most useful and healthy when it flows – otherwise it stagnates and the land dries out. The Renewable World we can choose to create will be a world of distributed energy: millions, even billions, of us becoming not just users of various forms of solar power, but its transformers, too, making the sun's energy useful to us all without depleting it.

By contrast, every ounce of fossil fuels we use means less is left for our children and grandchildren. Fossil fuels necessarily feed a presumption of scarcity – the deep fear of being without them that drives so much unhappiness and conflict in our world today. It is not so for solar sources. As World Future Council member Hermann Scheer reminds us, each day the earth receives 15,000 times the energy from the sun we are currently using. Its energy is effectively boundless.

As more and more of us participate in transforming renewable energy into a force that shapes our lives – as, for example, the 175,000 Danish household owners or co-owners of wind turbines have been doing – we may not only become less dependent on the concentrated physical power that fossil fuels embody, but on the limited social power connected to them as well. With this source of concentrated power diminishing, an open, living democracy may really start to flourish for the first time.

We are not suggesting that the end of fossil fuel will bring utopia, of course. But as the prospects of calamities come closer – for instance, cities and cultures submerged by flood or driven out of existence by drought – a reassessment of what we value is becoming unavoidable. As more of us realize that our 'privileged', fossil-fuel-dependent world is untenable, we're also starting to question just how happy it has made us. In 2008 University of Illinois psychologist Ed Diener reported that billionaires on the Forbes 500 list were not measurably happier than Maasai herdsmen of East Africa.[1] In fact, trend lines measuring happiness show no significant rise since fossil-fuel burning really got underway after World War II. Many groups are now exploring alternative indicators of happiness and wellbeing.

Some pundits tell us that we've had it too good – that we've been drunk on growth and now we must sober up and 'power down'. But what if the opposite is true? What if most of us during the fossil-fuel era have not been partying at all but have struggled in some form of bondage – the deprivation experienced by billions, and the bondage of competitive struggle for millions more? And consider that only a sixth of us were invited to this great 'party' of the fossil-fuel era anyway.

And what if part of the explanation is that what we have celebrated as growth – the ever-climbing GDP – and defined as essential to our happiness, is not growth at all? What if a large part of it is waste and destruction? If we begin there, things look very different. In the US, it is estimated that less than 10 percent of what is extracted, pulled into production and transformed actually ends up in 'products' that we use. Physicist Amory Lovins keeps pointing out that most of the energy used by a typical American is actually wasted. More than a third of global grain and fish catch goes into feed, using vast quantities of fossil fuels to produce and process it, wasting much of its potential to nourish. Only around 15 percent of the energy produced in a car's engine is usefully converted into motion, the rest is wasted in drive-train inefficiencies, heat loss, idling and so on.

The era of 'carboniferous capitalism' has been possible only on the basis of the systematic, relentless depletion of natural capital – fossil fuels, biodiversity, water, soil and a stable climate. The era promised stability based on enterprise, but most recently revealed itself as delivering chaos based on speculation.

Do we humans have what it takes?

A Renewable World postulates the possibility of change on a vast scale. But, let us be clear: it does not require that we change human nature. There is much evidence that human nature, even with all its complexity, contrariness and capacity for cruelty, has precisely the capacities most needed to make this turn. For one, to be happy most of us need to feel useful; to feel that our lives matter. What better way to feel useful than to know one's actions can contribute to planetary survival? Present generations have the dubious honour of being able to become heroes – to literally save the world!

Moreover, we are essentially cooperators. Neuroscience experiments examining our brain responses during competition and cooperation find that cooperating is deeply pleasurable. It stimulates parts of our brain in ways that are similar to what happens when we eat chocolate. A recent study also found that when people were divided into one group, given money and told to buy a gift for another, and another group was instructed to spend the same amount on themselves, it was the givers who were measurably happier. Anthropologists conclude that through most of human evolution – except for the last few thousand of some 200,000 years – *Homo sapiens* lived in societies where pervasive sharing of food was the norm. As food sharers, "especially among unrelated individuals", humans are unique, writes Michael Gurven, anthropologist at UCLA, an authority on hunter-gatherer food transfers. "Reciprocity is arguably the foundational basis

The World Future Council's 'Kid's Call' project compiled 20,000 letters and drawings by children from all over the world calling on politicians to take more care about looking after their future. This drawing was produced by the Maharisha Vidyar Mandir School, India.

of cooperation in humans."[2] Except in times of extreme privation, when some eat in hunter-gatherer society, all eat. If true, then the recent aberration, in which our species became characterized by extreme surfeit amid destitution, violates deep sensibilities inside us.

Highly useful in this time of enormous challenge is also the human need for basic fairness, arising out of a long history in which we understood both that our own survival depends on community and that unfairness tears community apart.

But perhaps most important in this pivotal moment is the human need for power as understood in its original Latin meaning: the capacity to act, to effect. Social philosopher Erich Fromm argued that we should discard the oft-repeated Descartes dictum "I think therefore I am." Instead, he realized that we humans experience our essence in action. "I am, because I effect."

No, we don't need to change our nature. But certainly, to bring about the transformations outlined here, we need to tap some of these deep capacities which have been ignored, denied and in many cases actively buried in the current order. What if we tapped our desire to share and contribute, and allowed our humanity to flourish?

Put another way, it is easy to focus solely on new technologies and new insights; but just as important is re-appreciating some very old capacities and patterns of living.

How do we do it?

To begin, we can reframe the concepts of growth and progress and ask: growth toward what purpose? Gross Domestic Product (GDP) (otherwise known as Gross National Product – GNP) is how our societies measure growth and progress, but what does GDP tell us? The quantity of production and consumption, surely, but not necessarily the quality of our lives. When our measure of progress values equally the amount of money we spend on educating our children, buying more pills because our fouled environment has made us sick, and on constructing more prisons, that's a fairly meaningless number. As Bobby Kennedy said of GDP over 40 years ago, "it measures everything . . . except that which makes life worthwhile."

Measuring, and thus valuing, our societies' wellbeing in this uni-dimensional way is another instance of how seemingly normal societies are in fact aberrant, hardly the norm of human existence. It is a relief to look to other eras for evidence that our materially-fixated, simplistically numbers-driven cultures is a detour, not a culmination. In ancient Greek philosophy, Aristotle used the word *eudaimonia* to express the good toward which all human endeavour strives, or the highest aim of human action and purpose. The term, roughly translated, means 'human flourishing', or the wellbeing of one's spirit.[3] Aristotle believed that *eudaimonia* did not flow from accumulating things but rather living a life in which honesty, friendliness, and even wittiness were far more 'valuable' than wealth.

To realize *eudaimonia* in our lives means, in part, feeling that we are contributing to an aim larger than our own material desires. But today, how often are we encouraged or even allowed to contribute to society in meaningful ways beyond the narrow strictures of our role as workers in an economy, adding to that GDP? And even when we do get involved civically, we face the worry that our contributions are effectively "random acts of sanity."

As Cicero said, "freedom is participation in power." But how do we ensure that our efforts are adding up, addressing root causes of today's terribly complex global challenges? If we feel that each of our individual actions are inadequate drops, is there a bucket that we can use to collect those drops so that they indeed become something powerful and lasting?

That 'bucket' could be the concept of open or living democracy – democracy not as simply a structure of government but as a way of life, manifesting shared values of inclusion, fairness and mutual accountability. People around the world are starting to let go of the failed notion that we must turn our fate over to an infallible, automatic market, or to leaders who will solve the climate crisis, and other problems, for us. We are seeing the possibility that we can all co-create our world – moment to moment. Many stories in this book are emblematic of this emergent culture of mutuality – for example, relocalizing energy patterns and social interactions via Transition Towns.

Another example of this emergent ethic of mutuality and co-creation is the astonishingly rapid growth of the 'open source' software movement. The Linux computer operating system was developed and is continually being improved by a community of volunteer programmers whose only reward is the knowledge that they are contributing to something useful. Instead of centralizing and professionalizing tasks, the open source approach allows anyone with ability and desire to contribute to the project. A decade ago, Linux was thought of as an intriguing but irrelevant experiment relative to the apparently unstoppable reach of Microsoft. Today it runs more than a third of the servers that make up the infrastructure of the internet.[4]

The success of Linux and other open source inspired projects like Wikipedia, proves that people are not merely motivated by economic factors. As Jeff Howe, author of *Crowdsourcing* writes, "Open source revealed a fundamental truth about humans that had gone largely unnoticed until the connectivity of the internet brought it into high relief: labour can often be organized more efficiently in the context of community that it can in the context of the corporation."[5]

Wikipedia and other open source-inspired

projects like it merely provide the bucket to collect diverse human contributions, allowing them to add up to something visible.

This is how many small changes can rapidly lead to something quite large and transformational. As law professor and author Cass Sunstein has put it: "If thousands of people are in a position to make small additions and improvements, an initial skeleton can rapidly become a full body."[6] The word 'wiki' itself comes from the Hawaiian term *wikiwiki* which means 'fast' or 'speedy'. Thanks to the open source movement, we now know that top-down, command and control hierarchy is not necessarily the only efficient way to solve problems.

Obviously, to solve the many crises engulfing us, online encyclopedias are not enough. To create A Renewable World we need rapid policy shifts all around the world, from the local to the international level. Is there a way to draw out and to weave together human ingenuity, as Wikipedia does, but toward actually solving real-world problems?

NEW MONEY TO SAVE CIVILIZATION
Jakob von Uexküll,
founder, World Future Council

Rapidly accelerating climate chaos threatens the wellbeing and very survival of many hundreds of millions of people in the near future. But only a tiny fraction of the trillions of dollars now provided to revive the economy and banks has been directed to support the urgent measures required to slow and reverse this overriding danger!

The transition to an equitable and sustainable global society will require a massive re-direction of money flows. Global climate negotiations are stalling because of the ostensible lack of money. Governments must now use their right to authorize the creation of
new interest- and debt-free money to fund the available solutions to the unprecedented threats facing us. Central banks in several countries have recently been authorized to create new money to buy up government debt. This process of 'quantitative easing' is meant to support a return to business as usual, after which it will be reversed to avoid the risk of inflation.

But new money creation causes inflation only when no new resources are produced in return – i.e. when too much money chases too few goods and services. In our current world of massive unemployment, over-production capacities and unmet needs, that is easily avoidable. Creating money is a legal agreement, a 'monetization' of expected future proceeds. Many governments have done this in the past, proving that new money created against performance, i.e. in payment for new goods and services, is not inflationary. This new money will not buy up existing debts. It will buy our future security by paying for the creation of a sustainable and equitable global order.

Does it really make sense that our sovereign governments should have to borrow the funds needed to protect our common future from private moneylenders, who create this money themselves through fractional reserve banking, and whom we as citizens and taxpayers have just rescued from bankruptcy?

The G20 agreement earlier this year to support a general allocation of IMF-created Special Drawing Rights (SDRs) is a first step in the right direction, which needs to be implemented quickly. The rules for SDRs need to be reformed, making them interest-free (as they originally were) and allowing them to be rolled over indefinitely, as they already are in practice. SDRs are convertible into national currencies of the holder's choice. Alternatively, the SDR itself could be made legal tender – as a new global currency.

Some critics have complained that SDRs constitute unconditional aid, which may be wasted. That may be so under the present system. But the proposed new SDRs would be paid only against performance.

There are two key global challenges justifying this unconventional approach which makes money again the servant and no longer the master of our civilization. One is our duty to assist those now suffering, first of all by funding the practical implementation of the UN Millennium Developments Goals. The other is our duty to our children and future generations to preserve a healthy planet. Growing climate chaos and ecosystems depletion are approaching tipping-points beyond which maintaining the planetary life-support system may become impossible at any cost. A healthy natural environment is the macro-system on which our security, health, food, water and economic wellbeing are totally dependent.

Naturally, the creation of this new money will change power relationships and must be carefully explained to maintain public trust. An experts' conference should be called to develop a global plan to maximize the global use of renewable energy, retrofit buildings for greater efficiency, build sustainable transport systems, protect water resources and promote the transition to sustainable systems of food production etc. The goals should be broken down into regional projects, for which competitive tenders should be sought from the private sector. The time frame should not exceed ten years, offering the greatest entrepreneurial opportunity of all time!

While the IMF is probably best equipped to organize the issue of these new SDRs, the UN Trusteeship Council could be revived with a revised mandate to supervise the project implementation.

Finding our voices, realizing our power

Today's thin democracy – something done for us or to us as solely representative democracy – is premised on the notion that most people don't have the time or the ability to do much more than vote. Voters learn that we must turn over our fate to representatives with access to information and who are capable of making decisions on our behalf. But today's problems are too complex, interrelated and pervasive to be solved by a few. They require a change in habits of billions of us and therefore the 'buy-in' of billions, which cannot be fostered by fiat. So we need a richer concept and practice of democracy to ignite the participation and collaboration needed – democracy that takes full advantage of the values, experiences, ingenuity – the 'fresh eyes' and the common sense of the lay person.

Credit: Herbert Girardet. In the Brazilian city of Curitiba, public displays tell people about the positive impacts of changes in their behaviour. This display board indicates how many trees have been saved as a result of their efforts at recycling cardboard and paper. Only through such public information campaigns can changes in personal behaviour be encouraged.

This richer democracy is emerging. Think of how the age of information facilitates inclusion of more voices: more than one billion of us can now access a huge share of global information via the internet. A strict division of labour between official and citizen no longer makes sense, if it ever did. With internet connection reducing communication costs to near zero, growing numbers of 'we the people' can share in the diverse knowledge and expertise that exists, to help craft far more effective public policy – and more broadly contribute to problem-solving at this time of great need.

Indeed, we must start to insist that our representatives actively involve us in the process of problem-solving. Russ Feingold, a US Senator from the state of Wisconsin has, since first elected in 1992, held 72 'listening sessions' across Wisconsin each year. In them, Feingold is able to sense the challenges people wish him to address to help him craft a legislative agenda reflecting these concerns. Thus Feingold engages his constituents in the policy-making process. As he says about his listening sessions,

Credit: Herbert Girardet.

"Except for my brief introductory remarks, I spend the entire time listening, taking notes and responding to questions. Wisconsinites give me great ideas for new legislation at these meetings."[7]

Whether blogging stories or opinions that otherwise would not have shown up in corporate media, whether engaging in micro-lending with individuals or communities unserved by international aid, or whether taking a direct role in policy-making, we are seeing the emergence of an 'open source society'. At the exact time that our economy has failed dramatically, the collective will of many visible hands can challenge the destructive will of an invisible hand.

We can see the global climate crisis as a problem in which we are all complicit. As Bill McKibben says, our use of fossil fuels creates "billions of little [explosions] every minute, as pistons fire inside engines and boilers burn coal".[8] In response to a challenge of this nature, we need a model of collective action that likewise allows every one of us to be a part of the solution. In this moment of urgency, we need all hands on deck.

KYOTO2 – breaking the deadlock
As this book sets out, we already know what we have to do to secure a stable future climate for our planet: halt greenhouse gas emissions by 2050, while conserving terrestrial ecosystems and enhancing their role as carbon sinks. Even if we succeed, greenhouse gases will rise to dangerous levels – but we must hope only for a short period before natural sinks draw carbon dioxide down into vegetation, soils and oceans, and a runaway global warming catastrophe is averted. But the Kyoto Protocol, the existing mechanism of international climate governance, is inadequate – as shown by the steeply rising curve of greenhouse gas emissions since it came into force.

And negotiations towards a successor agreement are stuck. This is mainly because national governments fear taking on emissions reductions targets that they might not meet, costing their taxpayers billions of dollars. They are also unwilling to accept targets that are stronger than those of their competitors, and put their industries at a competitive disadvantage. Rich industrial countries – responsible for the great bulk of historic emissions – therefore want poorer developing countries to take on targets too. But the developing countries want the rich countries to do much more first, and to pay up for developing country adaptation, technology transfer and so on. Meanwhile the Kyoto system is incredibly complex – and negotiators won't agree to changes whose consequences they do not understand.

It is with these problems in mind that I formulated the Kyoto2 proposals as a fair, effective and truly global mechanism of climate governance:

1. Define a global cap on emissions, and sell tradable permits up to that cap in a worldwide auction;

2. The permits have to be bought, then surrendered, by fossil-fuel producers based on the carbon content of their production;

3. The permit auction raises $1 trillion or more per year to spend on climate solutions, and most of that money is spent in developing countries;

4. The main expenditures are in renewable energy, energy efficiency, forest conservation, sustainable farming, water management, and adaptation to unavoidable climate change. A particular goal is to build entire new renewable energy infrastructures in developing countries, and leapfrog the carbon-intensive development path;

5. The core mechanism is backed up by direct regulation following the successful example of the Montreal Protocol, aimed at reducing costs and overcoming market failures.

In this way Kyoto2 would overcome most of the obstacles under the existing Kyoto Protocol system:

1. It is intrinsically straightforward;

2. All governments have to do is to supervise the system within their territories, without taking on commitments;

3. The core mechanism applies equally in all countries, avoiding competition issues;

4. The entire debate is shifted from the current negative discourse on 'burden-sharing' to a positive engagement on how to apportion the benefits of rapid and meaningful action on climate change.

More information is in Kyoto2 by Oliver Tickell, and on the website www.kyoto2.org

No time?

Some people don't buy it. They tell us that our dual challenge is not only solving incredibly complex problems but doing it now, so we don't have time to think about how we practice democracy, how we let private wealth determine public outcomes, or how our economic system fails to account for the true costs of our actions; after all, we are faced with a climate crisis that threatens to swamp (quite literally) all the other concerns on the table. And for better or worse, only top leaders can make things happen fast enough.

But this stance, however tempting, forgets core truths: the dire consequences, for example, when George W. "I'm the decider" Bush acted from this viewpoint. It also ignores the evidence that cultivating in ourselves the arts of living democracy – learning to work more collaboratively in and between communities – gives us a better chance at collecting the dispersed knowledge and willpower we need to effectively deal with the crisis in whatever forms it takes. Even if some of the worst predictions of climate collapse come true, investing in local decision-making and empowerment puts us in a more durable, self-sufficient position. All this means in part letting go of expectation that 'the' government will solve our problems, and recognizing that it must be 'our' government. And that means that we – all of us – need to bring our democracy to life.

We agree that humanity cannot wait for system-wide change before we try to put a price on carbon and shift the incentives in our economy away from fossil fuels towards clean energy. But we would be fooling ourselves to believe that we can achieve flourishing societies without decision-making bodies accountable to that goal, or that we can make this turn without remaking our failing forms of governance that have brought us to this crisis in the first place.

Igniting engagement on the scale needed, building trust and skills and a sense of a shared fate, can motivate each of us to help make the changes that are called for. This means, above all else, to reject what has become 'privately held government'.

In the United States, more than two dozen lobbyists pursue the interests of their sponsors, primarily powerful corporations, for every one representative sent to Washington by voters to represent the interests of American citizens. Fossil-fuel industries are among the biggest political players. Little wonder that vast sums are still spent on subsidizing fossil fuels even as the US government is pledging urgent action to fight climate change.

Confronting the vast waste and climate heating built into our economies requires new laws and standards, of course, and to enact them requires the public, rather than private wealth, to finance elections and to influence the legislative process. When campaigns are publicly financed, our representatives are more likely to listen to us and resist pressures from those continuing to benefit from planet-heating fuels and technology. It is that simple.

The pressure of time is real, but it need not paralyze us with anxiety if we also consider how quickly change has occurred in circumstances none might have predicted. Two examples come to mind, from Colombia and Niger.

In less than a decade, Bogota, Colombia – long considered a sadly dysfunctional city by many of its residents – has earned its place as global leader in sane, green transport. About a decade ago, city officials shifted the frame: Instead of continuing to reward the 15 percent of Bogota residents who own cars, they redirected city resources to benefit the majority of low-income people and the shared environment. They created broad corridors linking residents to schools, libraries and parks and geared towards buses, bicycles and pedestrians. Car gas emissions fell by 40 percent. Also stunning: the murder rate dropped by two-thirds as a more trusting and integrated community emerged.

Along with carbon emissions, the destruction of forests spells climate disaster, and one region that had been losing forest cover for decades was West Africa. Many considered that some of its degraded soils were virtually impossible to recover. Yet between 1975 and 2003 in Niger, 'regreening' efforts by farming communities resulted in the planting of some 200 million new trees, with the number of on-farm trees increasing 15- to 20-fold. This spectacular regreening achievement now covers 12.5 million acres, vastly improving the lives of farm families and sequestering significant amounts of carbon.[9]

THE CARBON TAX

Trisha Shrum

The idea of carbon taxes is to shift what is taxed, in order to produce a revenue-neutral boost for the climate and environment. Instead of earnings, a government could tax pollution. It could raise taxes on gasoline and waste, and lower them on renewables and efficiency. Redirecting money flows to environmental goods, rather than 'bads' is at the heart of the approach. It works best when applied equally to all sectors and all sources of greenhouse emissions. Excluding certain sectors such as fuels or greenhouse gases weakens the impact as they have the most potential for improvement. A tax can be applied 'upstream' or 'downstream' – for example at the first point of sale for a fossil fuel (wholesale), or at the last point of sale, on an electricity bill (retail). There is debate about whether these methods will change how much of the cost is borne by consumers or producers, but the tax burden is largely determined by how strongly consumers respond to the price increase by consuming less. Studies show that gasoline taxes, similar to carbon taxes, are split 50/50 between cutting into producer profits and adding to consumer costs. This split of the tax burden is important because it adds an incentive both for more efficient production and for more efficient consumption. This incentive spurs innovative technology, encourages the adoption of existing efficient technology, and encourages more efficient behaviour.

Ideally, the cost of a carbon tax per ton should be equal to the damages caused by a ton of carbon dioxide. This is complicated because science cannot predict exactly how much damage will result from climate change – estimates range from $6.60 to $2,400 per ton of carbon. Another method is to choose a quantity of reductions desired and gradually increase the carbon tax until those reductions are met. Starting small and ramping up over time gives people time to adjust their behaviour.

Carbon taxes have been implemented by a number of governments around the world. Norway, for example, has a high carbon tax, but exempted air and sea transport, fishing, high emission industries, and gave a large discount for pulp and paper manufacturers. You can see where this might cause a problem: if you tax gasoline, but not jet fuel, then you create an incentive for people to switch from driving to flying, which is obviously not going to help you bring down emissions. Denmark does not exempt industries, but does give them a lower rate. Their tax is much lower than that of Norway's, but they have seen much stronger drops in emissions. Their carbon tax of $14/t CO_2 has brought about a 15% reduction in emissions from 1990 to 2005. Sweden implemented a carbon tax in 1991. The Swedish government estimates that emissions would have been 20% higher without the tax.

Great Britain implemented a Climate Change Levy in 2001. This isn't a direct tax on carbon, but taxes fossil-fuel use – the largest contributor of greenhouse gases. They take the opposite approach and tax only industry and the public sector, while exempting households and transport. Energy-intensive industries get a discounted rate if they employ certain energy efficiency strategies. They recycle all the revenues back to industry through reduction in employer-paid social security taxes and incentives for energy efficiency and R&D. Estimates from the UK National Audit Office find that the policy is reducing emissions by about 3.5 million tons of CO_2 per year.

A determined stance of hope

In 2008, when San Francisco banned plastic

bags in groceries and pharmacies, calls started coming in to the city's supervisors. Other cities wanted to know: how did you do it? Soon cities such as Boston, Phoenix and Portland, Oregon started planning similar bans. Supervisor Ross Mirkarimi, who'd pushed the measure, said that Paris and London called, too. I think we've sparked "a wildfire of common sense," he said.[10]

The future of life as we know it rests on our capacity to ignite a vastly bigger wildfire of common sense. Throughout this book we've noted breakthroughs taking off that few would have predicted, so no one can know with certainty our chances of success. But what we each can control is our own focus, energy, and daring, motivated by what has always captured human hearts.

Hope is not what we find in evidence. It is a stance. At this pivotal point in history, acting from a determined stance of hope – that ignites hope in others – is a way to make your entry in that most important book of all, what Martin Luther King called the "invisible book of life that faithfully records our vigilance or our neglect".

THE FUTURE OF JUSTICE

The preceding chapters have set out many options for creating infrastructure and systems which do not harm the environment or the climate and which do not preclude options for future generations. But there is no doubt that they run counter to certain vested interests.

Our current development path, which is reinforced by deliberately created rules and political institutions, has thus far primarily served the interests of the individual – or a few select individuals. Thus the renewal of our biosphere and our energy system is obstructed by many fundamental barriers – inequitable and short-sighted behaviours which are causing resource depletion, pollution, extinctions of species, huge inequalities, poverty and climate change. A solid new foundation of 'future justice' – assuring the wellbeing of our descendants in the longer term – needs to be built that can also assure the wellbeing of those alive today as well.

The World Future Council has developed seven Future Justice Policy Principles to serve present and future generations. These are: 1. Sustainable use of resources, 2. Equity and eradication of poverty, 3. Precautionary approach, 4. Public participation, 5. Governance and human security, 6. Integration, and 7. Common but differentiated obligations. These criteria aim to put the values that are necessary to the creation of a sustainable, ethical world, at the heart of policies and policymaking. Future Justice is about remaking our governance frameworks – institutions, policies and laws

This is another drawing from our Kid's Call project, by the BAL Bhavan Society, India.

– to facilitate just cooperation, broad-based participation, and an equitable sharing of resources and benefits of progress between generations. This is 'Justice for all', as the American pledge of allegiance asserts – envisioning secure, free and creative lives for all of humanity in harmony with the Earth.

Where are the lands that used to be so green? Our Future Justice vision and agenda is based on the fundamental values of dignity, respect and mutual trust. Being treated fairly is a basic human need found in all cultures in the world and expressed as inviolable dignity in the universal declaration of human rights. What is fair may differ between contexts and times, and certain social structures are more conducive to fair behaviour than others.

Humanity is part of a greater biosphere comprised of a unique community of life and complex ecosystems following their own laws. Hunter-gatherers and nomads would find a lack of balance with nature to be fatal, but city people, now a global majority, are mostly insulated from the external effects of their behaviours – as long as there is water from the taps, food and clothing in shops, gasoline in the pump and electricity at the turn of a switch, city people tend to go about their lives without much consideration for the impacts of making these things available on a daily basis.

Humanity needs to reconnect with the earth's natural cycles. It seems important now to identify laws, rules and institutions that help to balance the needs of individuals with the stability of the planet and the needs of future generations. In this situation we see the need for collaboration between stakeholders from diverse backgrounds that do not usually cooperate: focusing on long-term concerns, they may see their interests converge – be they nature conservation, conflict prevention, migration, economic development, animal protection or human wellbeing.

Future Justice meets this challenge by engaging on all levels of societal change: From the bottom up we have 'thinking and acting', then 'laws and policies', and at the top is 'accountability and enforcement'. Bottom-up changes in the way people think and act, and what they publicly value, allows new laws and policies to come forward; these can then be enforced to create new norms and behaviours, with implicit values of fairness and sustainability built in.[11]

In the past, severe penalties existed for those found guilty of poisoning wells; in future we must develop more appropriate legal sanctions against those who betray and harm their fellow humans and the natural world – certain acts must be designated simply as 'taboos'. Bottom-trawling would be a clear example.

There are already many existing multilateral international agreements to be built upon, which concern the relevant areas of human rights and security, ecological integrity and peace. These include the UN Charter, the Earth Charter, the Declaration of Human Rights and the Rio Declaration on Environment and Development. However, when they do not suit certain interests they can be deliberately ignored or misapplied. This is why those who do not wish to abide by such social and legislative rules will see their behaviour criminalized.

Energy, ecology, equality

"There are times in history when to dare is the highest wisdom," wrote the American anti-slavery campaigner William Ellery Channing. The unavoidable transition that the world faces will demand a great deal from us all. 'A Renewable World' is a concept still in the making. With this book we have made a start, defining some of the key steps that humanity now needs to take. The energy systems that have made the modern world possible, based on the combustion of ever-diminishing amounts of fossil fuels, will also be the cause of its demise as it leads to ever-increasing amounts of greenhouse gases in the atmosphere. The rapid transition to renewable energy seems inevitable if humanity wishes to have a future. But at the same time we have to deal with the concentrations of greenhouse gases in the atmosphere, and the only realistic way to do this is to enhance the capacity of the biosphere to do absorb them. Many millions of jobs can be created in a world based on renewable energy, energy sufficiency, green manufacturing and recycling, sustainable water management, farming and forestry. But in this new departure the world yearns for equality of opportunity, with real benefits to people all over the world.

An anonymous contribution to the global debate.

The waters that used to be so pure? I fear for the world. I fear for the day I wake up and see no blue skies, feel no cool breeze, because they will all be destroyed by this menace, this evil cropping up which is global warming. Let us join hands to eradicate global warming once and for all.

Michelle, Kilmgu, Kenya, aged 14

This book is being finalized as the global discussion about the future of our planet and human life upon it is reaching an unprecedented intensity. Some commentators have been saying that it is too late to 'turn the ship around', that we are inevitably headed for the rocks on which the great ship we call home will falter. In this book we, with the help of many world experts and contributors, have asserted the view that 'A Renewable World' is still possible. But now the greatest challenge is to turn emerging ideas into a reality, and quickly. We would be delighted if we have been able to make a contribution to this process.

Acknowledgements

Frances Moore-Lappé *WFC councillior*
Jared Duval *WFC councillior*
Jakob von Uexküll *WFC founder*
Trisha Shrum *Researcher*
Oliver Tickell *Author*
Maja Göpel *WFC staff*
Ansgar Kiene *WFC staff*
Holger Güssefeld *WFC staff*

References

Chapter 1 –
Energy Change, Climate Change

[1] McCarthy, M. 'Sea levels rising twice as fast as predicted', *The Independent*, 11 March 2009

[2] Sieberle, R.P. (1982) *Der unterirdische Wald, Energiekrise und industrielle Revolution*, C. H. Beck

[3] Bailey, M., *Railway Regulation in the 19th Century*, www.mfbailey.co.uk/economics/papers/rail.pdf

[4] Barron Baskin, J., and Miranti, P. J. (2008) *A History of Corporate Finance*, Cambridge University Press

[5] Archives Hub, Edinburgh Uni. Library, www.archiveshub.ac.uk/news/02101803.html

[6] Ammonia Fuel Network, www.ammoniafuelnetwork.org/

[7] Berlin's history, www.berlin-geschichte.de/Historie/

[8] Goodwin, J. (2001) *Otis Giving Rise to the Modern City, A History of the Otis Elevator Company*, Ivan R. Dee Publisher

[9] World Resources Institute Washington, *Urban Growth*, www.wri.org/wr-98-99/citygrow.htm

[10] Our World, www.our-world-790395.html

[11] Wikipedia, en.wikipedia.org/wiki/Petroleum

[12] EE Times Asia, 2 April 2009, www.eetasia.com/ART_8800568569_499495 NT 0a8a4485.HTM

[13] Channel News Asia, 23 January 04, www.channelnewsasia.com/stories/afp asiapacific/view/67591/1/.html

[14] Alexanander's Gas and Oil Connections, 'China's private car ownership tops 10m', www.gasandoil.com/goc/news/nts32806.htm

[15] *China Daily*, 24 April 08

[16] US Energy Information Administration, www.eia.doe.gov/oiaf/ieo/coal.html

[17] Global Energy Industry Outlook 2009, http://www.freeenergyreports.com/

[18] Air pollution legislation, www.enviropedia.org.uk/Air_Quality/Legislation.php

[19] International Agreements on Acid Rain, www.ace.mmu.ac.uk/eae/acid_rain/Older/International_Agreements.html

[20] Reported by Al Jazeera, 18 April 2009

[21] Reported in *Daily Telegraph*, London, 20 April 2009

[22] UN (2008) *Realizing the Potential of Energy Efficiency*, United Nations Foundation Expert Report

[23] UK Energy Research Centre (2009) *Secure, Carbon-Free and Electric? The UK's Energy System in 2050*, April 2009

[24] World Bulletin, www.worldbulletin.net

[25] US Geological Survey *Estimates of Undiscovered Oil and Gas North of the Arctic Circle*, 2008

[26] Calculated by WFC staff member Axel Bree using the MAGICC/SCENGEN user manual, www.cgd.ucar.edu/cas/wigley/magicc/

[27] USGS *Arctic Oil and Gas Resource Report 2008*, geology.com/usgs/arctic-oil-and-gas-report.shtml

[28] NSIDC, *Arctic sea ice younger, thinner as melt season begins*, 6 April 2009; http://nsidc.org/arcticseaicenews/2009/040609.html

[29] World Future Council website, www.worldfuturecouncil.org

[30] IPCC (2005) *Special Report on Carbon Capture and Storage*

[31] McKinsey (2005) *Carbon Capture and Storage – Assessing the Economics*

[32] IEA (2007) *GHG R & D programme, CO_2 capture ready plants*

[33] Viebahn, P., et al (2006) *Comparison of Carbon Capture and Storage with Renewable Energy Technologies Regarding Structural, Economic and Ecological Aspects*, GHGT-8

[34] Mackenzie, K. *Use of Power faces first fall since 1945*, Financial Times, 22 May 2009

[35] Stern. N. (2006) *The Stern Review on the Economics of Climate Change*, HM Treasury, 2006 www.hm-treasury.gov.uk/sternreview_index.htm

[36] Sweet, W. (2006) *Kicking the Carbon Habit: Global Warming and the Case for Renewable and Nuclear Energy*, Columbia University Press.

[37] Report in *The Guardian*, London, 18 October 2008

[38] The 350 ppm campaign, www.350.org

Chapter 2 – Carbon and The Biosphere

1 Hansen, J., quoted in Climate Code Red, 2008, www.scribepublications.com.au/book/climatecodered

2 Friends of the Earth, Greenpeace and WWF, *Joint statement on offsetting carbon emissions,* www.wwf.org.uk/filelibrary/pdf/august06.pdf

3 Smith, K. *The Carbon Neutral Myth – Offset Indulgences for or Climate Sins,* Transnational Institute, 2007, www.tni.org/detail_pub.phtml?&know_id=56

4 Jones, C. *Increased Photosynthetic Capacity Reverses Global Warming,* www.amazingcarbon.com

5 Lovejoy, T., Flannery, T., and Steiner, A., *We did it, We Can Undo It,* New York Times, 28 January 2009, www.nytimes.com/2008/.../27iht-edlovejoy.1.17278077.html

6 WWF, *Living Planet Report 2008,* www.panda.org/lpr/08

7 Wikipedia, Carbon, en.wikipedia.org/wiki/Carbon

8 Global Carbon Project, www.globalcarbonproject.org

9 IPCC, *Climate Change, Mitigation of Climate Change,* UNEP, 2007

10 FAO (2003) *Extent of Forest Resources,* ftp://ftp.fao.org/docrep/fao/008/A0400E/A0400E03.pdf

11 Canadell, J. *Managing Forests for Climate Change Mitigation,* Science Magazine, Vol. 320, 13 June 2008

12 www.fs.fed.us/ecosystemservices/

13 Wikipedia, *Ecosystem Services,* en.wikipedia.org/wiki/Ecosystem_services

14 FAO, *Deforestation continues at an alarming rate,* www.fao.org/newsroom/en/news/2005/1000127/index.html

15 Stern, N. (2009) *A Blueprint for a Safer Planet,* Bodley Head, London, p25

16 CBD, *Biodiversity for Poverty Alleviation and Development,* https://www.cbd.int/doc/.../poverty-alleviation-booklet-en.pdf

17 Sukdev, P (2008) *The Economics of Ecosystems and Biodiversity,* UNEP

18 Mitchell, A. (2007) *Forests First in the Fight against Climate Change,* Global Canopy Programme

19 Stern, N. (2006) *The Stern Review on the Economics of Climate Change,* HM Treasury, 2006 www.hm-treasury.gov.uk/sternreview_index.htm

20 Bunyard, P., in Girardet, H., ed. (2007) *Surviving the Century,* Earthscan Publications, London

21 Makariaieva, A.M., Gorshkov, V.G. (2006) *Biotic pump of atmospheric moisture as driver of the hydrological cycle on land.* Hydrol. Earth Sys. Sci. Discuss., 3. 2621-2673

22 Phillips, O.L., *Drought Sensitivity of the Amazon Rainforest,* www.sciencemag.org/cgi/content/full/323/5919/1344

23 Global Canopy Programme, 6 March 2009, www.globalcanopy.org/main.php?m=120&sm=169&bloid=34

24 as 22

25 Global Timber Organisation, www.globaltimber.org.uk/congo.htm

26 Malaysian Palm Oil Council, www.mpoc.org.my/main_mktstat_export.asp

27 New York Times, http://query.nytimes.com/gst/fullpage.html?res=9A06E5DA143AF934A2575AC0A9659C8B63

28 Woods Hole Research Centre, www.whrc.org/southamerica/agric_expans.htm

29 Brown, L. (2006) *Plan B 2.0,* Earth Policy Institute, Washington

30 CNBC, European Business, *Green Heroes,* January 2009

31 Canopy Capital, www.canopycapital.co.uk/

32 Global Canopy Programme, www.globalcanopy.org/.../Forests%20Now%20Report_Nov%2008.pdf

33 Canadell, J., and Raupach, M., *Managing Forests for Climate Change Mitigation,* Science Magazine, 12 June 2008

34 Treehugger, ww.treehugger.com/files/2007/09/cuba_boosts_int.php

35 Jindal, R. (2006) *Carbon sequestration projects in Africa*, WRI, earthtrends.wri.org/features/view_feature.php?fid=68&theme=3

36 Lal, R. *Soil carbon sequestration to mitigate climate change*. Geodema, 123 (1-2): 1-22, 2004

37 unfccc.int/resource/docs/2008/smsn/igo/010.pdf

38 Smith et al., *Greenhouse Gas Mitigation in Agriculture*, Phil. R. Soc. London, B Biol Sci. (363)1492):789-813, 2008

39 Pimentel, D. (2008) *The Soil Erosion Threat*, www.news.cornell.edu/stories/March06/soil.erosion.threat.ssl.html

40 UN News Centre, *UN agency calls for inclusion of farming in talks on new climate change treaty*, 2 April 2009

41 FAO, *The carbon sequestration potential in agricultural soils*, August 18th 2008

42 UN News Centre, *UN agency calls for inclusion of farming in talks on new climate change treaty*, 2 April 2009

43 Map of Terra Preta Locations, terrapreta.bioenergylists.org/ubeyreuthdemap

44 Lehmann, J. and Joseph, S., editors (2009) *Biochar for Environmental Management, Science and Technology*, Earthscan

45 Courtesy of Craig Sams, Carbon Gold, www.carbon-gold.com

46 Harvey, F. 'Can You Dig It?', *Financial Times Weekend Magazine*, 28 February 2009

47 Fachhochschule Bingen, Landbauliche Verwertung von Klärschlammpyrolysat,

www.fh-bingen.de/Klaerschlammpyrolysat.2874.0.htm

48 Glenn, R., www.iconocast.com/.../R4/News1.htm

49 Madrigal, A. 'Food vs. Fuel: Saltwater Crops May Be Key to Solving Earth's Land Crunch', *Wired Magazine*, 4-12-08

50 Mangrove Action Project, www.mangroveactionproject.org/issues/climate-change

51 International Science Symposium. *The Ocean in a High-CO$_2$ World, Priorities for Research on the Oceans in a High-CO$_2$ World*, 2004

52 A Special Report of the German Advisory Council on Global Change, *The Future Oceans – Warming up, Rising High, Turning Sour*, 2006

53 Thorhaug, A. personal communication

54 Hansen, J., et al, Target Atmospheric CO$_2$: *Where Should Humanity Aim?* Open Atmospheric Science Journal, Volume 2, 217-231 (2008)

Chapter 3 – Renewable Energy

1 Makower, J., Pernick, R. and Wilder, C. *Clean Energy Trends 2009*, Clean Edge, March 2009

2 Renewable Energy Policy Network for the 21st Century (REN21). *Global Status Report: 2009 Update* (Paris: REN21 Secretariat)

3 REN21. *Global Status Report: 2006 Update*. (Paris: REN21 Secretariat and Washington, DC: Worldwatch Institute).

4 Makower et al., p2

5 REN21, *Global Status Report 2009 update*

6 World Wind Energy Association (WWEA). *World Wind Energy Report 2008*. www.wwindea.org/home/images/stories/worldwindenergyreport2008_s.pdf

7 REN21, 2009

8 Mehta, S. and Bradford, T. *PV Technology, Production and Cost, 2009 Forecast: The Anatomy of a Shakeout*, Executive Summary www.greentechmedia.com/GreentechMedia/Report/PVTechnologyProductionCost2009Forecast.html

9 REN21, 2009

10 REN21, 2006

11 REN21, 2009

12 REN21, 2009

13 Sustainable Business.com. *FPL To Reduce 2009 Wind Power Investments*. 29 October 2008. http://sustainablebusiness.com/index.cfm/go/news.display/id/17034

14 The Times. *Green energy plans in disarray as wind farm giant slashes investment*, March 26, 2009. http://business.timesonline.co.uk/tol/business/industry_sectors/natural_resources/article5977714.ece

[15] BBC news. 'Wind farm firm cutting 1,900 jobs'. 28 April 2009. http://news.bbc.co.uk/ 1/hi/business/8022688.stm

[16] Pagnamenta, R. 'Anger as Shell reduces renewables investment'. *The Times*, March 18, 2009. http://business.timesonline.co.uk/tol/business/indu stry_sectors/natural_resources/article5927869.ece

[17] Stern, N. (2006) *Stern Review: Report on the Economics of Climate Change.* Cambridge University Press. p366

[18] Mendonça, M. (2007) *Feed-in Tariffs – Accelerating the deployment of renewable energy.* Earthscan. pp17-18

[19] Mendonça, M., Jacobs, D., Sovacool, B. (2009) *Powering the Green Economy: The Feed-in Tariff Handbook.* Earthscan

[20] Mendonça, M., Lacey, S. and Hvelplund, F, *Stability, participation and transparency in renewable energy policy: Lessons from Denmark and the United States.* Policy and Society 27 (2009) 379–398

[21] For a detailed study and comparison of support schemes, see Mendonça, M., Jacobs, D. and Sovacool B. (2009)

[22] German Federal Environment Ministry, *Renewable energy sources in figures – national and international development*, June 2008

[23] German Renewable Energy Agency. *Current facts and figures.* www.unendlich-viel-energie.de /en/economy/current-facts-and-figures.html

[24] Ingenieurbüro für neue Energien. *Beschaffungsmehrkosten der Stromlieferanten durch das Erneuerbare-Energien-Gesetz 2008* (Differenzkosten nach § 15 EEG). www.erneuerbare-energien.de/files/pdfs/allgemein/application/pdf/ beschaffungsmehrkosten_bf.pdf

[25] Barringer, F. *Environmentalists in a Clash of Goals.* The New York Times, March 23, 2009. www.nytimes.com/2009/03/24/science/earth/ 24ecowars.html?_r=1&ref=us

[26] DESERTEC UK. *CSP: How to Reduce the Use of Water.* www.trec-uk.org.uk/csp/no_water.html

[27] Mendonça, M., Lacey, S. and Hvelplund, F. (2009)

[28] Cass, N. and Grindel. (2008) *Caton Moor Wind-farm Survey Report: A presentation and analysis of the findings of a small-scale questionnaire survey of residents of Caton, Brookhouse, and Halton.* Lancaster University. Available from the author

[29] German Wind Energy Association (BWE). *Mythen und Fakten der Windenergie.* www.wind-energie.de/fileadmin/dokumente/Kurzinfos/ BWE-Flyer_Mythen%2BFakten_web.pdf

[30] Stratton, A. 'Opposing wind farms should be socially taboo, says minister'. *The Guardian*, 24 March 2009. www.guardian.co.uk/environment/2009/ mar/24/wind-farms-opposition-ed-miliband

[31] United Nations Environment Programme (UNEP). *Reforming Energy Subsidies: Opportunities to Contribute to the Climate Change Agenda.* 2008. www.unep.org/pdf/PressReleases/Reforming_Energy _Subsidies.pdf

[32] Peter, S. and Lehmann, H. *Renewable Energy Outlook 2030 – Energy Watch Group Global Renewable Energy Scenarios.* Energy Watch Group. www.energywatchgroup.org/fileadmin/global/ pdf/2008-11-07_EWG_REO_2030_E.pdf

[33] Adam, D. 'International Energy Agency 'blocking global switch to renewables'.' *The Guardian*, 09 January 2009. www.guardian.co.uk/environment/ 2009/jan/08/windpower-energy

[34] Schlatter, E. *Welcome to Smart Grid City,* Colorado. High Country News, July 16, 2008 www.hcn.org/articles/17704

[35] Kourkounaki, D. (2008) *Will the public use 'Gridlights' to promote the efficient use of electricity? Graduate School of the Environment,* Centre for Alternative Technology, Wales

[36] MacKay, D. (2009) *Sustainable Energy – without the hot air.* UIT Cambridge Ltd

[37] Greenpeace (2007) *Energy [r]evolution – a blueprint for solving global warming.* www.greenpeace.org/raw/content/usa/press-center/reports4/energy-r-evolution-a-bluepr.pdf. Greenpeace (2009) *Energy [r]evolution – A sustainable global energy outlook.*

www.greenpeace.org/raw/content/international/press/reports/energyrevolutionreport.pdf. MacKay, as above. Rechsteiner, R. *Wind Power in Context – A Clean Revolution in the Energy Sector*. Energy Watch Group, December 2008

Chapter 4 –
Towards Energy Equality

1 Kanter, J. 'Could Small Nations Like the Maldives Lead in Renewable Energy?' *New York Times*, 16 March 2009. http://greeninc.blogs.nytimes.com/2009/03/16/could-small-nations-like-the-maldives-lead-in-renewable-energy/

2 The InterAcademy Council, *Lighting the Way: Toward a Sustainable Energy Future*, October 2007

3 REN21. *Global Status Report 2006*, p10

4 Runyon, J. *Researchers Explore Hybrid Concentrated Solar Energy System*. 3 November 2008. www.renewableenergyworld.com/rea/news/article/2008/11/researchers-explore-hybrid-concentrated-solar-energy-system-53981

5 Quaschning, V. (2005) *Understanding Renewable Energy Systems*. Earthscan

6 Which? Magazine. *Is Buying Used the New Green?* in Greener Driving. 2008

7 Carson, I. and Vaitheeswaran, V. V. (2008) *Zoom*. Penguin Books, pp216-217

8 UNEP. *Green Jobs: Towards decent work in a sustainable, low-carbon world*. 2008, pxxi

9 Stern, N. (2009) *A Blueprint for a Safer Planet*. The Bodley Head

10 Department for Transport. *Cycle to Work Scheme implementation guidance*. www.dft.gov.uk/pgr/sustainable/cycling/cycletoworkschemeimplementat5732

11 UNEP, 2008, p14

12 Wikipedia. *Transportation demand management*. http://en.wikipedia.org/wiki/Transportation_Demand_Management

13 Global Environment Facility (GEF), *Transfer of Environmentally Sound Technologies: The GEF Experience*. 2008 GEF, 2008, p6

14 REN21. *Global Status Report 2009*

15 Ibid.

16 World Bank, *RE Toolkit, 2009*. http://web.worldbank.org

17 GEF, 2008, p16

18 GEF, p17

19 Dechezlepretre, A., Glachant, M., and Meniere, Y. (2008) 'The Clean Development Mechanism and the international diffusion of technologies: An empirical study' Energy Policy, Volume 36, pp1273-1283

20 Lloyd, B. and Subbarao, S. (2008) 'Development challenges under the Clean Development Mechanism (CDM) – Can renewable energy initiatives be put in place before peak oil?' Energy Policy (2008) Volume 37, Issue 1, January 2009, pp237-245

21 Tyndall Centre for Climate Change Research (2007) *The Clean Development Mechanism: An assessment of current practice and future approaches for policy*. Tyndall Working Paper No. 114, October 2007

22 Crawford, W. *Fair Trade in Carbon*. The Converging World position paper

23 As per endnote 25

24 www.scadindia.org

25 Joint Research Centre of the European commission (JRC) (2008). *A new scheme for the promotion of renewable energies in developing countries – The renewable energy regulated purchase tariff*

26 Jacobs, D. (2009) *Promoting renewable energies in Africa – WFC Policy Position Paper*, April 2009

27 Ibid.

28 Grameen Bank. *Grameen Bank at a Glance*. February, 2009. www.grameen-info.org/index.php?option=com_content&task=view&id=26&Itemid=175

29 Grameen Shakti. *Programs at a Glance*. March 2009. www.gshakti.org/glance.html

30 Tryhorn, C. 'Nice talking to you … mobile phone use passes milestone'. *The Guardian*, 3 March 2009. www.guardian.co.uk/technology/2009/mar/03/mobile-phones1

Chapter 5 – Energy Sufficiency

[1] Brahic, C. *Humanity's carbon budget set at one trillion tonnes*, New Scientist, 29th April 2009

[2] Dürr, H.P., personal communication

[3] UN Foundation (2007), *Realizing the Potential of Energy Efficiency*, sefi.unep.org/

[4] International Energy Agency, *World Energy Outlook 2007*, p42

[5] Mainhardt-Gibbs, H., *Alternative Energy, Africa*, www.ae-africa.com/read_article.php?NID=666

[6] MIT, *Climate change odds much worse than thought*, web.mit.edu/newsoffice/2009/roulette-0519.html

[7] EREC, Greenpeace, (2007) *Energy Revolution, A Sustainable World Energy Outlook*

[8] McKinsey & Company, *What is energy productivity?*, www.mckinsey.com/energy/energy_productivity.asp

[9] World Business Council for Sustainable Development, *Energy Efficiency in Buildings*, www.wbcsd.org/includes/getTarget.asp?type=p...

[10] Lovins, A. Green Energy Conference, *The Negawatt Revolution*, www.ccnr.org/amory.html

[11] Wikipedia, *Negawatt Power*, en.wikipedia.org/wiki/Negawatt_power

[12] Lovins. A. (2004) *Winning the Oil Endgame*, Rocky Mountain Institute, p384

[13] www.loe.org/shows/segments.htm?programID=08-P13-00013&segmentID=4

[14] Roland-Holst, D. *Energy Efficiency, Innovation and Job Creation in California*

[15] www.scribd.com/doc/8066541/California-Ex-Sum-Energy-Efficiency-Innovation-and-Job-Creation-2008 The Californian Air Resources Board (2008), *Climate Change Proposed Scoping Plan*

[16] California's Long-term Energy Efficiency Strategic Plan, www.californiaenergyefficiency.com/

[17] *Next 10, California green innovation index*, www.next10.org/environment/greenInnovation.html

[18] Lorentzen, J. (2005) *How Denmark developed its DE, in: Cogeneration and On-Site Power Production*

[19] *Energy Performance Contracting*, www.energyservicescoalition.org/

[20] Strickland, J. *Transportation Energy Efficiency*, strickland.ca/efficiency.html

[21] Kenworthy, J. (2006), *The eco-city: ten transport and planning dimensions for sustainable city development*. Environment and Urbanization 18 (1) pp67-85.

[22] As 20

[23] Herring, H., *Encyclopaedia of the Earth*, The Jevons Paradox, www.eoearth.org/article/Jevons_paradox

[24] Illich, I. (1975) *Energy and Equity* clevercycles.com/energy_and_equity

[25] Wikipedia, *2000-Watt Society*, en.wikipedia.org/2000-watt_society

[26] Association for the Study of Peak Oil and Gas, www.peakoil.net; Energy Watch Group Report (2007) *Coal: Resources and Future Production*

Chapter 6 – The Green-Collar Economy

[1] MacMillan, D. *Switching To Green-Collar Jobs*. BusinessWeek.com. www.businessweek.com/managing/content/jan2008/ca2008018_005632.htm

[2] UNEP (United Nations Environment Programme), ILO (International Labour Organisation), ITUC (International Trade Union Confederation). *Green Jobs: Towards Sustainable Work in a Low-Carbon World*, preliminary version, ppxi and xiii

[3] Jones, V. (2008) *The Green Collar Economy*. Harper One

[4] Pinderhughes, R. *Green Collar Jobs – An Analysis of the Capacity of Green Businesses to Provide High Quality Jobs for Men and Women with Barriers to Employment*. Executive Summary. 2007, p3-4. http://blogs.calstate.edu/cpdc_sustainability/wp-content/uploads/2008/02/green-collar-jobs_exec-summary.pdf

[5] Apollo Alliance and Green For All. *Green Collar Jobs in America's cities – building pathways out of poverty and careers in the clean energy economy*. 2008, p3

[6] Worldwatch Institute. *Green Jobs. Worldwatch Report 177*, October 2008, p8

[7] American Solar Energy Society (ASES). *Defining, Estimating, and Forecasting the Renewable Energy and Energy Efficiency Industries in the US and in Colorado*, 2008

[8] American Solar Energy Society (ASES). *Renewable Energy and Energy Efficiency: Economic Drivers for the 21st Century*, 2007

[9] Kammen, D., Kapadia, K. and Fripp, M. *Putting Renewables to Work: How Many Jobs Can the Clean Energy Industry Generate?* Renewable and Appropriate Energy Laboratory, University of California, Berkeley, 2004

[10] German Federal Environment Ministry (BMU). *Renewable Energy*. www.bmu.de/english/ renewable_energy/aktuell/3860.php

[11] German Federal Environment Ministry (BMU). *Renewable energies create jobs and economic growth*. 15 March 2009. www.bmu.de/english/current_press_releases/pm/ 43536.php

[12] BMU, 2008, p21

[13] Ernst and Young. *Renewable energy Country Attractiveness Indices Quarter 1-2 2008,* www.ey.com/Global/assets.nsf/International/ Industry_Utilities_Renewable_energy_country_att ractiveness_indices/$file/Industry_Utilities_Renew able_energy_country_attractiveness_indices.pdf

[14] European Commission. *Buying green! A handbook on environmental public procurement*. 2004. http://ec.europa.eu/environment/gpp/pdf/ buying_green_handbook_en.pdf

[15] DEFRA. *Energy supplier obligations: Carbon Emissions Reduction Target (CERT)*. 2008. www.defra.gov.uk/environment/climatechange/uk /household/supplier/cert.htm

[16] Association for the Conservation of Energy (ACE). National and Local Employment Impacts on Energy Efficiency Investment Programmes Final report to the Commission April 2000 Volume 1: Summary Report, p7

[17] Shrum, T. (2007) *Greenhouse Gas Emissions: Policy and Economics*, A Report Prepared for the Kansas Energy Council Goals Committee, p5 www.vlib.us/kansasenergy/GHG_Review_FINAL.pdf

[18] UNEP, 2007, pxi

[19] Pinderhughes, p5

[20] Apollo Alliance and Green For All, p4

[21] New Economics Foundation (nef). *UK needs 'Green New Deal' to tackle 'triple crunch' of credit, oil price and climate crises*. 21 July 2008. www.neweconomics.org/gen/greennewdealneed edforuk210708.aspx

[22] UNEP. *Towards a Green New Deal: Economic stimulus and policy action for the double crunch*. www.unep.org/greeneconomy/docs/Green_New_ Deal_statement_20081202.pdf

[23] UNEP. *A Global Green New Deal*. 2009. www.unep.org/greeneconomy/docs/ggnd_Final% 20Report.pdf

[24] Financial Times. *Which country has the greenest bail-out?* March 2 2009. www.ft.com/cms/s/0/cc207678-0738-11de-9294- 000077b07658.html?nclick_check=1

[25] Apollo Alliance. *Clean Energy Is Foundation of Proposed Stimulus*. January 15 2009. http://apolloalliance.org/new-apollo- program/clean-energy-serves-as-foundation-for- proposed-reinvestment-bill/

[26] UNEP 2007, pxi

[27] Pinderhughes, 2007, p5

[28] Mendonça, M. (2006) *Policies to Change the World*. World Future Council. www.worldfuturecouncil.org/publications.html

[29] UNEP, 2007, pxiii

Chapter 7 – Renewing the City

[1] Information about all these towns can be found on the internet

[2] Girardet, H. (1996) *Getting London in Shape for 2000*, London First

[3] Girardet, H. (2004 and 2008) *Cities, People, Planet*, Wiley-Academy

[4] Dodman, D. (2009) *Blaming Cities for climate change? An analysis of urban greenhouse gas emissions inventories, Environment & Urbanization*, IIED, Volume 21, Number 1

5 Houghton, J., *Overview of the Climate Change Issue*, Forum 2002, St. Anne's College, Oxford

6 Vidal, J. 'World's biggest solar farm at centre of Portugal's ambitious energy plan', *The Guardian*, 6 June 2008

7 *Seville's Solar Power Tower*, www.inhabitat.com/2007/05/21/sevilles-solar-power-tower/

8 *Australia's solar cities*, www.environment.gov.au/.../solarcities/index.html

9 Cleantech.com. *India targets 609 solar cities*, cleantech.com/.../india-targets-60-solar-cities-catch

10 Renewable Energy world. *China's Solar City*, www.renewableenergyworld.com/.../chinas-solar-powered-city-48605

11 China Daily, *Himin sees more shine in Dezhou's Solar Valley*, www.china.org.cn/.../content_17247486.htm

12 The Guardian, *China launches green power revolution*, www.guardian.co.uk/.../2009/.../ china-green-energy-solar-wind

13 MacKay, M. *Whitelee Powers Glasgow*, withouthotair.blogspot.com/2009/05/ whitelee-powers-glasgow-again.html

14 BBCNews, 22 May 2009

15 Jones, J. Renewable Energy World, *London Array Given Green Light*, www.renewableenergyworld.com/rea/news/ article /2009/05/london-array-given-green-lgh

16 Girardet, H. (2008) *Cities, People, Planet* pp128-129, Wiley-Academy

17 C40 website, www.c40cities.org/about/

18 UN World Urban Campaign, www.rtpi.org.uk/download/6343/World-Urban-Campaign.pdf

19 ICLEI, www.iclei.org/

20 European Climate Alliance, www.klimabuendnis.org/

21 www.strategy-business.com/press/article/ 07104?gko=a8c38-1876-23502998

23 Owen, D. 'NYC is the Greenest City in America', *New Yorker*, 18 October 04

24 www.usmayors.org/climateprotection/

25 Texas wind energy, www.seco.cpa.state.tx.us/re_wind.htm

26 *The End of Suburbia*, www.endofsuburbia.com/

27 Lloyd-Wright, F (1932) *The Disappearing City*, William Farquhar Payson publishers

28 Brunner, P. Technical University, Vienna, personal communication

29 Wackernagel, M, and Rees W. (1996) *Our Ecological Footprint, Reducing Human Impact on the Earth,* New Society, Gabriola Island

30 The International Institute for Sustainable Development, *Urban and Ecological Footprints*, www.gdrc.org/uem/footprints/

31 Girardet, H., *Getting London in Shape for 2000*, London First, 1996

32 City Limits London, www.citylimitslondon.com

33 WWF, Living Planet Report 2002, Summary, www.panda.org/downloads/general/ LPR2002Summary.pdf

34 WWF, Living Planet Report 2008, www.panda.org/.../living_planet_report/

35 In Castells, M. (1996) *The Information Age, Volume 1, The Rise of the Network Society*, Blackwell

36 Folke, C. et al. *Ecosystem Appropriation by Cities*, Ambio, 1997

37 Climate Prosperity, www.climateprosperity.com/

38 Burgermeister, J. *Germany: The World's First Major Renewable Energy Economy*, Renewable Energy World, 9 April 2009

Chapter 8 – From Global to Local?

1 Taipale, K. (2009), *Cities for Sale, How Economic Globalization Transforms the Local Public Sphere*, Helsinki University of Technology, Centre for Urban and Regional Publications

2 Marglin, S. (2008), *The Dismal Science – How Thinking Like an Economist Undermines Community*, Harvard University Press

3 Von Thünen, J. (1826) *Der Isolierte Staat*, Perthes, Hamburg

4 Girardet, H. (2008) *Cities, People, Planet*, Wiley-Academy, 2004 and 2007

5 Priesnitz, W., *Counting our food miles*, 2007

6 Food Miles, http://en.wikipedia.org/wiki/Food_miles

7 'Locavores or globavores', *The Guardian*, www.guardian.co.uk/environment/2008/mar/23/ food.ethicalliving

8 Reuters, *Cuba exports city farming 'revolution' to Venezuela*, 22 April 2003, www.globalexchange.org/ countries/cuba/sustainable/651.html

9 Navdanya, www.navdanya.org

10 Merton Rule, http://www.merton.gov.uk/living/planning/planni ngpolicy/mertonrule.htm

11 Barcelona Energy Agency, Imma Mayol Beltran, *presentation to Fourth Municipal Leaders. Summit on Climate Change*. Barcelona City Council, 5-7 December 2005. Montréal.

12 www.publications.parliament.uk/pa/cm200607/ cmselect/cmtrdind/257/25707.htm

13 Hopkins, R. & Lipman, P. *Who We Are and What We Do*, Version 1.0., Transition Network 2009

Chapter 9 – Problem Technologies

1 One Million Europeans Against Nuclear Power. Homepage. www.million-against-nuclear.net/background/index.htm

2 Connor, S. *Nuclear power? Yes please...* The Independent, 23 February 2009. www.independent.co.uk/environment/green-living/nuclear-power-yes-please-1629327.html

3 Sovacool, B.K. and Cooper, C. *'Nuclear Nonsense: Why Nuclear Power is no Answer to Climate Change and the World's Post-Kyoto Energy Challenges.'* William and Mary Environmental Law and Policy Review, Volume 33, Issue 1, Fall 2008

4 Simms, A., Kjell, P. and Woodward, D. *Mirage and oasis – Energy choices in an age of global warming*. New Economics Foundation, 2005. www.neweconomics.org.uk/gen/z_sys_Publication Detail.aspx?PID=209

5 Brown, P. *Voodoo Economics and the Doomed Nuclear Renaissance: A Research Paper*. Friends of the Earth, 2009. www.foe.co.uk/resource/reports/ voodoo_economics.pdf

6 MacKerron, G. *Arguments against nuclear power*. Physics Education, (27) pp206-209, 1992. www.iop.org/EJ/abstract/0031-9120/27/4/007

7 Harrison, M. *Britain gets nuclear waste warning from energy chiefs*, The Independent, 02 March 2007. www.independent.co.uk/news/business/news/brit ain-gets-nuclear-waste-warning-from-energy-chiefs-438523.html

8 Socolow R. and Pacala, S. *A Plan to Keep Carbon in Check*. Scientific American, September 2006. www.princeton.edu/mae/people/faculty/socolow/ socdoc/carbonincheck.pdf

9 McCarthy, M. *Sea levels rising twice as fast as predicted*. 11 March 2009. www.independent.co.uk/ environment/climate-change/sea-levels-rising-twice-as-fast-as-predicted-1642087.html

10 Sovacool and Cooper, p8

11 Sovacool and Cooper, pp107-119

12 Sovacool and Cooper, p8

13 Sovacool, B.K. *'Valuing the greenhouse gas emissions from nuclear power: A critical survey'*. Energy Policy 36 (2008) 2940-2953, p2940

14 Sovacool and Cooper, p10

15 Sovacool, p2950

16 Sovacool and Cooper, p33

17 Wikipedia. *Fast breeder reactor*. http://en.wikipedia.org/wiki/Fast_breeder

18 MacKay, D. (2008) *Sustainable Energy – without the hot air*. UIT Cambridge Ltd, p173

19 Grice, M. *Seven years to save planet, says PM*. The Independent, 08 February 2006. www.independent.co.uk/environment/seven-years-to-save-planet-says-pm-465911.html

20 One Hundred Months.org. Homepage. www.onehundredmonths.org/

21 See notes 4, 5 and 6

22 Simms et al, p30

23 Gregory, S. S. *Devil's Advocate: 10 Green Arguments for Nuclear Power*. January 15th, 2008. http://planetsave.com/blog/2008/01/15/devils-advocate-10-green-arguments-for-nuclear-power/

24 Vince, G. *One last chance to save mankind*. New Scientist, 23 January 2009. www.newscientist.com/article/mg20126921.500-one-last-chance-to-save-mankind.html?full=true

25 Brown, P. *The Environmentalist's Nuclear Debate: (2) Mark Lynas*. 19 August 2008. http://thelazyenvironmentalist.blogspot.com/search?q=nuclear

26 Nuclear Consult.com. Homepage: *Energy Review*. www.nuclearconsult.com/

27 Renewable Energy World.com. *Biofuels*. www.renewableenergyworld.com/rea/tech/biofuels

28 Worldwatch Institute and Sierra Club. *Smart Choices for Biofuels*. 2009. www.worldwatch.org/files/pdf/biofuels.pdf, p5

29 Caldecott, J. (2007). Water – *Life in Every Drop*. Virgin Books

30 Worldwatch Institute and Sierra Club, p6

31 Ibid.

32 Searchinger, T. et al. *'Use of US Croplands for Biofuels Increases Greenhouse Gases Through Emissions from Land-Use Change.'* Science, 29 February 2008: Vol. 319. no. 5867, pp1238–1240. www.sciencemag.org/cgi/content/abstract/1151861

33 International Forum on Globalization and the Institute for Policy Studies. *The False Promise of Biofuels*. 2007, p23

34 Goldemberg, J. and Guardabassi, P. *'Are biofuels a feasible option?'* Energy Policy 37 (2009) p11

35 Ibid.

36 Ibid, pp11-12

37 Kho, J. *US Ethanol Industry Eyes Valero's Bid for VeraSun*. Renewable Energy World.com. www.renewableenergyworld.com/rea/news/article/2009/02/can-the-future-of-the-us-ethanol-industry-be-determined-by-verasun

38 Worldwatch Institute, p7

39 Ibid.

40 Wikipedia. Biofuel. http://en.wikipedia.org/wiki/Biofuels

41 Paul, H. 'Fuel from the Land', *The Ecologist* magazine, 14-21 February 2009, p17

42 MacKay, 2008, p43

43 Lal, R. *Land Area for Establishing Biofuel Plantations*. Energy for Sustainable Development, Volume X, Issue No.2, June 2006, pp67-79, p70. www.esd-journal.org/ESDvol10no2/landbiofuelabstractv10n2.html

44 Lal, p70

45 Paul, p16

46 Lal, p76

47 Lal, p78

48 Mathews, J.A. *'Carbon-negative biofuels,'* Energy Policy 36 (2008) 940–945, p940

49 Benemann, J. *Overview: Algae Oil to Biofuels*. Presentation, NREL-AFOSR Workshop, Algal Oil for Jet Fuel Production, Arlington VA, 19 February 2008. www.nrel.gov/biomass/pdfs/benemann.pdf

50 GreenFuel Technologies Corporation. *Applications*. www.greenfuelonline.com/technology.html

51 GreenFuel Technologies Corporation. Overview. www.greenfuelonline.com/technology.html

52 MacKay, p285

53 Renewable Energy World.com (REW). *Bionavitas Announces New Algae Growth Technology for Biofuels Production*. 25 February 2009. www.renewableenergyworld.com/rea/news/article/2009/02/bionavitas-announces-new-algae-growth-technology-for-biofuels-production

54 MacKay, p285

55 REW, *Bionavitas* www.renewableenergyworld.com/rea/news/article/2009/02/bionavitas-announces-new-algae-growth-technology-for-biofuels-production

56 Wikipedia, *Biofuel*

57 Massachusetts Institute of Technology. *Algae system transforms greenhouse emissions into green fuel*. http://web.mit.edu/erc/spotlights/alg-all.html

58 MacKay, pp285-286

59 Podewils, C. *Organized Wastefulness*. Photon International, April 2007

Chapter 10 –
Going Deeper, Looking Further

[1] Diener, E., and Biswas-Diener, R. (2008) *Happiness, Unlocking the mysteries of Psychological Wealth,* Wiley-Blackwell

[2] Gurven, M. (2008) *The evolution of contingent cooperation,* Current Anthropology 47:1

[3] http://en.wikipedia.org/wiki/Eudaimonia

[4] Sunstein, C.S. (2006) *Infotopia: How Many Minds Produce Knowledge,* Oxford University Press

[5] Howe, J. (2008) *Crowdsourcing: Why the Power of the Crowd Is Driving the Future of Business,* Random House

[6] Sunstein, C. *Infotopia,* p170

[7] http://feingold.senate.gov/listening/index.html

[8] McKibben, B., 'First Step Up', *Yes Magazine,* spring 2008

[9] The International Institute for Environment and Development et al. 2008. *Building on a Current Green Revolution in the Sahel: Some Lessons from Farmer-Managed Re-greening in Niger,* The International Institute for Environment and Development, Observatoire du sahara et du Sahel, VU University of Amsterdam, August 2008

[10] Gorn, D. *San Francisco Plastic Bag Ban Interests Other Cities* www.npr.org/templates/story/story.php?storyId=89135360

[11] World Future Council. *Future Justice.* http://www.worldfuturecouncil.org/futurejustice.html

Index

The World Future Council (WFC)

The World Future Council Initiative was launched in London in October 2004, having first been mooted by Swedish-German writer and activist Jakob von Uexküll in 2000. The idea was to create a global council made up of wise elders, thinkers, pioneers and young leaders who could collectively become a voice of future generations.

The project was developed by Jakob von Uexküll and Herbert Girardet as a response to the apparent inability of global politics to take the necessary steps to secure a liveable world for future generations. It was apparent there was no shortage of good proposals for tackling the problems we face, but that the existing institutions seemed incapable of making the most of these ideas.

In May 2007 the WFC was formally founded in the town hall of Hamburg, Germany. Thirty-four Council members from twenty-two countries solemnly declared that "we will do everything in our power to help sustain life on earth with all its beauty and diversity for future generations."

There are now 50 councillors. The WFC has offices in four countries and a total staff of 25. It is actively supported by an international Board of Advisors. The WFC aims to match global challenges with appropriate solutions: what are the most effective polices for accelerating renewable energies, for creating sustainable cities, for regulating international financial markets, for assuring justice for future generations? How can best policy solutions be transferred from one country to another?

The most important WFC bodies are its *Expert Commissions* – 'think-and-do tanks' – comprised of Council members, external experts and WFC staff. The commissions set up so far focus on Climate and Energy, Cities and Climate Change, Future Justice, Future Finance, and Living Economies.

The Climate and Energy Commission aims to spread effective legislation for climate protection. In seminars and websites (such as www.onlinepact.org) it offers support to policy-makers keen to introduce appropriate legislation. Since 2006 the WFC has promoted 'Feed-in Tariffs' (FITs) which deliver renewable energy faster, cheaper and more equitably than any other policy. Several countries and US states have now introduced FITs, clearly referring to the influence of the WFC.

The *Cities and Climate Change Commission* seeks to improve urban resource efficiency and increased use of renewable energy through suitable policies and improved city planning. As cities consume some 80 percent of global energy resources and emit the largest share of greenhouse gases, a change in the way cities function is of critical importance for a sustainable world.

The *Future Justice Commission* has the goal of protecting the rights of Future Generations through best policy promotion and worst behaviour denunciation. The WFC has developed Future Justice indicators, principles and standards which integrate human rights and security, ecological integrity and peaceful relations, and which guide the work of the Commission.

The *Future Finance Commission* is working on a new vision of the global financial system. It is developing concrete policy proposals on the global challenges of poverty, climate change and the destruction of natural resources. Money should serve people and the planet, and financial markets should assure human security and wellbeing for all – including future generations.

The *Living Economies programme*, closely related to the topics Future Finance and Justice, is working to develop new economic thinking and governance proposals based on respect of and responsibility for natural and social wealth and fundamental human freedoms.

Through its Council members and advisors, the WFC is able to reach national and international decision-makers, and members of the international community, promoting a sustainable, just and peaceful future where the dignity of human beings, and our connectedness to the integrity of life on earth, is universally respected and supported.

For further information please access our website: **www.worldfuturecouncil.org**

About the Authors

Prof. Herbert Girardet is an author, consultant and film-maker. He is co-founder and director of programmes of the World Future Council. He is author and co-author of 12 books and 50 TV documentaries on many aspects of sustainable development. In recent years he has focussed mainly on the challenges of sustainable urban development. He has been a consultant to UNEP and UN-Habitat and has developed sustainability policies for major cities such as London and Vienna. In 2003 he was 'Thinker in Residence' in Adelaide, developing sustainable development strategies for South Australia. He has also been a senior adviser to the Dongtan Eco-City project on Chongming Island, Shanghai.

For 12 years Herbert was chairman of the Schumacher Society UK, which stages the annual Bristol Schumacher Lectures to commemorate the work of E. F. Schumacher. He is a recipient of a UN Global 500 Award 'for outstanding environmental achievements'. He is an honorary fellow of Royal Institute of British Architects, a patron of the Soil Association, UK, and a visiting professor at the University of the West of England. In 2004 Wiley-Academy published his book, *Cities, People, Planet – Urban Development and Climate Change*. In 2007 he edited *Surviving the Century – Facing Climate Change and other Global Challenges*, published by Earthscan for the World Future Council.

Miguel Mendonça is the World Future Council's Research Manager. His background is in forestry, horticulture, geography, history, journalism, social science and environmental ethics. He is a UK-based researcher, writer and advocate, and has spoken and campaigned successfully on four continents on the subject of the most effective renewable energy policy: feed-in tariffs. He has also introduced a variety of initiatives to improve international knowledge-transfer and discussion on them. Miguel focuses on social and political aspects of renewable energy policy, working for the rapid deployment of renewable energy around the world, and public participation in this process. He writes books, papers, articles, commentaries and reviews on sustainability issues, is author of the influential *Feed-in Tariffs – accelerating the deployment of renewable energy* (2007), and co-author of the follow-up, *Powering the Green Economy: The Feed-in Tariff Handbook* (2009).